Women in Computing

Edited by
Rachel Lander and Alison Adam

intellect™

EXETER, ENGLAND

First Published in 1997 by
Intellect Books
EFAE, Earl Richards Road North, Exeter EX2 6AS

Consulting editor: Masoud Yazdani
Copy Editor: Wendi Momen
Proofreading: Julie Strudwick
Production: Robin Beecroft

A catalogue record for this book is available from the British Library

ISBN 1-871516-58-7

Printed and bound in Great Britain by Cromwell Press, Wiltshire

Contents

Section 1. Research Perspectives

Section 2. Women in Computing - Professional Roles

Section 3. Education and Training Practice

Section 4. Women and the Internet

Introduction

This book presents the series of papers given at the Women into Computing Conference held at De Montfort University Milton Keynes and entitled 'Progression: From Where to What?' Women into Computing (WiC) is a national organisation which is committed to encouraging more women to participate in computing education, to take up work in the computing industry and to be involved with professional bodies and research. Regular conferences have been held since the organisation's inception in 1988.

The 1997 conference aims to provide a forum for discussion for those concerned with issues for women entering or working in computing. The papers collected in this book demonstrate that gender related research in computing is of increasing interest to a variety of disciplines and that this work is of international significance. The Programme Committee of the conference accepted 20 full papers and a selection of workshops or short presentations; not all of the latter appear in these proceedings. The published contributions represented the following eight countries:

| Australia | 2 | Austria | 1 | Canada | 2 | Germany | 1 |
| Ireland | 1 | Sweden | 2 | USA | 1 | UK | 12 |

In organising this collection of papers, it became clear that it was not appropriate to make a sharp distinction between mature research and reports of work in progress. In any case, we have encouraged our authors to make explicit the nature of their research, to indicate whether it is still at a planning stage or whether they are reporting the results of a study. We believe this approach is warranted owing to the problems inherent in gender and computing research, which, as any emerging field, suffers from difficulties in obtaining recognition for funding of substantive projects in the many areas meriting serious research. However, there are promising signs that perceptions in funding bodies are shifting and the papers here reporting research in progress reflect this change.

Janet Stack, the current Chair of WiC, opens the collection with an article about the organisation originally featured in the journal *ACM Interactions*. The conference papers are then presented in four sections. The first, Feminist Perspectives on Computing Research, includes the WiC keynote speech to the conference in which Frances Grundy assesses how far we have come and the problems and issues that remain to be confronted. The other papers in this section illustrate the range of new research approaches and ideas emerging, including interesting analyses of gendered styles of language usage. This demonstrates that research on women and computing is moving forward both on the theoretical and the empirical front.

The section on Education and Training contains our guest speaker Gerda Siann's contribution on researching the reasons for the continued decline in numbers of women enrolling on computer science courses in the UK. This section contains the greatest range of contributions from international authors. This allows for interesting comparisons to be made and for solutions and ideas from one country to be made available for use in, what is possibly, a very different cultural and geographical setting.

Our section on Women and the Computing Profession covers both research into women working in the industry or using technology in their work and wider international perspectives on barriers to women entering the field. Within this section Eva Turner and Fiona Hovenden present thought-provoking research on the portrayal of women in computing advertisements.

Our final selection of papers is on women and the Internet. This demonstrates the range of interactions which currently takes place as well as optimistic views of the way that women can take charge of networked ICTs.

In bringing these papers together for the conference proceedings, we were aware of some of the problems which have been highlighted at past conferences. The most obvious of these is the continuing problem of numbers of women at all levels in computing, the very problem which provided much of the rationale for the founding of WiC in the first place. But, although the research reported here acknowledges that this concern has certainly not disappeared, it does not dwell on the negative aspects of the research domain. Rather it offers maturer theoretical perspectives, well-planned empirical studies and a sense of optimism. This is a change of mood and emphasis; the feeling that women can and do take control of information technology for positive ends.

The papers in the conference went through a three stage refereeing process. Initially abstracts were refereed and comments fed back to authors. Each full paper was then refereed anonymously by two members of the programme committee. Finally, members of the programme committee met to reconcile referees' reports and add further comments. We are extremely grateful to all members of the programme committee for all their hard work in this process. We are particularly grateful to members of the organising committee, especially for their willingness to respond, often instantly, to anxious emails. Indeed their responses were often so immediate that we have wondered if some colleagues are surgically attached to email and if we now have instances of the much quoted 'cyborg'.

More information on Women into Computing can be found at our web site [http://osiris.sund.ac.uk/wic/wic-home.htm] or by contacting:

Janet Stack, WiC Chair, Computing Science Department, 17 Lilybank Gardens, University of Glasgow, GLASGOW G12 8RZ, Scotland.
E-mail: jstack@dcs.glasgow.ac.uk

We would like to thank British Telecommunications for sponsorship of the publicity for the conference and the School of Computing Sciences at De Montfort University for institutional support of the conference. For the cover design, and design of the conference leaflets and poster we would like to thank Suheila Tavacol.

Women into Computing

Janet Stack

(Chair)

The national UK organisation Women into Computing (WiC) was formed in November 1987 as a result of widespread concern at the drop in female participation in computing. The need for action to increase the number of women applying to computing courses became apparent to universities when statistics showed that the percentage of women accepted by UK universities had fallen from 24% in 1980 to 10% in 1987.

WiC has no full time workers, only members who volunteer their time, and is committed to encouraging more women to participate in computing education and research, to take up work in the computing industry and to be involved with professional bodies. The members are mainly women working in UK educational institutions, but membership is open to any interested individual. Organisations and educational institutions can be affiliated members. Members meetings are held four times a year in different locations around the country which encourages a geographic spread of members, each meeting having a particular discussion theme. WiC is a network which maintains contact by email and the Web. A quarterly newsletter contains news of events, articles for discussion, reports from relevant meetings, profiles and reports of initiatives in progress. During the ten year existence of WiC, several very successful conferences have been held. Selected proceedings have been published and form an invaluable source of reference material.

In the early days of WiC it was hoped that initiatives such as awareness campaigns, workshops and recruitment drives targeted at school girls would remedy the situation. Ten years later, it is realised that the situation is far more complex. The problem is still unresolved but progress has been made.

Culture plays a large part in the low uptake of computing both at school and universities but gender issues in a wider context are now seen to be relevant. The discipline of computing science itself is a large part of the problem: it is mainly 'man-made' and has been developed to reflect the male ownership, seeking affirmation in engineering constructs.

A principal aim of WiC is to encourage research into the reasons for the gender imbalance in order to influence the development of Computing Science as well as to open doors to women who have previously been marginalised. WiC recognises that until research into gender-related issues in computing is validated by the computing community, progress will be slow. Interdisciplinary research is essential.

For ten years WiC has provided a unique forum in the UK for the dissemination of research findings in this area, and has been instrumental in encouraging a new area of interdisciplinary research, bringing together social scientists, educationalists and computing scientists. It is essential that computing scientists understand the implications of results in this research. With this in mind, members of the Conference of Professors and Heads of Computing (CPHC) are committed to supporting WiC initiatives. The CPHC represents all university departments of computing and is encouraging departments to adopt good practice within the department and to support individuals, male or female, in relevant research projects. Computing scientists must recognise the validity of social science research, and both disciplines should refrain from using terminology exclusive to its discipline.

There are other UK organisations whose purpose is to encourage women into Science, Engineering and Technology (SET). Although computing should be well represented in these, as it occupies all three fields, in practice it falls between them. Some of these organisations have been set up as a result of Government proposals, but still there is often a failure to realise the particular position of computing. It is not recognised as a science by pure scientists, nor as engineering by engineers, and neither does technology fit. WiC endeavours to redress this situation by maintaining a presence within these organisations and encouraging links with them, so creating an awareness of the inherent problem. The nature of the computing discipline itself needs to be addressed by its participants: what is computing science? This need is slowly being recognised but the variety of answers reflects the problem.

Recent conferences organised by WiC have reflected this change of emphasis from the early days when the hope was that all that was needed was to tell school girls that computing was fun and challenging. The title of this conference is *Progression: From Where To What?* which reflects some of the concerns discussed above. This conference provides an essential meeting place for the different disciplines to exchange ideas, for isolated individuals to feel supported, and for much needed publicity. Computer Science is still evolving and WiC intends that women will be in a position to influence the evolution.

A version of this paper appeared in *ACM Interactions* Vol. iv. 3, and is reprinted with permission of *ACM Interactions*.

WiC Conference

WiC Conference Chair

Rachel Lander   *Department of Computer and Information Science, De Montfort University*

WiC Programme Committee

Alison Adam   *Department of Computation, UMIST*

Kay Dudman   *School of Computing Science, Middlesex University*

Judy Emms   *Open University*

Christine Fidler   *School of Computing Sciences, De Montfort University*

Frances Grundy   *Department of Computer Science, University of Keele*

Barbara Kitchenham   *Department of Computer Science, University of Keele*

Anne Leeming   *Director MBA [IT & Management], City University*

Sue Lees   *Department of Computer Science, University of Keele*

Gillian Lovegrove   *School of Computing, Staffordshire University*

Greg Michaelson   *Department of Computing and Electrical Engineering, Heriot Watt University*

Wendy Milne   *Department of Computer Science, Exeter University*

Anne Moggridge   *Department of Computing, University of West of England*

Louise Moses   *Mount Union College, USA*

Daxa Patel   *Centre for Educational Technology Development, De Montfort University*

Wendy Pattinson   *Department of Mathematical and Information Sciences, Coventry University*

Pat Pearce   *School of Computing, University of Plymouth*

Simon Rogerson   *Director, Centre for Computing and Social Responsibility,*
                          School of Computing Sciences, De Montfort University

Barbara Segal   *Open University*

Janet Stack   *Department of Computing Science, University of Glasgow*

Eva Turner   *School of Computing Science, Middlesex University*

Sue Williams   *School of Computing, Staffordshire University*

Author Biographies

Alison Adam is a lecturer in the Department of Computation at UMIST (University of Manchester Institute of Science and Technology) where she teaches courses on artificial intelligence and IT and society. Prior to this she spent a number of years in industry. She has published a number of papers on gender and information technology and her book, *Artificial Knowing: Gender and the Thinking Machine* is to be published by Routledge in 1998. Email: A.Adam@co.umist.ac.uk

Malcolm Atkinson is Professor of Computing Science at the Department of Computing Science, University of Glasgow.

Martin Beirne is a senior lecturer at the Department of Management Studies, University of Glasgow

Christina Bjorkman holds an MSc in Engineering Physics from the Royal Institute of Technology, Stockholm, Sweden. Since 1985 she has been a lecturer at the Department of Computer Systems at Uppsala University, Sweden. Email: tina@docs.uu.se

Ivan Christoff received his PhD in Computer Science from Uppsala University in 1990. He is a senior lecturer at the Department of Computer Systems, Uppsala University, and is also co-ordinator of the Computer Science Programme. Email: ivan@docs.uu.se

Barbara Crow is an assistant professor at the University of Calgary. She is a self-taught computer user and has been on the Internet for over a decade. She teaches in Women's Studies and one of her courses is on Gender and Technology. Her most recent publication is a forthcoming edited collection of primary documents on US radical feminism to be published by New York University Press, Autumn 1997.

Anne Davidson is a lecturer in Women's Development and Training at the Women and Work Programme based in the School of Health and Social Sciences at Coventry University. She was formerly Senior Information and Training Officer in the Computing Services Department at Coventry. She became interested in IT as a woman returner herself – in her previous employment area as a researcher in chemical pathology.

Kerstin Fischer has an MA in English linguistics from the University of Bielefeld. After being employed on faculty positions and in the Verbmobil project in Bielefeld, she spent the last academic year at the University of California, Berkeley. Currently, she participates in the 'Graduiertenkolleg *Aufgabenorientierte Kommunikation*' at the University of Bielefeld where she works on the lexical representation of discourse particles.

Frances Grundy has been employed in computing continuously for over 30 years, first in industry and subsequently in a university setting; she has been a lecturer in computer science at the University of Keele since 1982. She is a former chair of Women into Computing and is currently employed in the teaching of traditional computing topics such as databases and system development. Her book,*Women and Computers*, was published by Intellect in 1996. Active in her trade union for many years, she has sought to promote the cause of women, particularly in the universities. This has included work in front of industrial tribunals. Email: frances@cs.keele.uk

Andrew Halkett was involved in secondary education, in the production of interactive and group-work materials and in staff training. He has acted as tutor on the Information Technology and Vocational Information Technology courses at St Andrews for several years.

Kevin Hammond holds a PhD in Computer Science from the University of East Anglia where he taught Computing Science at all levels, and was formerly at Glasgow University. He is course coordinator for the first year Computer Science module, and for the honours level *Professional and Social Aspects of Computing* course, a course assessed entirely by continuous assessment, with no exam component.

Fiona Hovenden is a research fellow in computing at the Open University. Her current work is concerned with the social construction of software, focusing specifically on software quality, and on object oriented technology. Gender is a particular interest and she is a co-organiser, with Laurie Keller, of the Open University's Gender and Technology study group. Email: f.m.hovenden@open.ac.uk

Ita Kavanagh is the course director for BSc. in Information Systems at the Regional Technical College, Limerick. She graduated with MSc (Machine Learning) from University College Dublin. Her work experience includes research into machine learning algorithm for subject classification of full text documents (ESPRIT Project SIMPR 2008), and software engineer with Lotus Development Ireland. Ita is a former executive member of Women in Technology and Science. Email: itak@rsl.rtc-limerick.ie

Colin Mason was formerly senior lecturer in Biomedical Sciences at Bradford University. He has published papers on, and run both local and national workshops on a variety of teaching and learning strategies in higher education. His recent appointment at St Andrews has coincided with the University's involvement in several SHEFC staff development initiatives which are relevant to increased participation of women in Science, Engineering, and Technology.

Anne Moggridge is a Senior Lecturer in Information Systems in the Department of Computing at UWE, Bristol where she has worked for many years. Her research interests in recent years have been based around human inquiry and community information systems. She is committed to engaging in research which is relevant to and contributes to her experiences as a woman and as an academic; hence 'research' seems both part-time and perpetual.

Wendy Nightingale holds a PhD in Neurophysiology and a Postgraduate Certificate in Vocational Training in Information Technology from St Andrews University. She has acted as tutor on the Information Technology and Vocational Information Technology courses at St Andrews for several years and also taught undergraduate neurophysiology modules.

Fredrik Palm is completing his MSc thesis in psychology at Uppsala University, Sweden. He is planning to continue with postgraduate studies in social psychology with a gender perspective.

Androniki Panteli is a research fellow at the University of Glasgow Business School and the project co-ordinator of the research cited in the paper.

Margit Pohl has degrees in psychology and computer science and is currently university lecturer at the University of Technology Vienna. Her research interests include hypertext, educational software, women and computing. Email: margit@iguwnext.tuwien.ac.at

Harvie Ramsay is Professor of International Human Resource Management at Strathclyde University.

Ita Richardson lectures with the Department of Computer Science and Information Systems at the University of Limerick. She graduated with an MSc (Applied Maths and Computing) in 1993 and is currently researching into the application of quality techniques to software process improvement. She previously worked with Wang Laboratories B.V. where she had responsibility for development, maintenance and support of various information systems. Ita is a member of Women in Technology and Science. Email: ita.richardson@ul.ie

Paula Roberts teaches computing in the School of Communication and Information Studies, Faculty of Humanities and Social Sciences, in the University of South Australia. She previously taught computing in Reception to Year 12 schools, where students as young as five years were encouraged to write with computers. Her research interests include writing with computers, the social and ethical implications of computer use, and women and computing. She hopes this year to complete her doctoral thesis which is entitled, *Why can't a computer think more like a woman?: the gendered nature of the computer culture and its consequences for girls and women.*

Minna Salminen-Karlsson is a PhD student at the Department of Education and Psychology at Linköping University. The subject of her thesis is *The creation of computer engineering curriculum in the gendered context of technical universities.* Her interests include gendered occupational choices and gender perspectives on higher education. Email: Minsa@ipp.liu.se.

Leslie Regan Shade is finishing her PhD this year at McGill University's Graduate Program in Communications. Her dissertation is titled 'Gender and Community in the Social Constitution of the Internet.' Her consulting work concentrates on the social, policy and design issues surrounding new technologies. Clients include Industry Canada/Faculty of Information Studies, University of Toronto, with the Universal Access projects (see http://www.fis.utoronto.ca/research/iprp/ua). She has also written widely on the social and policy issues in a variety of publications. Previous work experience includes freelance researching , law and advertising agency librarian and administrative work. Email: shade@well.com

Gerda Siann holds the NCR Chair of Gender Relations at the University of Dundee. She has published widely in the field of social psychology and is the author of numerous papers, articles and three books, the latest being *Gender, Sex and Sexuality: contemporary psychological perspectives* which was published in 1994 and reprinted earlier this year.

Janet Stack is lecturer at the Department of Computing Science, University of Glasgow and is the chair of Women into Computing.

Linda Stepulevage is a senior lecturer in the Department of Innovation Studies at the University of East London. Her research and teaching deal with women's relationship to science and computing, and the development of technical skills, such as database design. Her classes are taught within two interdisciplinary degree programmes: BSc (Hons) Women and New Technology, and BA (Hons) Women's Studies.

Eva Turner is a senior lecturer at the School of Computing Science at Middlesex University. She has been involved in the area of women in computing for a number of years, organising retraining programmes for women returners and being active in WiC and the university's Gender Research Centre. She is currently on sabbatical, conducting research into gender bias in computing. She is interested in programming, teaching and working with visual languages and object orientation. Email: eva1@mdx.ac.uk

Anna Vallin is completing her MSc thesis in psychology at Uppsala University, Sweden. She also studies Information Systems and plans to combine the two disciplines in her future career.

Fiona Wilson is a lecturer in organisational behaviour in the Management Department at the University of St Andrews. She is the author of 'Language, Technology, Gender, and Power', *Human Relations 45:9*, 883–904 (1992), a study of how language is used to exclude women from careers in computer-related areas and also of *Organisational Behaviour and Gender*, McGraw-Hill (1996).

Britta Wrede studies computational linguistics, computer science and psychology at the University of Bielefeld and works for the SFB 360 'Situierte künstliche Kommunikatoren'. Her research interests are phonological aspects of speech recognition.

Rosemary Wright received her PhD in Sociology in 1994 from the University of Pennsylvania and is an Assistant Professor in the Department of Social Sciences and History at Fairleigh Dickinson University in Madison, New Jersey, USA. A former computer professional with 15 years of experience as a programmer, systems analyst, manager and consultant, she left her computing career in 1986 to return to graduate school to study computing from a social perspective. She has published widely on women and computing and her book entitled *Women Computer Professionals: Progress and Resistance* is published this summer.

Amina Znaidi has worked as a modern languages teacher, translator, interpreter and development worker. She is currently based at the Centre for People and Systems Interaction, South Bank University. Email: znaidia@sbu.ac.uk

Where Do We Go From Here?

Frances Grundy

Department of Computer Science, University of Keele, Keele, Staffordshire ST5 5BG, UK

Abstract

This paper is a sequel to *Women and Computers* in which I defined three levels of solution to the women in computing 'problem', namely the 'add-more-women', liberal and radical levels of change. I now look in more detail at how these three levels should be introduced. Should they be introduced in sequence or in parallel? Examination of this question leads to a discussion of a critical mass (of women) and critical flow (their rate of influx). It also involves an examination of the effects of the existence of token women and their likely impact on change. The second part of the paper re-presents the impact of change, or rather lack of it, at the liberal and radical levels, this time from the point of view of a potential recruit – I have called her Pauline.

1. Feminism and the Three Levels of Change

I would like to discuss with you some further thoughts I have had on what would count as a solution to the women into computing 'problem', what needs to be done and how it should be done. I say 'further thoughts' because they lead on from ones expressed in my book *Women and Computers* (Grundy 1996) and the reactions of some readers to what I have said there. I am sorry if some of you are already well acquainted with what I have to say in this introduction but, obviously, many of you will not have read it.

We need to start with my deliberately simple definition of 'feminism'. First, *minimal feminism*, i.e., the set of beliefs that are the least that are required for a position to be described as feminist. These beliefs are that there is no difference between the intelligence, abilities and aptitudes of women and those of men and that all jobs should be open to everyone regardless of their gender, people being chosen for jobs strictly on their merits. In theory, at any rate, the outcome of this set of beliefs would be that there should be as many women as men in computing at all levels (with the correlative that there should be as many men as women at the lowest levels as well). Minimal feminism is, as it were, a set of premises the logical conclusion of which is that we ought to add more women to those few already there, in theory, up to the point where there are equal numbers.

Optimal feminism is a more complex set of beliefs than minimal feminism and goes beyond minimal feminism by asserting that by training and upbringing, but not inherently, women bring to their work standards which are preferable to those that men bring. Clearly I am not talking here of all women and all men; I am saying that the preponderance of women and the preponderance of men have distinctively different standards.

What are these standards and motivations that women bring? Women bring a caring and nurturing disposition which is the antithesis of the competitiveness of men. For example – and an important example – men tend to encourage unnecessary hierarchies with managers overseeing people's work when they can manage quite well by themselves. Men tend to disempower in order to gain submissive control, whereas women prefer to empower others through negotiation in order to achieve consensual control. Another example: many women and those men of a similar disposition enjoy spending time sorting out misunderstandings between individuals in the computing workplace. In an academic environment women want to ensure that students understand what they are required to do and that they have proper access to the facilities they need. Women are often happier when engaged in this type of activity than when they ignore it – unlike most men (and some women) who concentrate on research and attracting money and hence promotion and self-aggrandisement. Women are unlikely to want to become 'hard-nosed', as a male colleague urged me to do recently when we were discussing just this kind of thing. Similarly, in a commercial environment, I have observed that women show a greater tendency to be sensitive to the needs of end-users than do men. It is part of the spirit in which they do their work to 'remain behind' and encourage the end-users and ensure that a newly introduced system is working to their satisfaction rather than rushing on to the next activity which will probably involve exploiting the most up-to-date software.

For completeness, when establishing my hierarchy of feminism, I identified a third version which I labelled *drastic feminism*. This asserts that women are inherently superior to men and that in future they should therefore be allowed to dominate much as men dominate at present. This final version I repudiate and it plays no part in generating my programme of changes.

Having established these types of feminism, I now go on to identify three levels at which change is needed. I made the value judgement that the cluster of attitudes women tend to bring to their work is superior to that brought by men. I want to make a further value judgement: that we should not simply add more women to men's world of work at the expense of losing the valuable ethos women bring to work. Given that we accept these value judgements, there is then a moral obligation to alter the workplace in a way that incorporates these differences rather than getting women to abandon them and to think and behave like men. It is not enough to add more women without parallel changes to the ethos and the environment in which we live and work. Clearly this generates a set of objectives alongside, and indeed beyond, adding more women. I called these two different sets of aims the *add-more-women* and the *liberal* levels of change. For instance, at the liberal level, one objective would be to abolish redundant hierarchies and have people co-operating on an equal footing rather than be coerced by so-called 'superiors'.

Changes at the liberal level help to ensure that women do not have to compromise their identity when they enter computing. This is also true at my third or *radical level*. Although liberal and radical level changes merge into one another, the liberal level is more about the setting in which the changes take place. The radical level, on the other hand, is more about the activities themselves. An example of this is the difference between a 'bricolage' or 'tinkering' approach – people building software the way it suits them in contrast to following an approach dictated by others (Turkle 1996). Identifying gender bias that might be deeply embedded in an area of activity as some allege it is in AI, and proposing alternative approaches to and uses for this new AI are further examples of change at the radical level.

Thus we have three levels at which change needs to be made – 'add-more-women', liberal and radical. The need for change at all of these three levels is generated by just the two types of feminism – minimal and optimal. I have, as I say, repudiated so-called drastic feminism. It has nothing to do with my radical solution which, like the liberal level, is generated by optimal feminism.

I want now to examine how we could implement change at these three levels and bring about solutions to the problems characteristic of each.

There are two interrelated questions which need addressing. The first is a composite one. In what sequence, if any, will the three levels occur? Is success at the add-more-women level a pre-requisite for any change? Does the liberal level have to precede the radical level? Or should, not merely could, all three occur simultaneously?

The second question I shall address is: Are there any constraints on the speed at which these changes must be implemented if the lot of womankind is to be improved?

2. The Sequence of Change

There is already a sufficient number of women in the profession to get things moving. Rather than suggest that we should increase that number and make other changes at the add-more-women level before making any changes at the liberal level, I am suggesting that changes at the liberal level must occur in parallel with further changes at the add-more-women level.

In my view the liberal level is generated alongside 'add-more-women' because they are reciprocally dependent on one another. Progress has to be made at both these levels if progress is to be made at either. Until the work environment caters for the female motivations which I have just highlighted, there will be a dearth of good women applying for computing posts.

One plausible view of the relationship between adding-more-women and the other levels is that one should aim at adding more women until a critical mass is reached. Once this critical mass is reached, liberal and radical level changes would follow almost automatically.

From this perspective, below a certain level of women in the faculty it is impossible to effect the liberal level changes that would attract more women students into the subject and hence more good women applicants for faculty places. Even if the demand side is right and departments are willing to appoint more women, not enough good women would be attracted to apply unless changes are made at the liberal level. It is no good getting the demand side right and ignoring the state of the supply side. There is perhaps some plausibility in the response so often heard: 'We would appoint more women if only they would apply'.

How do we overcome this impasse of women being unlikely to apply while the jobs for which we would like them to apply are set in such a hostile environment? But of course the hostile environment can't be changed while there aren't enough women. So we appear to be caught in a vicious cycle. The frustration which this can cause was neatly expressed by a sympathetic male colleague from another university who commented to me: 'What else can we do beyond putting yet more potted plants in the entrance to the department?' This feeling that we are stuck at the present state of affairs – and indeed if anything it's getting worse – is one with which I believe a good proportion of my female colleagues would agree.

2.1 The Critical Mass

What is this 'critical mass' which I just mentioned? Rosabeth Moss Kanter (1977) suggests that in order to become more than a mere token, an under-represented group like women should constitute 15% or more of an organisation's population. Below this critical mass women are isolated, uninfluential and perceived in one or more of the various female roles which society expects of them: 'mother', 'seductress', 'pet', 'iron maiden'. Kanter suggests that once the critical mass is reached, members of such a group can form alliances, affect the culture and are perceived as individuals in their own right rather than as representatives of women.

I have already said I think there are enough women in the academic profession to get things moving. Rosabeth Moss Kanter's figure for the general run of organisations is 15% and this is very close to the 13.9% which represented the total female population amongst UK computing academics in 1991/92 (USR 1988-94).

2.1.1 The Composition of the Critical Mass

The idea that there is a critical mass looks more plausible if it includes senior women. One might well think that if women are distributed, not necessarily evenly, throughout the population but certainly including some at the senior level, then there is more likely to be a change to a woman-friendly environment and consequently a further rise in the number of women overall.

2.2.2 The Influence of Personalities

The notion of a critical mass is extremely complex and depends not only on sheer numbers and their distribution but also on the personalities of those involved. First, do the senior women really want change? Henry Etzkowitz *et al* found in their research into the dynamics of increasing participation of women in 30 science departments that 'as the number of women faculty members in a department increased, they divided into distinct subgroups that could be at odds with each other. Senior female scientists typically shared the values and work styles of older men; their narrow focus failed to meet the needs of most younger women' (Etzkowitz, Kemelgor, Neuschatz, Uzzi and Alonzo 1994, p51).

Whilst realising that there are honourable exceptions, it is my belief that many senior women inside the profession do not want change. The dominant competitive ethos encourages us all, men and women alike, to stand out and to distinguish ourselves. One easy way in which women can do this is to be one of a very few women at a senior level. It is in the interests of such women to maintain this set of values and restrict their number high in the hierarchy, otherwise they will not stand out.

It is also in their interests to maintain the fiction that in general women aren't as able as men at science but these successful senior women are the exception and thus distinguished. These women may find computing exciting and challenging, however I have serious doubts as to whether they are really interested in empowering other women on a scale sufficient to challenge the supremacy of these distinguished exceptions.

The women who have been promoted so far have been awarded their promotion by the existing patriarchy. These women have been selected because they are unlikely to show 'ingratitude' and 'disloyalty' for their senior positions by criticising their department in suggesting that all is not well with the world. This is particularly true for women who wish to go yet further up the hierarchy. Indeed, it is likely that these women often do genuinely believe that all *is* well with the world – the proof of this is their personal success! And the patriarchy can itself point to the promotion of these women as proof that all is well. This is a phenomenon neatly put by Adrienne Rich when she spoke about 'the decoy of the upwardly mobile token woman' (Rich 1987, p37).

I would like to emphasise that I am not talking here about all women and, the truth should be told – I have not been averse to seeking promotion myself.

2.2 Critical Flow

Critical mass implies a certain level of women in an organisation at and above which change occurs almost automatically. But the critical mass of women cannot be critical in this sense without what I shall call *critical flow*. If change is too slow and merely a trickle of additional women is admitted over decades, then these entrants will be sucked into the patriarchal way of thinking and will simply endorse the *status quo*.

Figure 1 shows the changes in the numbers of women in the UK academic computing profession between 1987/88 and 1993/94. In percentage terms this represents a change from 11.0 to 12.8% for the period shown. This rise of 1.8% over seven years is indeed a trickle and this in itself could well be having a deterrent effect on the influx of women – in the last two years for which USR statistics exist, there has been a drop in the overall number of women from the highpoint of 13.9% in 1991/92 (USR 1988-94).

At the same time as we have this slow rate of increase, other male-friendly aspects of computing are becoming increasingly entrenched and difficult to shift. This is particularly true of language. The well-known words that connote sex and violence which are now in common use are becoming increasingly difficult to change.

2.3 The Interaction of Critical Mass and Critical Flow

It is not easy to disentangle the effects of low numbers of women and their lack of 'mass' at a particular point from the effects of a low rate of influx. This interaction of mass and flow is nicely illustrated by the following story.

After offering an MSc entitled 'Data Engineering' for some eight years, my department decided that there should be a major revision of the syllabus. This revision gave us the occasion

Figure 1: Computer Studies Female Staff (UK)

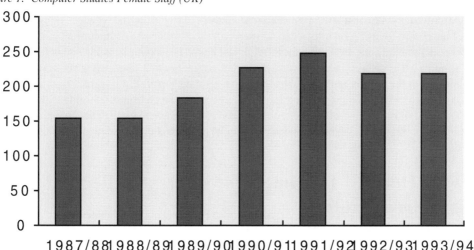

to examine the course title. As Course Tutor in the early years of the course had some anecdotal evidence of women being deterred by its name from applying, I was one of two women (amongst a total of nine people) involved in the choice of a new title and I did not fight hard for change because I knew from experience that the chance of success would be exceedingly small and the likelihood was that I would expend a considerable amount of energy fruitlessly. In the end the voting came down heavily in favour of 'Data Engineering' again.

It is possible that had there been a greater number of women asserting with me that the word 'engineering' is a deterrent for women, as I believe it is, and had we been able as a group to bring pressure to bear for more detailed discussion of this, the title might have been changed. *Prima facie* that is an argument about critical mass. But it is also an argument about critical flow. That title is going to be very difficult to change, the name of the course will be closely linked to its reputation. So long as sufficient students come forward to take this course (although lip-service is paid to gender imbalance, nobody in a position of influence is actively bothered about it) it will continue and will continue under this name. Had the rate of influx of women since the course started been greater, then it is possible that those who wanted change could have achieved it.

There must be an influx of women at such a rate that by their sheer numbers and consequent ability to make alliances to initiate change, they can make these changes come to pass. What seems to be happening at the moment is that the overall number of women is virtually static and that the only increase is in the number of women at senior level, with the implication that, as they are promoted from junior to senior level, they are not replaced by other women at the junior level. This is likely to reduce the call for liberal level changes because of the divisive and defusing effects that promoting women to senior levels tends to have. These now senior women are unlikely to make alliances that will bring about change.

Seen in this light it looks even more likely that for change to occur, stimulus from outside the discipline will be needed. Indeed, it is doubtful if change at the liberal or radical levels can occur without external stimulus.

2.4 Add-More-Women and the Radical Level

So far I have been focusing on add-more-women and the liberal level. Much of what I have said applies equally to add-more-women and the radical level. For example, if the subject were more influenced by ideas originating from radical level changes, good women students would take more interest in the subject and approach it with an enthusiasm and in numbers that at present we just don't see. They would feel that the subject belonged to *them* and would therefore feel more involved in it and part of it in ways which do not occur at present. Following on from this, there would be greater numbers of recruits for faculty posts and in this way more women would be added …

3. What Does All This Imply for a Potential Recruit? or 'The Perils of Pauline'

There is an alternative way of looking at all this and that is from the point of view of a potential recruit – let us call her Pauline. She certainly faces enough hazards. From a very early age she has to survive the tendency of parents to buy computers for her brothers and see them play games for which she has no inclination and the tendency of teachers in mixed schools to focus their attention on the boys and to assume that the boys will be better at this subject. She has to survive the ridicule of boys in the playground and classroom and being elbowed off the computers in the classroom. The GCSE (General Certificate of Secondary Education) computer studies examinations in which girls did well in spite of these difficulties – 40.5% achieving top grades in 1993 – has now been abolished. With this introductory level gone, she will find little to encourage her to embark on an 'A' level course. Even when GCSE computer studies were in place, only 17.6% of those attempting 'A' level in 1993 were girls (SOE 1994). The explicit encouragement of girls by teachers, while welcome in some respects, must also make Pauline wonder 'What's wrong? Why haven't other girls been taking this? I don't want to stand out like that. I want to be like all the others.'

Most people are conformist. While, as I have already suggested, we live in an environment where we are encouraged to distinguish ourselves, such distinguishing activity must lie within a very narrow band. You take a considerable risk of being labelled 'extremist' if you step outside these societal bounds. So a girl leaving school immediately after her secondary education is not going to find it easy to enter into computing work outside the service fields of secretarial work, data entry, telephone answering services and so on.

Such conformism will also apply to a new undergraduate who might consider entering computing (and she can do that in the UK without computer studies or maths 'A' level). Pauline will quite likely choose not to embark on a computing course because the whole scene – staff, buildings (even with their potted plants), labs, fellow students, subject matter – simply puts her off. Or she *will* choose it. But if she does, she's not going to have the confidence and is not going to risk the ridicule she is likely to attract if she were to suggest that the subject has no meaning for her as a female. She is unlikely to ask that the syllabus be changed in any way to suit her female disposition, even if she could articulate what that meant. In fact, more likely the opposite will occur: she will want to show that she can keep up with the others who are, of course, predominantly male.

The question of the value of role models arises here. For many undergraduate female students, the faculty women, even the high fliers, are not people on whose lives these students wish to model their own. Rather than looking to these people as ones who might clarify what women students are looking for to make the subject more women-friendly, they see these 'role models' as people who have carefully avoided the question. Our Pauline may well see them as messengers for the patriarchy, telling her how things must be done, reinforcing the idea that there is no room for questioning the basis on which the subject is founded.

National statistics on the relative success rates of men and women at undergraduate level in 'pure' computing are hard to come by. But my experience is that women do well. For example, in my own department for at least the past three years a greater percentage of women have achieved 2.1 or above as compared with men. Assuming that women do do well in first degrees, how much encouragement are they given for going on to work for a higher degree? Ten years ago I saw women with first class degrees given none and men with low 2.1s given lots. This picture has to some extent changed: women are now demanding more and I believe there is more encouragement for them to do research and work for a higher degree. Currently (1997) 15% of the PhD students in my department are women.

It is extremely difficult for women embarking on research in computer science to study anything that is remotely radical – in the sense of working towards radical level changes. It will be more than their careers are worth. Anyway, they need a good supervisor and sympathetic mentor in one person and these are hard to come by. So, while Pauline may submit an excellent PhD, it's not going to be a shatteringly ground- breaking one. Even if she does pursue traditional research and has a sympathetic supervisor and mentor, it can be unnerving if the supervisor fails in her career in some way. For example, if the supervisor fails to get promotion because her ideas about women are considered to be too advanced, then the graduate student, no matter how good the supervisor, is going to feel let down and undermined. Such setbacks will do the student's confidence in her own ability no good and will not encourage her to apply for academic posts and pursue an academic career.

If Pauline does apply for a faculty post, she won't face the more overt discrimination that was prevalent in the fairly recent past. For example, I doubt if nowadays she would be asked at interview, as I was nearly 30 years ago, if it wouldn't be better for my daughter if I stayed at home and looked after her. Nor would she be told by a colleague just after she had accepted a new post, 'X shouldn't have employed you if you are pregnant.' Nor is she likely to be asked, as I was in 1965, by an interviewer at a blue-chip computer manufacturer, if I had a boyfriend. People are more wary about saying such things nowadays. But underground the sexism is just as strong. Indeed, I think some people think it is their duty to maintain these standards.

Assuming she gets a post, our heroine has, sooner or later, to face the task of gaining promotion. This is a chapter in her life to which I alluded earlier and have written about elsewhere.

I do not claim that anything I am saying here is new; I am presenting you with an alternative way of slicing the cake. I am re-presenting my three levels, but this time from the point of view of how what I have discussed in relation to the three levels impacts on one individual. What can we do to remove some of the perils facing our intrepid Pauline?

I am in no doubt that there are in the schools some young high-fliers who, with the help of inspiring teachers, could begin to identify and articulate what it means to study subjects in ways which 'suit their female disposition' (without turning to needlework and cookery).

Amongst all these perils, there are some over which we, in the universities, have no influence, like the decisions of parents to give their sons rather than their daughters computers. We have no control over what computer games are available for girls and boys. We might have grave reservations about, but no control over, the demise of GCSE computer studies in that this has closed off computing for many girls.

But over other matters we do have some control. We *can* get changes made in our university syllabuses. But we have to decide what these changes should be and then face the huge task of getting them accepted. If students in the sixth-form (i.e. 'A' level standard) caught wind of radical level changes in the universities where there was new scope for real debate on the masculinity of computing, then they might start to show an interest. I suspect that some girls would enjoy studying the philosophy of AI. But first we have to capture the imagination of some school teachers, who in turn have to engage the interest of these girls.

We can also influence the attitudes of senior women. We can point out to them, loudly and clearly, that the subject may have attractions for them but there is no evidence in the numbers of women coming forward to enrol on undergraduate degrees that the broad mass of women think the same. They could also do more to encourage the idea that it is *proper* research to investigate gender issues. They could be more pro-active in encouraging the recognition of pastoral work as an activity worthy of commendation and reward. And most importantly of all, because this could influence the schools, they could join with us in discussing revision at the radical level.

4. A Prognosis For Pauline

The beginning of these deliberations sounded rather gloomy. I painted a picture of a vicious cycle in which the profession now has some women and societal and economic forces are such that, in spite of or even perhaps because of this, change is unlikely. There are some women in the profession but the rate of change is so slow that the current patriarchal system is solidifying and change is becoming increasingly difficult to achieve.

But as I have developed these thoughts, I see some reason for optimism. We need to help Pauline at as early an age as possible. Changes in the universities would, I am sure, influence the schools and it is up to us to ensure that these changes come to pass. It is our responsibility not to let the situation crystallise any further.

Notes

1. In my book, I include other changes in 'add-more-women': changes in language, reducing the use of jargon, the names and labels we use to describe techniques, software, pictures and images, games. In fact, their inclusion at this level is not quite as clear cut as I made it appear in my book. On the one hand, these can be viewed as superficial changes which act like fancy packaging of goods to attract the consumer. On the other, they can be regarded as changes at the liberal level in that they alter the ethos and setting in which computing operates. They therefore fall on the borderline between the two levels and intersect them.

2. All these statistics refer to staff employed in the so-called 'old' universities in the UK; that is, those that were universities before the former polytechnics gained university status.

3. The data for this is given in the following three sets of figures. In each set I give, first, the academic year, second, the total number of students involved, third the percentage of women gaining 2.1 or above and fourth the pecentage of men gaining 2.1 or above.

1993/4	61	53%	34%
1994/5	42	75%	50%
1995/6	40	67%	59%

Clearly these samples are extremely small and this data is further complicated by the fact that almost all of these students will be taking joint honours and studying another subject which will have contributed towards their final result.

References

Etzkowitz, H.; Kemelgor, C.; Neuschatz, M.; Uzzi, B. and Alonzo, J. (1994). 'The Paradox of Critical Mass for Women in Science'. *Science* 266: 51-4.

Grundy, F. (1996).*Women and Computers*. Exeter: Intellect Books.

Kanter, R. M. (1977). *Men and Women of the Corporation*. New York: Basic Books.

Rich, A. (1987). *Blood, Bread and Poetry: Selected Prose 1979—1985*. London: Virago Press.

Turkle, S. (1996). *Life on the Screen: Identity in the Age of the Internet*. London: Weidenfeld & Nicolson.

SOE (1994). *Statistics of Education 1992/3. Public Examinations*. Department for Education.

USR (1988-94). University Statistics 1988-9, 1989-90, 1990-1, 1991-2, 1993-4; vol. 1, Students and Staff.

Feminist Perspectives in Computing Research: A Place for Human Inquiry?

Anne Moggridge

Department of Computing, University of the West of England, Bristol BS16 1QY

Abstract

The focus of this paper is the processes by which knowledge is constructed and used in the contexts in which we live and work. The contributions to our understanding of these processes of feminist perspectives and of participative 'human inquiry' approaches to research are examined. It is suggested that feminist human inquiry offers women working in computing an approach to defining our own research questions and methods and hence to undertaking research which is inclusive of our own meanings and experiences. The paper concludes with an invitation to participate in such an inquiry.

1. Introduction

In this paper I introduce the main strands of a research perspective to which I am personally and intellectually committed. In particular, I explore links between feminist approaches to research and other participative approaches to research which I shall refer to collectively as human inquiry. In attempting to articulate my own perspective I shall suggest ways in which the various strands might help us find new meanings from our experience of working as women in computing.

1.1 My perspective

My focus throughout is with the processes by which knowledge is constructed and used in the contexts in which we live and work. In broad terms this perspective has much in common with the constructionist framework proposed by Flis Henwood (Henwood, 1993). Technologies are viewed as part of, not separate from, the social contexts in which they are developed and used and they take on a variety of meanings as different people encounter them at different times and in different places: in education, in work and increasingly in everyday life.

The call for papers for this conference explicitly includes a request for contributions on the topic of feminist perspectives in computing research. I have labelled myself a feminist throughout my adult life, although the meaning of that label has not always stayed the same for me or others (whether used positively or pejoratively, by men or by women). In my work as an academic in a computing department, I have experienced many of the comments, criticisms and general disclaimers described by Frances Grundy (Grundy, 1996) and I have had decidedly limited success in developing effective strategies for dealing with them. The framing of recent debates about gender related research in computing (WiC Newsletter, Dec 96) reminds me that, even for women, the role of feminist perspectives in computing research is still a highly contentious issue. Speaking as a feminist is a risky business; so too is speaking any kind of truths which are incompatible with dominant frameworks or uncomfortable for those whose assumptions and ways of working are challenged by what is said.

2. Human inquiry and feminist perspectives

I begin by identifying some key characteristics of human inquiry and feminist perspectives. Both have contributed to the broader search for alternatives to the traditional approaches to research which have dominated the social sciences. It is not my purpose here to enter into the many academic debates within either approach. Rather it is my intention to explore some shared commitments, concepts and practical implications for identifying research questions, participating in research, creating knowledge and making sense of experience. Woven into this exploration are some tentative suggestions for research for women in computing. Finally, I invite others to share ideas about how we might engage in participative feminist research in our work environments in the future.

2.1 Research as human inquiry

I use the term human inquiry to embrace all those approaches to research which have at their heart a commitment to learning that is undertaken with and for people. To fulfil this commitment requires that research is conducted through the active involvement of participants for mutually beneficial practical purposes. Participants engage in cycles of action and reflection and through these processes create knowledge which is grounded in their individual and collective experiences and is of practical benefit to the extent that it helps them act more effectively in directing their own lives. Hence human inquiries are primarily concerned with knowledge that is created in and for action (Reason, 1988). Research from this perspective is no longer seen solely as an academic affair, the preserve of an educated (and otherwise privileged) elite; rather it is part of the lived experience of the participants.

2.2 Feminist perspectives in research

In line with many feminist writers (Stanley & Wise, 1990; Maguire, 1996), I do not see feminism as a single monolithic perspective but as a tapestry of standpoints and research approaches reflecting the many ways in which women's voices and women's meanings have been excluded, suppressed or otherwise marginalised. Women's experience of and responses to these manifestations of oppression are as diverse as the historical and cultural contexts from which they emanate; hence feminism to me is both a collective endeavour and an honouring of this diversity. The collective commitment is to understand, challenge and work to transform the many systems and structures that silence our voices and restrict our choices, including but not isolating those which are gendered.

3. Implications for research

In the following sections I explore some of the implications for the conduct of research as feminist human inquiry.

3.1. Research as personal and political process

For many of us, research is both a personal process (Reason & Marshall, 1987) and a political process. It is personal in the sense that we seek to explore topics which are relevant to our own lives and political in that we are often motivated by a desire to transform some aspects of the situations that we study (Marshall, 1992). Similarly, much feminist research starts from questions which have personal origins and seeks to effect some kind of social change (Reinharz, 1992). The research process in either case is a lived experience not separate from other parts of life or observed without impact upon the researcher herself.

A shared concern for most participants in this conference is assumed to be the 'problem' that only a minority of the people working as or training to be computing professionals are women. As in most occupational areas, the proportion of women decreases as the measurement is made higher up the hierarchy. Many people would agree that there is something 'not right' about this situation and a variety of arguments and strategies for effecting change have already been developed. However, there is little evidence that either national or organisational initiatives have been successful in meeting women's needs (Adler *et al*, 1993; Tanton, 1994; Marshall, 1995). Few women reach senior positions in computing and there is growing evidence that fewer are training to enter the profession (Grundy, 1996). So from the 'outside' there is clearly something wrong but there have been few explanations offered from 'inside' computing. The more personal and political perspectives that we could bring to research as women working in computing seem to me to offer a basis for developing more grounded understandings of our experiences in computing.

3.2. Participation in research

A common concern in the practice of feminist research is to establish open relationships and work in ways which are non-exploitative of others. This is also a key commitment of human inquiry. The implications for the conduct of research contrast sharply with established methods in computing research where the responsibility for research design and management lies solely with the initiating researcher. In human inquiry approaches such as co-operative inquiry (Heron, 1981b; Reason, 1988; Reason & Heron, 1995), all those involved in the research contribute to the generation of ideas about what is to be researched, in designing and participating in action to further the research and in reflecting upon and drawing conclusions from the experience. Hence, although the inquiry may be initiated by a single researcher, for the research to progress in a manner which honours the contribution that each person can make to the learning process, it is necessary for the distinction between 'researcher' and 'subject' to give way as each participates in the action which is being researched.

This does not mean that the quality or frequency of each individual's commitment need or will be identical or that they will all participate in the same action. However, it does suggest that a possible (and perhaps rather different) starting point for women wishing to understand and change their situations within computing might be to work together to frame our own research questions and design ways in which we could take them into our working lives. As discussed in the next section, we would be less concerned with traditional theorising than with understanding and trying to change the patterns which constrain, devalue or otherwise have a detrimental effect upon our lives. These might include the articulation of women's experience of various aspects or forms of technology, of working in computing departments and of attempting to challenge received wisdom in our organisations.

3.3. Extending our view of knowledge

Most research in computing emphasises the intellect as the primary means of knowing and conceptual language as the primary means of demonstrating knowledge. Statements about research outcomes are presented as detached from the human contexts in which the research was conducted and untainted by the researchers' subjective experiences. Heron (1981a; 1996) refers to this type of research outcome as propositional knowledge. He distinguishes this from practical knowledge, knowledge which is demonstrable in the application of the skills and competencies that the researchers have developed rather than in published accounts of the research. This is not the place to discuss the details of his work in this area but one further aspect warrants consideration.

The distinction between the propositional and the practical (knowing that and knowing how) will be familiar to many researchers in computing through the work of Dreyfus and Dreyfus (1986). From a human inquiry perspective, Heron points to the additional dimension of experiential knowledge, an inner knowing which can only be acquired through direct face-to-face encounter with people, places or things. Each of these forms of knowledge is important in informing our understanding and choice of available actions. Practical and experiential knowledge are grounded in our lived experience and may be felt rather than thought in any articulatable language. Feminist research calls us to attend to and value those aspects of our inner knowing which present themselves as emotions, intuitions and bodily felt sensations. In their extensive work on women's ways of knowing, Goldberger *et al* (1987) distinguish between subjective knowledge, or the inner voice, and procedural knowledge, the voice of reason. The challenge for us is to find ways of integrating these voices to maintain emotional and intellectual life in some meaningful whole.

4. Women in computing today

Most women (in the UK at least) in computing today work in organisations and with technologies that have largely been defined by male dominated cultures. We belong to minority groups in our departments and in our work teams. We are 'under-represented' as researchers, academics and managers. Our attempts to construct our own knowledge and speak out from our own perspectives are at best subject to multiple (mis)interpretations by those around us and too often dismissed as or forced back into polarised gender stereotypes. Our position as researchers is weak, particularly if we feel unable to subscribe to the view that computing technology and the processes by which it has been developed and used is value free.

4.1. A way forward?

I believe that feminist human inquiry offers us an approach to defining our own research questions and methods and to doing research that is relevant to our lives. I also believe that such an approach is entirely in line with the notion of social responsibility which is an underlying theme of this conference. More specifically, I believe that those of us in education and other arenas of employment in computing have a responsibility to explore ways in which we can effect change in our organisations and our technologies to make both more respectful of women's experiences and inclusive of women's meanings. This feels important for the quality of our remaining years in employment; for the experience of women in the future as they consider and perhaps enter the computing profession and for everyone whose life is affected by technology. Some might feel that things have moved too quickly, that it is too late for us. Yet if we look around at the powerful decision-makers in our organisations and funding bodies and at the structures that maintain their influence, I see little prospect of change unless we develop some momentum ourselves.

4.2. Making sense of experience

When we research, talk about or write about our experiences, there are many available perspectives from which the material can be viewed (Marshall, 1995). These include those based upon and those which challenge theories about organisations and technology which are presented as gender-neutral. Many of them constitute what Stanley and Wise (1990) refer to as our intellectual autobiography. Being explicit about the analytical frameworks which researchers bring to and employ in design and sense-making of research is important for the coherence and quality of the research process itself. For example, whilst human inquiry draws our attention to the role of power in the construction of organisations, technology and associated theory, feminism draws attention to gender relations in these contexts. Although we may be clear that many of the assumptions, structures and patterns created in our organisations make it difficult for women to be included in research and decision-making, we must remain open to having our own assumptions challenged as well. Being clear about available perspectives is also important when we seek to communicate our ideas to others so that they can judge our interpretations in context rather than solely in relation to their own preferred frameworks.

Our validity as meaning-makers in computing rests both on our ability to articulate our own perspectives and our ability to persuade others to entertain them. Hence part of our commitment is to engage in what Liz Kelly *et al* (1994) refer to as consciousness raising – using our experiences to build explanatory frameworks which will inform future negotiation, contestation and transformation of our roles and our technologies. Here I find myself sharing another of Flis Henwood's conclusions: our task should be focused on constructing our own knowledge of technology and work, knowledge which is grounded in our experiences of both.

5. Conclusion

In announcing my own perspective at the start of this paper I have perhaps made the ground seem a little firmer than it does as I stand on it. I have not presented solutions; rather I have tried to be clear about the many issues and challenges with which those willing to undertake feminist human inquiry must be prepared to work. I have also made some tentative suggestions about possible starting points but research approached in this way needs to be our research, not mine alone. I invite others to join me.

Acknowledgements

I would particularly like to thank Rachel Lander and Frances Grundy for encouraging me to participate in 'Women into Computing' and other members who have since made me feel welcome.

References

Adler, S.; Laney, J. and Packer, M. (1993). *Managing Women*. Buckingham: Open University Press.

Dreyfus, H.L. and Dreyfus, S.E. (1986). *Mind over Machine*. New York: The Free Press.

Goldberger, N.R.; Clinchey, B.McV.; Belenky, M.F. and Tarule, J.M. (1987). 'Women's ways of knowing: on gaining a voice', in P. Shaver and C. Hendrick (eds.). *Sex and Gender*. Newbury Park, CA: Sage Publications.

Grundy, F. (1996). *Women and Computers*. Exeter: Intellect Books.

Henwood, F. (1993). 'Establishing Gender Perspectives on Information Technology: Problems, Issues and Opportunities', in E. Green, J. Owen and D. Pain (eds.). *Gendered by Design?* Taylor and Francis, 31-49.

Heron, J. (1981a). 'Philosophical basis for a new paradigm', in P. Reason and J. Rowan (eds.). *Human Inquiry, a sourcebook of new paradigm research*. Chichester: Wiley.

Heron, J. (1981b). 'Experiential research methodology', in P. Reason and J. Rowan (eds.). *Human Inquiry: a sourcebook of new paradigm research*. Chichester: Wiley.

Heron, J. (1996). 'Quality as Primacy of the Practical', *Qualitative Inquiry*, 2 (1), 41-56.

Kelly, L. Burton, S. and Reagan, L. (1994). 'Researching Women's Lives or Studying Women's Oppression? Reflections on What Constitutes Feminist Research', in M. Maynard and J. Purvis (eds.). *Researching Women's Lives from a Feminist Perspective*. London: Taylor and Francis, 27-48.

Maguire, P. (1996). 'Considering more Feminist Participatory Research: What's Congruency Got to do with it?', *Qualitative Inquiry*, 2 (1), 106-18.

Marshall, J. (1992). 'Researching women in management as a way of life', *Journal of Management Education and Development*, 23 (3), 279-87.

Marshall, J. (1995). *Women Managers: Moving On*. London: Routledge.

Reason, P. (eds.) (1988). *Human Inquiry in Action*. London: Sage Publications.

Reason, P. and Heron, J. (1995). 'Co-operative inquiry', in R. Harre, J. Smith and L. Van Langenhove. *Rethinking methods in psychology*. London: Sage Publications.

Reason, P. and Marshall, J. (1987). 'Research as personal process', in D. Boud and V. Griffin (eds.). *Appreciating Adult Learning*. London: Kogan Page.

Reinharz, S. (1992). *Feminist Methods in Social Research*. New York: Oxford University Press.

Stanley, L. and Wise, S. (1990). 'Method, methodology and epistemology in feminist research processes', in L. Stanley (ed.). *Feminist Praxis: Research, Theory and Epistemology in Feminist Sociology*. London: Routledge, 20-60.

Tanton, M. (ed.) (1994). *Women in management: A developing presence*. London: Routledge.

What should we do with cyberfeminism?

Alison Adam

Department of Computation, UMIST, P.O. Box 88, Manchester M60 1QD

Abstract

This paper begins by discussing the need to establish theoretical perspectives for gender and computing research. It explores the possibilities inherent in cyberfeminism as one potential theoretical position for bringing together feminist theory and gender and computing research. I look to the intellectual roots of cyberfeminism in cyberculture and Donna Haraway's (1991) writing before describing Sadie Plant's views on cyberfeminism. I conclude that cyberfeminism, in its present form, appears too problematic to be rescued for those seeking feminist theoretical positions on which to base gender and computing research. The reasons are as follows. Cyberfeminism shows little engagement with the growing body of empirical research which shows many negative aspects of women's experiences of ICTs. It adheres to a technological determinism which takes the technology as given and immutable and even mystifies it to the point of being inaccurate about its capabilities. It barely engages with mainstream feminism. Most importantly, in standing apart from politics, it offers an escapism which cannot substantiate its claim to make women's lives better. Nevertheless cyberfeminism offers valuable lessons in thinking about a way forward in gender and computing research.

1. Establishing Theoretical Positions

This paper takes it for granted that women working in computing, particularly those undertaking research on gender, no longer want to be told what they already know in 'doom and gloom' scenarios of women's absence from the world of computing. This is not to deny the continuing value of empirical case studies and reports both of harassment and inequality and of empowerment and success. I acknowledge the increasing maturity of gender and computing research, at least at an international level, if not so much in the UK, but at the same time it is still a very small enterprise. Instead of asking the traditional question of how we can get more women into computing, I want to explore the possibility of a theoretical basis for gender and computing research.

This is not to suggest that there should be only one such stance for research. In many disciplines, clearly much of the best research emerges from the creative synergy resulting from different viewpoints. However, I argue that there is now a pressing need to establish appropriate theoretical bases for gender and computing research. Why should this be so? Part of the reason can be found in the understandable response of assuming that arguments from feminist theory, social sciences and philosophy do not really belong to gender and computing research which emanates from computing departments. This view is predicated on the idea that such research will be tainted by too much social science input and will not be taken seriously amongst computing peers. Even if lip-service is paid to the importance of interdisciplinary research, in an academic world where formal assessments of the value of research are increasingly the order of the day, interdisciplinary research is much harder to evaluate and understand. As Susan Leigh Star (1995: 89), a sociologist who has spent a number of years working closely with computer scientists, so aptly puts it:

> . . . most computer scientists are contemptuous of social science, especially qualitative social science and especially sociology. . . . The values of quantification . . . are deeply embedded in that community. Numbers, algorithms, abstractions are valued over qualities, emotions, and deep descriptions. These values are linked with precision, portability, and speed.

Yet as Star points out in her essay, computer scientists need social scientists, not least in the analysis of mistakes and, worse, disasters created in the wake of large-scale information systems problems. Somewhat uneasily, computer scientists are turning to social scientists to learn about social change, organisations and the ethical consequences of the systems they engineer.

Now it seems to me that there is an, albeit milder, version of Star's problem at work in gender and computing research. Anyone tackling research on gender, within an academic computing environment, will have trouble being taken seriously anyway amongst mainstream peers, no matter what their theoretical position. This is one of the battles that organisations such as WiC (the UK's Women into Computing) have fought over the years and it is to WiC's credit that it has succeeded in having the topic aired on a number of occasions with senior (usually male) colleagues. But what I am arguing here is that a view of gender and computing research which shies away from the help it can get from the social sciences, in order to try to locate itself more in mainstream computing, is limiting itself and threatens to move into a downward spiral. Gender and computing research get no degree of comfort from mainstream computing. Other than performing more headcounts, an activity which is statistical rather than computational, gender and computing research is not amenable to the formal, parametrised, algorithmic expression enjoyed by mainstream computer science. Furthermore, gender and computing research which avoids social science and tries to remain in the mainstream itself disguises a tendency towards a particular political position. This is the position of *liberal feminism* which has been criticized by Flis Henwood (1993), amongst others.

Liberal feminism takes the view that science, technology, and hence information and communications technologies too, are inherently neutral. It is based on the idea that it is enough to find ways of getting more women into the various science and engineering disciplines for a situation of equality to prevail. This is broadly the view that various women into science and engineering (WISE) campaigns have taken over the years. The problem with such a view is that it is essentially conservative and undertheorised. It does not offer a substantial analysis of why technical disciplines should be unattractive to women in the first place. It asks for no change to be made in the parent disciplines, nor indeed in the men who dominate these disciplines. The onus is all on women to make changes and they are seen to be somehow at fault for not entering technical professions in droves. This suggests that initiatives to get more women into science and engineering, based on this view, are likely to be limited in their success unless they can somehow effect a consciousness-raising exercise on men and indeed schoolboys (e.g., perhaps we should have 'get your son to do the housework' days alongside 'take your daughter to work' days).

I have, perhaps, presented the liberal feminist position in its extreme form and I am aware that much gender and computing work, even if it started off from such a position, has moved to a stance which is much more aware of the subtleties of the forces at work in 'gendering' computing and other technical domains. Nevertheless, I believe that this view acts as a kind of 'common sense' base point which is still widely prevalent in the computing profession. The problem is, then, that if measures to improve the lot of women in computing are only, at best, partially successful and if research based on this view reports time and time again the same situations prevailing, then this is a position which does not move gender and computing research forward. It retells the same story with no obvious means of improvement and hence the downward spiral.

2. Is There an Alternative to Liberal Feminism?

It is, of course, all too easy to criticise a liberal position without being able offer convincing alternatives. However, I believe that alternatives are appearing and that those involved in gender and computing research, especially the traditional WiC audience, are in a good position to evaluate the alternatives. But I think that this is more than just an intellectual exercise. It is actually extremely important that gender and computing researchers critically evaluate new theoretical positions. This is partly because such positions make claims about how women are using information and communication technologies, in other words, things that are very dear to the heart of a WiC audience. Additionally and importantly, theoretical positions may make claims about the capabilities of the technology which technically informed women are in an advantageous position to evaluate.

3. The Intellectual Roots of Cyberfeminism

With this in mind I consider what is on offer in 'cyberfeminism', a feminist position in relation to gender and computing. This is by no means the only theoretical position on offer, and as will be clear from what follows, I do not believe ultimately that it offers a substantial enough basis for gender and computing research. Nevertheless, it has received attention both in the media and in academic circles, and at least for that reason cyberfeminism deserves critical appraisal.

The intellectual parentage of cyberfeminism can be examined from the twin areas of cyberculture and the cyborg imagery of Donna Haraway's (1991) much quoted, *A Cyborg Manifesto*. Sadie Plant, as cyberfeminism's main British exponent, suggests that women are using the new technology to their own ends, with the pleasing image of women subverting the internet for their own ambitions in a cyberfeminism that, following cyberculture itself, tries to set itself above and beyond politics. Yet, tellingly, empirical studies do not support Plant's arguments and there are a number of distinct problems which I wish to explore. Despite this, Plant suggests that it offers several valuable lessons in the process of bringing feminist theory to bear on gender and computing research, even if it cannot be rescued in its present form.

3.1 What is Cyberculture?

It is difficult to elaborate a discussion of cyberfeminism without first examining the concept of cyberculture to which, in an intellectual sense, it bears such a strong affinity. Cyberculture is the term often used to describe the upsurge of interest in cultures developing around virtual reality (VR), the internet and artificial intelligence. There is a futuristic tone to cyberculture, although it does not speak with a uniformly utopian voice. It is noteworthy that, for social scientists, the computing 'problem' of the immediately preceding intellectual generation in the shape of office automation spawned only a limited amount of interest within the social sciences. Yet cyberculture has proved to hold an enormous appeal and has speedily generated a number of anthologies (e.g. Dovey 1996, Ess 1996, Shields 1996). It also makes good copy for daily newspapers which in reporting the latest 'cybercrime' are clearly not averse to playing on the salacious nature of harassment of women on the internet (see, for example, *The Guardian*, tabloid section, 7 January 1997).

Cyberculture occupies a curious intellectual position in relation to other cultural movements, not least of all feminism. In setting itself up as a youth centred counter-culture which apparently challenges the established social order, we might expect that it would align itself with a more general world view which is critical of the progress of science and technology. Yet cyberculture is nowhere to be found in these debates, either on the popular front or in the academy. In a sense, this is not perhaps surprising, as for all cyberculture's counter-cultural pretensions, it is deeply conservative, not least in its acceptance of all that computer technology apparently has to offer. Such a position rests squarely on a technological determinism which is uncritical of technological advances, which accepts as inevitable that technology will be used in a particular way and which also relies on developments in technology which may or may not ever happen; e.g., intelligent computers or completely realistic virtual reality environments. For cyberculture to be overly critical of science and technology would be to bite the hand that feeds it.

Cyberculture is a youth culture and in particular appeals to young men. It conjures up the idea of cybercafes and alternative cyberculture magazines. It has been strongly influenced by cyberpunk science fiction novels such as William Gibson's (1984) *Neuromancer*. Cyberpunk visions of the future are distinctly negative. These are views of a future where technology has gone wrong, where the only alternative to living in the vast urban sprawls or desolate no-go areas in between is to 'jack in' to 'cyberspace' as a way of transcending the mere 'meat' of the body, suggesting a particularly masculine form of a retreat from bodies and places where bodies exist.

The concept of transcending the 'meat' of the body is not confined to science fiction. It is also seriously considered amongst some computer scientists who see it as a way of creating computational offspring. We only have to look to the writing of a well-known mainstream AI roboticist, whose work developed apparently quite separately from and rather earlier than cybercultural influences. Hans Moravec (1988) proposed the idea of *Mind Children*. His views on this are more akin to science fiction than pragmatic engineering as he imagines a 'postbiological' world where we have downloaded our minds and where our children are machines rather than human beings. Sue Curry Jansen (1988:6) has pointed to the way in which several AI scientists express their dream of creating their own robots, of 'becoming father of oneself'.

The second aspect of a meat-free existence, and one which does seem to be more important to the rhetoric of cyberculture than artificial birth, is the idea of transcendence and escape. This point is so important that some authors (Schroeder 1994) suggest that this explains much of cyberculture's appeal as a means of producing new psychic and artistic experiences which seem to go beyond ordinary uses of technology. Most obviously this provides a seemingly healthy and legal alternative to drug culture where virtual reality and internet technologies offer an endless supply of new experiences. Ralph Schroeder (ibid.: 525) sees a tension between the technical problems which may or may not ever be solved (e.g. the way that virtual worlds are still cartoon versions of reality) and the world view of human wish-fulfilment which has been projected onto the technology. Added to this tension is apparent contradiction of the bleak view of the future which cyberpunk offers. But if the dystopia of cyberpunk is to be believed, then there is perhaps all the more reason to escape into cyberspace. Yet escape and transcendence seem to be particularly masculine views. Women's lives involve so much invisible labour in the looking after of bodily material things it is hard to imagine them having the time, let alone the inclination, to drift about in cyberspace in this way.

3.2 Cyberculture and feminism

I do not think it would be surprising if cyberculture, as I have described it above, held but limited appeal for women. Before exploring this I want to make it clear that I am not saying that women cannot or should not use whatever cyberculture has to offer by way of self fulfilment. However, I argue that there are several reasons for the apparent lack of appeal. The first aspect concerns the transcendence of the body, which is a particularly masculine form of reasoning. This has generated a central argument in feminist philosophy against forms of reasoning which split the mind from the body and elevate mental reasoning over bodily knowledge (Lloyd 1984). I do not wish to suggest that women are somehow more in touch with their biologies than men are, as such a view is in danger of slipping into an essentialism which sees women as having essential fixed characteristics determined by their biology. Yet several authors (Harding 1991; Rose 1994) have noted that women's work often involves looking after bodies, cleaning and feeding the young, old and the sick. It involves looking after men's bodily requirements too in what Hilary Rose (ibid.) has termed, women's 'compulsory altruism' which is also an invisible altruism. Looking after bodily needs is a process which sinks into invisibility and leaves men free to live the higher status life of the mind. Small wonder that transcending the body should have become associated with masculinist modes of reasoning and should be reflected, not only in the work of AI roboticists but also in the desire of cyberculture enthusiasts to leave the body behind in cyberspace.

Bodily transcendence is one problem with cyberculture, but a potentially more important issue for the development of new theoretical approaches to gender and computing is cyberculture's pretence to exist beyond the reaches of political concerns. This shows up as a style which lacks criticism and which, in turn, is demonstrated in several different ways. First of all, popular cyberculture rests on a technological determinism against which both modern science and technology studies, and gender and technology research have argued. For cyberculture, technological determinism is a view which takes technological development as inevitable, as having its own inner logic, and sees technology as having immutable effects on society, rather than, possibly, the other way round. Cyberculture makes predictions about the sort of technology we will have ten, twenty or fifty years in the future. But, importantly, such technological predictions also carry along with them predictions of how technology will be used. For instance, the prediction that the widespread availability of teleshopping will mean that women will sit at home making purchases is an empirical issue which can only be determined by studies of spending patterns as the technology becomes available. Statements about the availability of intelligent robots fifty years hence does not mean that we *have* to use them in any particular way or that we must download our minds into their bodies. Such views ignore the ways in which technology may be used which its originators did not predict. There are many examples of this. In this respect Judy Wajcman (1995) sees the relationship between technological and social change as fundamentally indeterminate. Women often have the means to disrupt the original purposes of a technology.

> The designers and promoters of a technology cannot completely predict or control its final uses. There are always unintended consequences and unanticipated possibilities. For example, when, as a result of the organized movement of people with physical disabilities in the United States, buildings and pavements were redesigned to improve mobility, it was not envisaged that these reforms would help women manoeuvering prams around cities. It is important not to underestimate women's capacity to subvert the intended purposes of technology and turn it to their collective advantage. (ibid.: 199)

3.3 Cyborgs

I have argued that popular cyberculture may not be very appealing to women because of its desire to transcend the body and its lack of criticism of technological determinism. However, cyberfeminism has a second intellectual parent in the cyborg imagery developed in Donna Haraway's *A Cyborg Manifesto* (1991). Haraway writes of the cyborg, or cybernetic organism, a fusion of human and machine. The idea of the cyborg comes from cyberpunk fiction and film but also predates it in older images of the fusion of human and machine, e.g. as in Frankenstein's monster. The cyborg is hardly a feminist invention, indeed in its manifestation in films such as *Terminator* and *Robocop* it represents masculine destruction. In Haraway's writing the cyborg becomes a blurring, a transgression and a deliberate confusion of boundaries of the self and machine, a concern with what makes us human and how we define humanity. In our reliance on spectacles, hearing aids, pacemakers, dentures, dental crowns, artificial joints, not to mention computers, faxes, modems and networks, we are all cyborgs, 'fabricated hybrids of machine and organism' (ibid.). The cyborg is to be a creature of a post-gendered world. As the boundary between human and animal has been thoroughly breached, so too has the boundary between human and machine. Although it might not be clear, at first sight, why this should be important, the notion of boundary transgression in Haraway's writing has been taken up by feminist writers who have seen it as a way of blurring troubling dualisms of masculine–feminine, body–mind and so on.

Although the idea of transgressing boundaries in Haraway's work has been extremely influential in recent feminist writing, it does not seem to have permeated gender and computing research to a great degree, at least gender and computing research in the UK which situates itself in computing. Part of this may be the language she uses, but it also may relate to the rather abstract nature of the cyborg which may not, on the surface, seem to have much to say to the pragmatic concerns of a WiC audience. But rather than assuming that Haraway's *Cyborg Manifesto* is somehow 'not for us', considering its influence in cyberculture and feminism in general, it may yet have something to offer more empirical gender and computing research.

4. What is Cyberfeminism?

Both popular cyberculture and Haraway's writing, in its role in generating interest in feminist cyborg studies, have been involved in producing the offspring of cyberfeminism. But what is cyberfeminism? Sadie Plant (1996: 182) describes it as 'an insurrection on the part of the goods and material of the patriarchal world, a dispersed, distributed emergence composed of links between women, women and computers, computers and communication links, connections and connectionist nets'. Shields (1996: 9) argues that cyberfeminism takes advantage of the ambiguities of boundaries and the amoral nature of cyberspace. It is the transgressing of and the process of making ambiguous boundaries which it inherits from Haraway's cyborg feminism. 'Rather than new relations between women and men, the amoral quality of Net ethics throws into question essentialized identities and dualistic sexual categories. . . . Instead, notions of authenticity, of essential femininity and of the self are displaced in favour of multiple roles, alternative personae and a matrix of potentialities.' (ibid.)

Yet Judith Squires (1996: 195) has been particularly critical of what this offers:

> . . . whilst there *may* be potential for an alliance between cyborg imagery and a materialist-feminism, this potential has been largely submerged beneath a sea of technophoric cyberdrool. If we are to salvage the image of the cyborg we would do well to insist that cyberfeminism be seen as a metaphor for addressing the inter-relation between technology and the body, not as a means of using the former to transcend the latter.

Squires argues that cyberfeminism tends to the same position with regard to the transcendence of the body, as cyberculture in general, and it also shares with cyberculture the unrealistic desire to be apolitical, to stand outside traditional moral boundaries. Squires's critique of cyberfeminism centres round the writing of Sadie Plant, self-declared cyberfeminist. There is no doubt that Plant has done more than possibly any other writer, at least in the UK, to bring issues of women and cybernetic futures to a more popular audience (see for example Plant (1993)). Squires describes Plant's approach as one which 'shares the apoliticism of the cyberpunks but also invokes a kind of mystical utopianism of the eco-feminist earth-goddesses'. (Squires 1996: 204) Part of the problem is the tendency to see women's experiences as universal, which on the one hand denies the individuality of experience and on the other distances itself from actual empirical findings. This is demonstrated in statements such as: 'Women . . . have always found ways of circumventing the dominant systems of communication . . .' (Plant 1993: 13); 'they [women] are . . . discovering new possibilities for work, play and communication of all kinds in the spaces emergent from the telecoms revolution'. (Plant 1995: 28); 'Women are accessing the circuits on which they were once exchanged . . .' (Plant 1996: 170)

4.1 What's Wrong with Cyberfeminism?

I shall return to the question of how far cyberfeminism takes on board, wholesale, cyberculture's transcendence of the body, its apoliticism and technological determinism, towards the end of this section. First of all I want to look at the question of who are the women and what is the technology addressed in cyberfeminist writing.

In the absence of empirical evidence it is difficult to know who the women are in Plant's writing. This is particularly important as there is a rapidly growing number of studies looking at the ways in which women are using information and communications technologies. The possibilities for women to turn technologies towards their own ends and uses – an important positive message arising from feminist studies of technology – is considerably diluted and is also open to criticism if we merely assume that women are subverting technology without empirical evidence to back it up.

Empirical studies suggest that the picture is extremely complex and ambivalent. On the one side there is evidence of women feeling empowered by their use of information technology. For instance, witness the responses to the formation of a direct-action feminist group against internet censorship at Carnegie Mellon University, picturesquely styled the 'Clitoral Hoods': 'We're big girls who don't need to be protected from horny geek fantasies.' (Riley 1996: 159)

On the other hand, there are negative experiences and some authors take the view that, for example, the internet reinforces and magnifies stereotypical gendered behaviours rather than smoothing them out and acting as the great leveller that some desire. Susan Herring's (1996) well-researched study of interactions on the internet shows that computer-mediated communication does not neutralize gender. She found women as a group are more likely to use supportive behaviour whilst men were more likely to favour adversarial interactions. These she linked to men favouring individual freedom while women favour harmonious interpersonal interaction. Such behaviours and values can be seen as important in reinforcing male dominance and female submission. Carol Adams's (1996) study of cyberpornography supports Herring's research. Adams found that interactions on the internet magnified and reinforced inequalities found in real life.

If those whose intellectual home is computing find Haraway's cyborg writing challenging, they may find Plant's rather mystical style of writing heavy going. Nevertheless, it is important that the 'technically informed' analyze what is being claimed in the name of information and communication technologies in cyberfeminism. There is a reverential tone with which Plant describes 'complex dynamics, self-organizing systems, nanotechnology, machine intelligence'. (Plant 1995: 28) The 'connectionist machine is an indeterminate process, rather than a definite entity. . . . Parallel distributed processing defies all attempts to pin it down, and can only ever be contingently defined. It also turns the computer into a complex thinking machine which converges with the operations of the human brain.' (Plant 1996: 174—5) Attributing an almost mystical quality to aspects of computer design or technology is more pervasive than one might imagine and seems to be a rhetorical trick favoured by cyberculture. On the one hand this side-steps the necessity of having to understand the actual workings of the technology and on the other it leaves untouched a determinism which regards the technology as having a will of its own.

This can be seen, for instance, in the concept of 'emergence' to which Plant alludes.

Emergence is the idea that higher-order behaviours emerge from computer systems programmed with lower-order behaviours. In the artificial life domain (Helmreich 1994), which is related to artificial intelligence, populations are modelled in a computer environment and such populations may thrive or dwindle according to a kind of artificial evolution. For instance, artificial birds might be programmed with the low-level behaviours of avoiding obstacles and keeping close to the next nearest artificial bird. When 'released' in their artificial environment these artificial bird show a tendency to 'flock' like real birds. Flocking is an emergent phenomenon. But the philosopher Daniel Dennett warns against efforts to mystify emergence which make it seem somehow more than the sum of its parts. (Crevier 1993) This is not a version of HAL in 2001 taking over from less efficient humans; it is merely a convenient level of describing computational phenomena.

The question of women's actual experiences and the mystification of technology are problematic enough for cyberfeminism. However, I argue that the most important problem with cyberfeminism, at least in the version that Plant describes, is the loss of the political project. It seems to adhere to a version of liberal feminism which I criticize towards the beginning of the paper as maintaining the status quo without challenge. In fact, Kira Hall (1996) describes two possibilities for cyberfeminism in terms of *radical cyberfeminism* and *liberal feminism.* Radical feminism refers to the development of the numerous women-only on-line bulletin boards and newsgroups in response to male harassment. Liberal feminism, Hall identifies, is a view involving a gender-free utopia influenced by feminist science fiction where women's sexual liberation is seen as all that is necessary for equality and where freedom of self-expression is emphasized. However, it is far from clear why this should produce a better world for women.

One of the problems is that cyberfeminism just does not engage with mainstream Anglo-American feminism. If it did, I argue that it could not possibly maintain its apolitical stance. In fact, it is odd, in a way, that the phenomenon is called 'cyberfeminism' at all, as it seems to set itself apart from feminism's politics. The apparent absence of a political agenda is reinforced by the alliance of cyberfeminism to cyberpunk, science fiction versions of cyberculture which are deliberately alienated from politics, albeit thinly disguising a masculinist view underneath. Far from giving a setting where women can take charge and subvert the original technology, Stephanie Brail's (1996) report of being stalked by anonymous email messages and Carol Adams' (1996) study of cyberpornography suggest that cyberspace reproduces and magnifies many traditional aspects of male and female interaction. For critics such as Squires (1996: 208), this is the most disturbing part of cyberfeminism. Cyberpunk does not pretend to hope for a better world, in fact much of its force seems to derive from the vivid picture it paints of negative, alienating future technology. Plant is claiming that cyberfeminism offers women a better future, but how could a movement so strongly linked to something as negative as cyberpunk offer a better future for women without the addition of a strongly positive political input — something which is currently missing.

5. Conclusion – Can Cyberfeminism be Saved?

I argue that cyberfeminism in its present form appears too problematic to be rescued for those seeking feminist theoretical positions on which to base gender and computing research. My reasons are based on the preceding discussion. Cyberfeminism shows little engagement with the empirical research which demonstrates many negative aspects of women's experiences of ICTs. It adheres to a technological determinism which takes the technology as given and immutable and even mystifies it to the point of being inaccurate about its capabilities. It offers a version of escapism rather than trying to include the role of the body. It barely engages with mainstream feminism. Most importantly, in standing apart from politics, it cannot substantiate its claim to make women's lives better.

However, attempting a critical exercise such as this at least allows us to draw some valuable lessons in beginning the process of establishing theoretical positions in gender and computing research. The first lesson concerns the need to keep hold of the value of empirical research which reflects the changing experiences of women using information technologies. The second lesson involves the need to relate empirical studies to feminist theory and there is evidence that this is already happening in gender and computing research (e.g. see Adam et al. 1994, Green et al. 1993, Grundy 1996, Vehvilainen 1997). This point also relates to the question of politics. The best kind of feminist research involves a strong sense of political project which exposes and chips away at inequalities and offers scope for change. To pretend to be beyond politics leaves the whole process open to market forces and such an argument cannot be used to substantiate a claim that women's lives could be made better. The final points relate to technology. As so much energy in feminism has been directed towards studies of the body, gender and computing, research needs to find ways of incorporating women's bodily work and presence rather than slavishly following the masculinist cyberpunk desire to leave the body behind. Accepting this would also be a step towards transcending technological determinism, particularly as feminist studies of technology (e.g. Wajcman 1991) have done so much to banish determinism in showing that women have real choices about how they may use technology.

References

Adam, A.; Emms, J.; Green, E. and Owen, J. (eds.) (1994). *IFIP Transactions A-57, Women, Work and Computerization: Breaking Old Boundaries — Building New Forms.* Amsterdam: Elsevier/ North-Holland.

Adams, C. J. (1996). '"This is not our fathers' pornography": sex lies and computers', in Ess, C. (ed.) *Philosophical Perspectives on Computer-Mediated Communication*, 147-170. Albany, NY: State University of New York Press.

Brail, S. (1996). 'The price of admission: harassment and free speech in the wild, wild west', in Cherny, L. and Weise, E. R. (eds.) *wired_women: Gender and New Realities in Cyberspace*, 141–70. Seattle, WA: Seal Press.

Crevier, D. (1993). *AI: The Tumultuous History of the Search for Artificial Intelligence.* New York: Basic Books.

Dovey, J. (ed.) (1996). *Fractal Dreams: New Media in Social Context* . London: Lawrence and Wishart.

Ess, C. (ed.) (1996). *Philosophical Perspectives on Computer-Mediated Communication.* Albany, NY: State University of New York Press.

Gibson, W. (1984). *Neuromancer.* London: Harper Collins.

Green, E.; Owen, J. and Pain, D. (eds.) (1993). *Gendered by Design? Information Technology and Office Systems.* London: Taylor and Francis.

Grundy, F. (1996). *Women and Computers.* Exeter: Intellect Books.

Hall, K. (1996). 'Cyberfeminism', in Herring, S. (ed) *Computer-Mediated Communication: Linguistic, Social and Cross-Cultural Perspectives*, 147-70. Amsterdam and Philadelphia: John Benjamins Publishing.

Haraway, D. (1991). 'A cyborg manifesto: science, technology and Socialist-feminism in the late twentieth century', in Haraway, D. *Simians, Cyborgs and Women: The Reinvention of Nature*, 149-81. London: Free Association Books. (Originally published in Socialist Review 80 (1985): 65–107.)

Harding, S. (1991). *Whose Science? Whose Knowledge?: Thinking from Women's Lives*. Milton Keynes: Open University Press.

Helmreich, S. (1994). 'Anthropology inside and outside the looking-glass worlds of artificial life'. Unpublished paper, Department of Anthropology, Stanford University, Stanford, CA. (Available from author at this address or by email on stefang@leland.stanford.edu)

Henwood, F. (1993). 'Establishing gender perspectives on information technology: problems, issues and opportunities', in Green, E., Owen, J. and Pain, D. (eds.). *Gendered by Design? Information Technology and Office Systems*. 31-49. London: Taylor and Francis.

Herring, S. (1996). 'Posting in a different voice: gender and ethics in CMC', in Ess, C. (ed.). *Philosophical Perspectives on Computer-Mediated Communication*, 115-45. Albany, NY: State University of New York Press.

Jansen, S. C. (1988). 'The ghost in the machine: artificial intelligence and gendered thought patterns'. *Resources for Feminist Research* 17: 4-7.

Lloyd, G. (1984). *The Man of Reason: 'Male' and 'Female' in Western Philosophy*. Minneapolis: University of Minnesota Press.

Moravec, H. (1988). *Mind Children: The Future of Robot and Human Intelligence*. Cambridge, MA and London: Harvard University Press.

Plant, S. (1993). 'Beyond the screens: film, cyberpunk and cyberfeminism'. *Variant* 14 (Summer 1993): 12-17.

Plant, S. (1995). 'Babes in the net'. *New Statesman and Society* (27 January): 28.

Plant, S. (1996). 'On the matrix: cyberfeminist simulations', in Shields, R. (ed.). *Cultures of the Internet: Virtual Spaces, Real Histories, Living Bodies*, 170-83. London, Thousand Oaks, CA and New Delhi: Sage.

Riley, D.M. (1996). 'Sex, fear and condescension on campus: cybercensorship at Carnegie Mellon', in Cherny, L. and Weise, E.R. (eds.). *wired_women: Gender and New Realities in Cyberspace*, 158-68. Seattle, WA: Seal Press.

Rose, H. (1994). *Love, Power and Knowledge: Towards a Feminist Transformation of the Sciences*. Cambridge: Polity Press.

Schroeder, R. (1994). 'Cyberculture, cyborg post-modernism and the sociology of virtual reality technologies: surfing the soul in the information age'. *Futures* 26 (5): 519-28.

Shields, R. (ed.) (1996). *Cultures of the Internet: Virtual Spaces, Real Histories, Living Bodies*. London, Thousand Oaks, CA and New Delhi: Sage.

Squires, J. (1996). 'Fabulous feminist futures and the lure of cyberculture', in Dovey , J.(ed.). *Fractal Dreams: New Media in Social Context*, 194-216. London: Lawrence & Wishart.

Star, S.L. (1995). 'The politics of formal representations: wizards, gurus and organizational complexity', in Star, S.L. (ed.). *Ecologies of Knowledge: Work and Politics in Science and Technology*, 88-118. Albany, NY: SUNY Press.

Vehvilainen, M. (1997). *Gender, Expertise and Information Technology*. Faculty of Economics and Administration, University of Tampere, Finland.

Wajcman, J. (1991). *Feminism Confronts Technology*. Cambridge: Polity Press.

Wajcman, J. (1995). 'Feminist theories of technology', in Jasanoff, S. , Markel, G., Petersen, J. and Pinch, T. (eds.). *Handbook of Science and Technology Studies*, 189-204. Thousand Oaks, CA, London and New Delhi: Sage.

Transparent Relations in Research on Women and Computing

Linda Stepulevage

Department of Innovation Studies, University of East London

Abstract

One of the main approaches used by feminist social scientists to explain women's relationship to computing is its social construction as a masculine site of knowledge, skills and high status employment. In these analyses, women are seen to struggle to maintain an identity that is locally appropriate to their situation as women in a male domain. In this paper, I take a lesbian perspective that is informed by educational background and working experience in both the social sciences and computer science, to explore how a social construction of computing as masculine may keep some women out of computing, and can sometimes even fail to take account of the experiences of women computer scientists themselves.

Studies on women's positioning in the domain of computing tend to be grounded in a perspective of gender that implicitly assumes heterosexuality. In this paper I refer to this perspective as hetero-gendered, i.e. one in which gender is socially constructed as a masculine / feminine dualism, embedded in heterosexuality. In exploring the gendered construction of computing, I want to show how a feminist analysis of its social construction as masculine that examines gender relations with reference to heterosexuality can contribute to an understanding of how the field retains existing power relations between women and men.

1. Introduction

One of the main approaches used by feminist social scientists to explain women's relationship to computing is its social construction and reconstruction as a masculine site of knowledge, skills and high status employment (Gill and Grint 1995; Wajcman 1993). In these studies, the experiences of the women who work as computer professionals, in design, programming, network management, etc. and in academia do not tend to be the focus of explorations of computing knowledge, practice and culture. The women referred to in most of these studies are usually end-users and/or operators of computer systems, such as data entry clerks or operators of word-processors (there are exceptions such as Webster 1996). When women computer professionals are the focus of discussion, it is usually from a perspective concerned with equality issues, i.e. the numbers of women taking computer science courses or in working in professional computer jobs. Some women computer professionals have written about their own experiences (e.g. Bodker and Greenbaum 1993; Grundy 1994), but a discourse of women's invisibility persists in feminist social science research on women and computing.

In this paper, I explore a possible link between women's invisibility and the masculine construction of computing. It moves outside the taken-for-granted discourse of gender relations in social construction studies, and questions whether research focused on the social construction of computing as masculine, and therefore excluding of women, adequately explains why some women are *in* computing.

The concept of transparency is standardly used in computing with reference to considerations of interface design and the attempt to make the complexity of the underlying processes transparent or invisible to the user of the computer system. In this paper, I hope to show how explanations of women's positioning that identify the domain of computing as masculine tend to be grounded in a perspective of gender that implicitly assumes heterosexuality as a *transparent* relation. I refer to this perspective as hetero-gendered, i.e. one in which gender is socially constructed as a masculine/feminine dualism, embedded in heterosexuality. In hetero-gendered analyses, women tend to be seen as struggling to maintain an identity that is locally appropriate to their situation as female in a male domain. The only subjectivity ever presented as an alternative to this dynamic positioning is to become 'one of the boys'. In my past experience as a programmer and systems designer, and currently as a tutor, I am in contact with women who approach computers as a familiar technology. In most social construction studies, however, it is usually the women who consider computing as something alien who are implicitly taken as the norm. Women who have a different sort of relationship to computing are usually described, explicitly or implicitly as 'one of the boys', embedding their identity in a hetero-gendered norm. This taken-for-granted dualism offers a limited and limiting view of how women construct their identity. I argue that an alternative perspective, located outside this dualism, be used to explore how women might locate themselves within the male dominant domain of computing.

2. Lesbian Positioning

Just as the social relations of the creation of scientific knowledge construct 'truths' that can be held in place through practices based on reduction, abstraction and rationality (Harding 1986), the taken-for-granted duality of masculine/feminine gender relations can be seen to be held in place or constituted through practices based on heterosexuality (Butler 1990). It is not heterosexuality itself that I focus on as the problem, but how it is used to regulate and maintain power relations. It is these hetero-gender relations that I think can help explain why women remain invisible in examinations of computing as a masculine domain, and may help explain why women choose or reject computing as an area of study and/or as an employment possibility.

The explanations in feminist writings about why so few women choose computing, when not concerned with equity issues, usually deal with the social construction of women's needs, wants and preferences within a taken-for-granted heterosexual world, e.g. one where women have domestic and family responsibilities and men do not have them. Kitzinger (1993) discusses how this construction contributes to the invisibility of lesbians and gay men through an analysis of students' common responses to the mention of lesbians. Most students in her classes assert that lesbians are the same as everybody else, the everybody else being heterosexual. (10) This treating everyone as the same, i.e. as heterosexual, is also the common practice in the feminist literature on computing. That the world of lesbians and gay men is profoundly different is beginning to be documented and discussed (see Wilton 1995). While it seems reasonable to assume that all women move within a heterosexual world, some women, i.e. lesbians, negotiate relationships outside it as well. Lesbians have become used to interrogating what is assumed for others as the taken-for-granted way to be. (Wilkinson and Kitzinger 1993) As Phelan (1993) notes, those of us who identify as lesbians have had to invent or fashion ourselves out of 'a whole network of identity and power relations'(775), and the very process of 'becoming' lesbian in a hostile world can offer insights that may be invisible to many heterosexuals. It is from this lesbian positioning, one which interrogates the assumed and transforms the taken-for-granted, that I argue for research studies to consider the interrelationship between computing and gender and heterosexuality. By making feminist analyses of the social construction of computing that take hetero-gender relations into account, we can build on the contributions already made and further develop an understanding of how the computer field retains its existing power relations.

3. Transparency in Gender Relations

In another paper, I examine research dealing with women's experiences on conventional computer science courses (Stepulevage in press), and show how questions concerning women's hesitancy to aspire to scientific and/or technical competence and expertise usually deal with the hetero-gender relations that constrain women, even though the analyses do not identify this constraint as such. I interpreted these studies as implying that if women are to keep their feminine gender identity, they must remain 'other' in relation to men. The logical extension of this relation is that women must be vigilant in their performance of heterosexuality, or at least should not transgress the boundaries of the local heterosexual culture, otherwise they lose their identity as women.

Mahony and Van Toen (1990), in discussing women's relationship to computing, ask the question, 'Who, after all, would want to go into a field that privileges and admires the stereotypes of the obsessional and anti-social hacker and the techno-freak who uses his technical mastery as a form of macho posturing?' (326). Their question provides a clear example of this dualism. Analyses like these imply that any woman who moves outside what is locally deemed to be 'normal' is in danger of being identified in terms of deviance (in this case, anti-social behaviour, etc.). The affect on women of constructing an identity associated with deviance is significant in a world of masculine/feminine duality. In this world, a linkage of biological sex, gender role, gender identity and sexual object choice, i.e. heterosexuality, is implicit, and deviance from gender role indicates deviance from heterosexuality (Phelan 1993). Phelan goes on to warn that this linkage sometimes leads to the conflation of feminism with lesbianism, i.e. if you do not behave as a girl/woman should, you are on the road to becoming a lesbian. Rather than conflating deviance from local gender roles with women being lesbian, I agree with other researchers who show that the threat of being labelled lesbian is used to keep women in their place (Sheppard 1989; Epstein and Johnson 1994).

In the next section, I offer a few brief examples of how this hetero-gendering is applied in a computing magazine and in feminist writings about the experience of women computer professionals. I use the concept of lesbian positioning to begin to unpick the gender-computing relationship. The individual sexualities of any women in the studies discussed below are not the subject. The subject is the constraint for women of a continual maintenance of hetero-gendered relations and continual renegotiation within hetero-gendered positions.

4. Women in Computing

It is a well-documented association for women that being employed in 'men's work' means continual work at reproducing femininity, if you are concerned not to be seen as 'masculine' (Sheppard1989). Van Oost (1991) documents the ascription of deviance to women not performing their expected local heterosexual role. She quotes from a 1950's company study made prior to the computerization of a company's systems, in which the researcher

> '...found that there are a number of unmarried female managers who give rise, due to the character of their leadership, to tense relations with the personnel. Married men with children in particular complain about the lack of warmth in their style of leadership. The researcher would like to assume that in general male employees are not against female superiors, provided that they lead with a warm and somewhat motherly style.' (416)

Female managers were seen as one of the labour relations problems in this researcher's study. Van Oost cites this study to demonstrate sex-typing in jobs. In analysing this text from outside a hetero-gendered perspective, however, I believe it demonstrates what Wilton (1995:30) identifies as one of the commonalities in the definitions of 'a lesbian': lesbians as pseudo-males. An analysis of these female managers in relation to computing can also be seen to be about hetero-gender relations, especially as the writer of the study is overt in identifying unmarried women (the women who are not doing as they should) and married (the men who complain about them).

Mortberg (1994) raises the issue of sexuality in organisations, specifically male heterosexuality. She references researchers who have studied the reproduction of male dominance and power within organisations through practices such as sexual harassment. In discussing her research, she details how aspects of women's lives, such as responsibility for the family, present obstacles to their professional life. She considers the possibility of men changing their roles in family life as one way to deal with this 'family' obstacle. Even though she identifies male heterosexuality as problematic, this analysis is rooted in heterosexuality and heterosexual relations remain the norm. She makes an association between masculinity and technology/computing, and asks an interesting question: 'Do men take more responsibility for their children and domestic work because their masculine identity cannot be questioned because of their occupations' (381). She wonders whether some men can transgress the boundaries of traditional male spheres because of a secure masculine identity, one rooted in their computing work.

If we apply the logic of her question to women, it becomes problematic. When looking at the question from a hetero-gendered perspective, women's identity as female is secure only in the domestic sphere. This security in their identities as female, however, does not empower them to transgress the boundaries of traditional female spheres, gender relations being asymmetrical. Woman's identity as female comes into question when she positions herself in a masculine domain. Men doing 'housework' at home, on the other hand, would be seen favourably by women in employment. The option left open to women who wish to work in a masculine domain, then, is to reconstitute their identity as female by continuing to perform their role in the domestic sphere. If this analysis of gender relations had explored heterosexuality as a constraint rather than conflating heterosexuality with female subjectivity, it might have explored more possibilities for challenging and transforming the gender-technology relation. The next example of hetero-gendering, from the computing press, clearly demonstrates the 'family' situation discussed by Mortberg.

5. On the job with…

This section is based on quotes from an occasional series in *Computing* (1996) entitled 'On the job with…'. The series depended on the contributions of volunteers who work in computing. It consisted of text and photos of the people at their workplaces. The texts quoted below are from the beginning and end of day descriptions of an IT manager (9 May 96), a computing lecturer (13 Jun 96), an IT coordinator (21 Mar 96), and a network consultant (25 Jan 96).

IT manager

'07.00:   I spend an hour reading the trade press before catching my lift to work….'
'18.45:   I've had enough, and a glance at the clock confirms it's time to go home. It's a long day and it's hard graft, but working for a charity is incredibly worthwhile and beats a commercial IT job any day.'

Computing lecturer

' 06.15:   At home, I rise, get dressed and make breakfast for my family….'
'17.30:   …My working day is over, and it's time to drive the 21 miles back home. Hopefully, my husband will have cooked dinner.'

IT coordinator

'06.30:   Before I arrive at the office, I've already done what feels like a full day's work. …feeding hungry children and dogs, and sorting laundry…'
'17.00:   Finally, I head for home and the prospect of tired children—bathtime, bedtime, preparing supper and sorting laundry. Work? That's the easy part.'

Network consultant

'06.30:   A quick look in the diary to check what I've got arranged for the day. Today there area two meetings….'
'17.45:   The end of another day—almost. I often do some paperwork when I get home. After that it's a trip to my local pub for a quick drink and then back home to relax with my family.'

Three of the four people can be easily located within the heterosexual norm, the computing lecturer, the IT coordinator, and the network consultant. This is confirmed by the introductory paragraphs of the pieces (written in the third person) which describe each as married with various numbers of children. The IT manager, however, is not located within a domestic sphere. The introductory paragraph describes her career path in detail, but we are given no information on her personal life. I think it is significant that we are given details of the other three people. The computing lecturer and the IT coordinator, both women, carry the double load that is well-documented in feminist studies such as Mortberg's, that of domestic responsibility for themselves and their family, and a full-time paid job. The network consultant, a man, has a full-time paid job and relaxes at home.

Rather than focus on the IT manager and the absence of her personal details, the point I would like to make relates to the presence of heterosexual details of the three other people in these texts. We can only read these 'days in the life' as texts rather than as the lived days of these four people since they are a construction of the features editor and the people who volunteered for the series. Within a hetero-gendered world, that two of the women have husbands and children seems both significant and taken-for-granted. Perhaps we are told about their husbands and children to show that women can do responsible computing jobs and have domestic responsibilities as well. It might also be to show that when women are in paid employment, they must be prepared to take on two 'jobs' instead of one. I would like to give a different reading, one that problematises hetero-gender relations rather than focusing on problems within the norm of heterosexual relations. In this reading, the text shows that women who work in computing are still part of the binary norm of female/male relations. They, therefore, remain 'real women' rather than becoming pseudo-men. The one woman who is not presented as part of this norm, the IT manager, is asexual by default. And if she's not asexual, the less said in the text about other aspects of her life the better. It is the heterosexual norm that needs reconstitution. I think these 'day in the life' constructions are useful in demonstrating how, when woman is conflated with wife and mother, maintenance of these 'family' relations implies at the very least a double load for women.

The pervasiveness of hetero-gender relations as an unproblematic norm is clearly demonstrated in these texts. I argue that it is important for us as feminists to problematise this discourse when we carry out our research, for as long as it is seen as unproblematic, there may be little room for transformation of the gender-computing relation.

6. Positioning via conversation

The final piece I provide an alternative reading of is a feminist computer scientist's impressions based on her personal experience of gender relations in a computing workplace. Grundy (1994) provides a valuable analysis of a number of differences between the men and women in the department where she worked on a project. Her discussion focuses on how the men maintain their power through various practices, both technical and non-technical. One of the areas she examines, and I would like to focus on, is topics of conversation. The author demonstrates differences between women and men in relation to the dichotomy of computing and non-computing topics. Consistent with most of the literature on IT and gender, the link between masculinity and computing topics is evident. When non-computing topics are discussed, the author again notes difference. Topics recognised as appropriately male were the ones the men discussed, i.e. 'cars, car insurance, social drinking, football, aircraft, cricket, etc.' (352) She goes on to say that when women participated in these discussions "they did so as supplicants, only very rarely with deep-seated interest. If that interest was well-founded, then they might be accepted as 'one of the boys'." (352) Some women, she noted, '… refused to earn their credentials by showing interest in male topics.' (352)

In analysing the gender relations of these conversations, women seem to have three possible positions: 1) feigning interest in order to be included in the conversation; 2) joining due to active interest; 3) not showing interest. Position 1 is described in terms of normative femininity, with women 'as supplicants'. Position 3 is interpreted as one that rejects the location of authoritative power. Grundy says that these women were seen as more of a threat to the male power base than those in the other two positions. It would be interesting to explore further why this lack of participation is seen as threatening to the status quo and rejecting of the site of authoritative power. Is these women's lack of interest interwoven with a refusal to play the locally acceptable gender role and is seen as such by the men? This line of inquiry could explore the links between deviance from gender role and deviance from heterosexuality (Phelan 1993). Regarding the site of authoritative power identified by the author, is the lack of any alternative locations for this power linked to the women's own subjectivities? Are they constrained due to the threat and/or danger of being identified as deviant, i.e. lesbian?

The second position identified by the author presents some women as being accepted as 'one of the boys', but, she notes, they are still without access to central power-making functions. Within a hetero-gender perspective, these women are therefore positioned as asexual, as 'one of the boys'. They can not really be 'one of the boys' , however, because, the author says, they are still under the control of the men with whom they conversed. By setting up a dichotomy of male/female topics, women who are interested in sports, etc. can only be seen as 'one of the boys', thus reconstituting the norm of hetero-gender relations.

In the sentence which concludes the paper, the author has made a direct, if implicit, link between heterosexuality and women's positioning in computing. 'It is very convenient for those in power to make the subject of sex discrimination as taboo as explicit discussion of sexual intercourse.' (362) As long as continual reconstitution of heterosexual relations remains transparent, it will be difficult to challenge this link.

7. Conclusion

Heterosexual relations are constituted in a dynamic that in turn reinforces the existing power relations of technology. A continual maintenance of hetero-gendered relations and continual renegotiation within hetero-gendered positions points to a key question: does investment in heterosexuality implicate some women in colluding in a discourse of computing that excludes them in practice and ignores them in research?

By examining how these asymmetrical gender-technology power relations are maintained through a discourse of heterosexuality, we can make a richer analysis of the positioning of both lesbians and heterosexual women, and perhaps discover new possibilities for women that enable them to transform the social relations of technology. This approach shifts the focus from women struggling to maintain an identity embedded in a transparent heterosexuality, whose only alternative is to become 'one of the boys' to a focus on how the practice of heterosexual relations constrains women in challenging and transforming gender-technology relations.

References

Bodker, S. and Greenbaum, J. (1993). 'Design of Information Systems: Things versus People', in Green, E. et al (eds.). *Gendered By Design? Information Technology an Office Systems.* London: Taylor and Francis.

Butler, J. (1990). 'Gender Trouble, Feminist Theory and Psychoanalytic Discourse', in Nicholson, L. (ed.). *Feminism/Postmodernism.* New York: Routledge.

Computing (1996). 'On The Job With. . .' 25 January, 35; 21 March, 35; 9 May, 36; 13 June, 50.

Epstein, D. and Johnson, R. (1994). 'On the Straight and the Narrow: The Heterosexual Presumption, Homophobias and Schools', in Epstein, D. (ed.). *Challenging Lesbian and Gay Inequalities in Education.* Buckingham: Open University Press.

Gill, R. and Grint, K. (1995). 'Introduction', in Grint, K. and Gill R. (eds.). *The Gender-Technology Relation: Contemporary Theory and Research.* London: Taylor and Francis.

Green, E. et al. (1993) (eds.). *Gendered By Design? Information Technology an Office Systems.* London: Taylor and Francis.

Grundy, F. (1994). 'Women in the Computing Workplace: Some Impressions', in Adam, A. et al. (eds.). *Women, Work and Computerization: Breaking Old Boundaries - Building New Forms.* Amsterdam: Elsevier Science.

Hall, M. (1989). 'Private Experiences in the Public Domain: Lesbians in Organizations', in Hearn, J. and Sheppard, D. (eds.). *The Sexuality of Organization.* London: Sage.

Harding, S. (1986). *The Science Question in Feminism.* Ithaca, NY: Cornell University.

Kitzinger, C. (1993). 'Not Another Lecture on Homosexuality'. *Young People Now.* March, 10-11.

Mahony, K. and Van Toen, B. (1990). 'Mathematical Formalism as a Means of Occupational Closure in Computing—why "hard" computing tends to exclude women'.*Gender and Education*, 2 (3), 319-331.

Mortberg, C. (1994). 'Women's ways of acting - possibilities and obstacles', in Adam, A. and Owen, J. (eds.). *Proceedings of the 5th IFIP International Conference on Women, Work and Computerization.* Manchester.

Phelan, S. (1993). '(Be)Coming Out: Lesbian Identity and Politics'. *Signs,* 18(4), 765-790.

Sheppard, D. (1989). 'Organizations, Power and Sexuality: The Image and Self-Image of Women Managers', in Hearn, J. and Sheppard, D. (eds.). *The Sexuality of Organization.* London: Sage.

Stepulevage, L. (in press). 'Sexuality and Computing: Transparent Relations', in Griffin, G. and Andermahr, S. (eds.). *Straight Studies Modified: Lesbian Interventions in the Academy.* London: Cassell.

Tijdens, K. (1991). 'Women in EDP Departments', in Eriksson, I.V. et al (eds.). *Women, Work and Computerization.* Amsterdam: Elsevier Science.

van Oost, E. (1991). 'The process of sex-typing of computer occupations', in Eriksson, I.V. et al (eds.). *Women, Work and Computerization.* Amsterdam: Elsevier Science.

Wajcman, J. (1993). 'The masculine mystique: a feminist analysis of science and technology', in Probert, B. and Wilson, B. (eds.). *Pink Collar Blues: Work, Gender and Technology.* Melbourne: Melbourne University Press.

Webster, J. (1996). *Shaping Women's Work: Gender, Employment and Information Technology.* Harlow: Addison Wesley Longman Ltd.

Wilkinson, S. and Kitzinger, C. (1993) (eds.). *Heterosexuality: A Feminism & Pyschology Reader.* London: Sage.

Wilton, T. (1995). *Lesbian Studies: Setting An Agenda.* London: Routledge.

Discourse Particles in Female and Male Human-Computer-Interaction

Kerstin Fischer and Britta Wrede

University of Bielefeld

Abstract

This paper presents an investigation of the differences between human-to-human and human-to-computer communication with respect to discourse particles. In particular, quantitative and functional analyses were carried out for the distribution and functions which discourse particles fulfil in two large German corpora. It was found that the number of discourse particles does not simply decrease as suggested by Hitzenberger and Womser-Hacker (1995), for instance. In particular, female speech does not follow the predictions. Furthermore, many discourse particles were found to undergo a strong functional shift. Functional analyses are therefore indispensable for the study of the role of discourse particles in the human-computer interface.

1. Introduction

During the last 20 years, there has been increased interest in the communicative behaviour of speakers in interactions with artificial communicators. More recently, an independent register *computer talk* was postulated (Krause and Hitzenberger 1992, Marx 1996). The hypothesis is that an artificial communication partner consistently influences the properties of the speaker's communicative behaviour. These properties concern certain aspects of human-machine communication, in contrast to human-to-human communication (Hitzenberger and Womser-Hacker 1995: 56 (translation ours)):

- increase in differences compared to normal speech
- modification of syntactic constructions
- increasing number of overspecifications
- increase in instances of formal code
- decreasing number of framing elements in dialogues
- decreasing number of politeness formulae
- decreasing number of partner-oriented dialogue signals
- decreasing number of particles

The register *computer talk* is only defined negatively, in opposition to human-to-human communication. Furthermore, the authors do not consider socio-linguistic variables, particularly gender, and they do not make any distinctions within the linguistic structures they describe. Moreover, their predictions mainly concern the quantitative distribution of properties of speech.

In this paper, we will look at the features of *computer talk* concerning the use of discourse particles in human-machine interaction. In the list provided by Hitzenberger and Womser-Hacker (1995), it is not entirely clear how the last four features can be distinguished and where discourse particles are located since framing, partner-orientation and the creation of a harmonious and polite atmosphere belong to the many functions discourse particles fulfil in spontaneous spoken language dialogues (Schiffrin 1987, Fischer and Drescher 1996). It is certain, however, that irrespective of whether discourse particles are included in the framing elements, politeness formula, partner-oriented signals or in the class of particles, the *computer talk* hypothesis asserts that in human-machine communication the number of discourse particles decreases.

Discourse particles (Schiffrin 1987), i.e. segmentation markers and interjections such as *oh, yes, well, ah, now,* as well as hesitation markers like *er* and *um,* fulfil many different functions in spontaneous spoken language dialogues. For example, they segment and connect utterances in spoken language and support the turn-taking system; they mark important information; they provide the speaker with time to think and give the hearer time to adjust to the voice quality of the speaker. Moreover, they establish a harmonious atmosphere between communication partners and smooth potentially problematic information. They introduce new topics and help to structure the argumentation in the dialogue, as well as the construction of the dialogue itself. In human-to-human communication, discourse particles are therefore multifunctional.

The aim of this paper is, firstly, to determine how far predictions about the distribution of discourse particles are true of our corpora of German spontaneous spoken language dialogues. We will see that while many discourse particles are distributed in accordance with the predictions of the computer-talk hypothesis, others are not, i.e. discourse particles cannot be considered a homogeneous class in this respect.

Secondly, we want to find out whether the register *computer talk* can be equally identified for female and male speakers. Again, with respect to discourse particles, severe differences could be found which cast doubt on the validity of the computer-talk hypothesis as it is formulated by Hitzenberger and Womser-Hacker (1995).

2. The Corpora

Two corpora serve as the basis for the following analyses (Sagerer et al. 1994, Brindöpke et al. 1995); both were recorded in the same domain and are therefore comparable. The task the participants had to fulfil was in both cases to instruct someone to build a model aeroplane. The two corpora differ, however, in that the constructor in the first setting was another human communicator; whereas in the second, the participants believed they were talking to an automatic speech processing system. The data therefore provide a basis to compare human-to-human communication with verbal human-computer interaction.

The dialogues were recorded on DAT. The human-to-computer dialogues were transcribed according to Fink et al. (1995); the human-to-human dialogues are currently retranscribed according to the same transcription conventions. The transcriptions form the basis for the investigations presented.

2.1 The Human-to-Human Scenario (Sagerer et al. 1994)

The 22 probants in this scenario had to solve two tasks: first, they were asked to construct a model aeroplane themselves, following an illustration. Then each probant had to instruct another person to construct this aeroplane in a relaxed, face-to-face situation. In most of the dialogues, the communication partners could not see each other. Sometimes they were restricted to having a look at the other's construction; sometimes they could not see their communication partners at all. However, no systematic variation with respect to sight could be found concerning the distribution of discourse particles. Consequently, in the following the dialogues are treated as one corpus.

Furthermore, to ensure comparability with the dialogues in the human-to-machine scenario where the constructors' utterances consisted in prefabricated units, in the following only the instructors' utterances are considered.

The 22 dialogues altogether comprise 25914 words, with a mean length of 1178 words per dialogue. There was an equal number of male and female participants all of whom were university students.

2.2 The (Simulated) Human-to-Computer Scenario (Brindöpke et al. 1995)

The tasks the 40 probants had to solve in this experiment were almost the same as in the previous one with the difference that they had to instruct an artificial system via a microphone to build the model aeroplane. In fact, the behaviour of the artificial intelligent system was simulated by two people (*wizards*) in another room. One person built the model aeroplane according to the participant's instructions, the other selected verbal messages to simulate the speech processing system's output.

After every instruction, a snap-shot of the resulting state of construction was taken by a camera controlled by the second person. The picture was then transferred to the screen in front of the probant. In the meantime, the other person could send a message to a text-to-speech synthesizer which the probant could hear through overhead phones.

In order to make the simulated behaviour of the artificial intelligent system more convincing, the *wizards* had to decrease their level of cooperation in line with the following restrictions:

- reject instructions that contain words that one would assume an artificial system would not understand;
- randomly reject a certain number of instructions to simulate recognition errors;
- reject instructions that require memory;
- ignore instructions concerning objects that are not precisely specified by the instructor;
- reject instructions which are too global or underspecified.

In addition, the probants were asked to fill out a questionnaire giving their opinion about the characteristics of the artificial system. Only three of the 40 probants answered that they had doubted the existence of such an intelligent system during the recording. The remaining 37 probants believed that they had indeed communicated with an artificial system.

The corpus comprises 40268 words. The mean length is 1007 words per dialogue. Although the number of male and female participants is not exactly equal, the corpora are big enough to ensure reliable results. The speakers were all enrolled as students at the University of Bielefeld.

3. Analyses and Results

Preceding the quantitative analyses of the corpora, the normalized rate of occurrence of each discourse particle was computed for each dialogue:

normalized rate of occurrence =
    absolute number of occurrence * 100 / total number of words

The normalized data provide the basis for the quantitative investigations. These analyses were carried out half-automatically by means of tools which, for instance, counted the word frequencies in each dialogue and computed the distributions according to each group of speakers. Considering the total number of occurrences of discourse particles in the two corpora, it turns out that although there is a difference in the total number of discourse particles for male and female speakers, the total number of discourse particles decreased considerably in the simulated human-machine-scenario for both groups (Figure 1). The analyses of variances provide a significant effect for the different scenarios with p<.01.

However, the data for individual discourse particles reveal that only a small portion of the eleven German discourse particles investigated (*ach, äh, ähm, also, gut, hm, ja, nee, nein, oh, okay*) reacted wholly in accordance with the computer talk hypothesis (for instance, *ja, also, okay*); again the analyses of variances show a significant effect of the variable *scenario* for each discourse particle with p<.01:

In human-to-human conversation, German *ja, also* and *okay* typically fulfil functions with respect to the dialogue structure on the one hand, and signal a positive speaker attitude (Fischer 1996) on the other. In example (1) below, *ja* and *okay* display positive feedback and furthermore

Figure 1. Discourse particles per 100 words

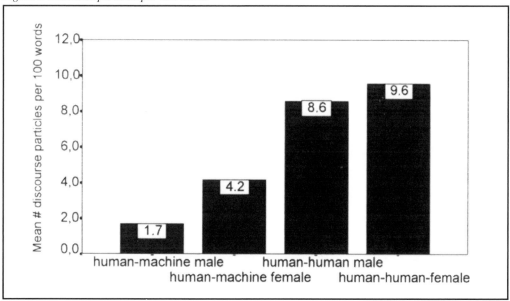

can be interpreted as turn holding and yielding signals. Moreover, second position *ja* relates the current utterance to the previous one, connecting the utterances in the dialogue.

(1)   *ah ja, gut, die grüne Schraube, wenn Du es schon drangeschraubt hast <-> okay <->*
        'oh yes, good, the green screw, if you have fixed it already <-> okay <->'

The structuring properties of *ja* and *also* become apparent in example (2) in which they connect the two utterances. More commonly, however, they occur initially and relate the respective utterance to the one the communication partner has just uttered, signalling contact, perception and understanding, as well as the idea that one is going to utter something relevant and is therefore taking a turn, as in example (3).

(2)   *<-> von <-> äh rechts nach links, ja, also ganz re/ ganz rechts ist eins*
        '<-> from <-> uh right to left, yes, so very far ri/ right far right is one'

(3)   *So ja und jetzt habe ich noch die eine rote Schraube mit der Kerbe*
        'well yes and now I still have the one red screw with the notch'

        Ja und den Fünferstab
        'yes and the five-hole bar'

Ja is often used in this function when the content of the utterance may constitute a possibly offending speech-act, for instance in questions like (4):

(4)   *<-> ja was passiert mit dem zweiten Teil des Flügels?*
        '<-> yes what happens with the second part of the wing?'

Ja is necessary here to establish an atmosphere of basic agreement between the speakers, to smooth the force of the utterance. Furthermore, in this example, *ja* is also used to introduce a new

Figure 2. ja, also, okay

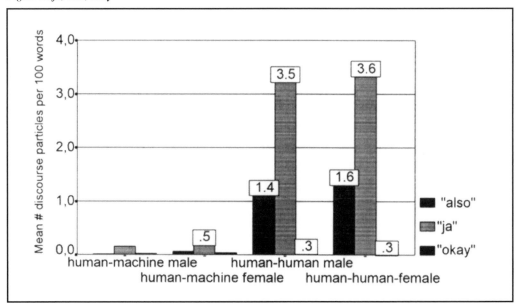

topic. The main functions of *ja, also* and *okay* are therefore located in the interactive as well as the discourse structuring domain.

Since the number of instances of *ja, also* and *okay* decreases so much, it can be concluded that speakers seem to expect that either computers do not need any positive feedback and signals of positive speaker attitude, or that they do not expect computers to recognize their discourse structuring functions, or both. Further analyses show that the interactive functions of discourse particles are particularly reduced in human-computer interaction.

The quantitative results so far, as well as the functional considerations, are in full accordance with the predictions of Hitzenberger and Womser-Hacker (1995).

In opposition to this, as can be seen in Figure 3, the discourse particle *hm* shows a completely different tendency. The use of *hm* increases considerably in human-computer-interaction (significance of the effect for the different settings: p<.01).

Although this result contradicts the predictions of the computer-talk hypothesis, it is not very surprising if it is taken into account that *hm* signals beginning divergence (we distinguish here between *hm* which signals beginning divergence and *mhm* which is used as a positive feedback signal, usually with fall-rise intonation). In human-human interaction it is rare since politeness constraints do not normally allow speakers to express their dissatisfaction so openly (cf. Lindenfeld 1996).

The distribution of instances of *gut* does not provide supportive data for the computer-talk hypothesis for female speakers: for women, there is no statistically significant difference between the different scenarios. However, the two-way interaction of the variables *sex* and *scenario* is p<.01. Here, functional analyses have to be carried out to explain the results.

Figure 3. hm

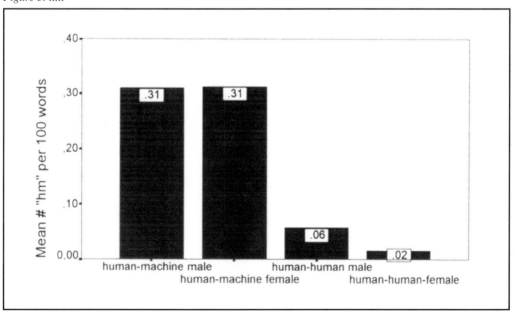

That the number of instances of *gut* does not decrease for the female speakers in human-computer interaction can be explained by two facts: firstly, almost half of the occurrences of *gut* occur in combinations which limit, by default, the positive speaker attitude as it is conveyed by *gut* in human-human interaction (5), for instance *na gut, schon gut, nun gut* (6). Secondly, another half occurs in deliberations, i.e. uttered to oneself, not oriented towards the communication partner (6). The rest of the occurrences is used in framing functions, marking the end of a construction phase (7). This latter function can also be found in the human-to-human dialogues.

(5)   *Auf beiden Seiten festgeschraubt, gut.*
        'fixed on both sides, fine'

(6)   *<attrib> ach so soll das sein, na gut </attrib: leise>*
        '<attrib> oh that's how it is supposed to be, oh well </attrib: quiet>'

(7)   *gut <-> <hum: atmen> mein Gott. Sie nehmen <-> die gelbe Schraube*
        'okay <-> <hum: breathing> my god. You take <-> the yellow screw'

So while *gut* is used in human-to-human-communication to provide positive feedback to the communication partner or to conclude a topic, it is used in human-computer-interaction mainly without partner-relation, or in connection with a signal of resignation. Consequently, the functional analysis can support the predictions of the computer-talk hypothesis on the decreasing interactive functions while the quantitative analysis cannot explain the distribution in the corpora, at least not for the female speakers.

Concerning the discourse particle *nein*, the quantitative analysis shows that while male and female speakers start off from different numbers in human-to-human communication, the number of occurrences of *nein* does not decrease in the speech of the women in human-

Figure 4. gut

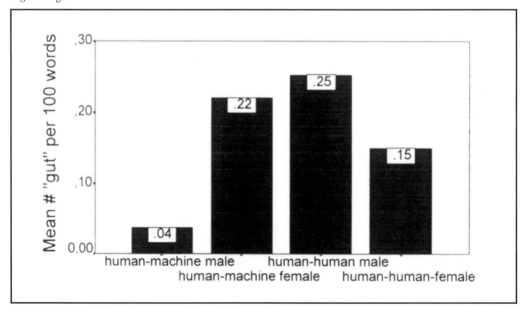

computer interaction. The Man-Whitney U-test shows no significant difference between the female human-human group and the female human-machine group while a difference between the male human-human group and the male human-machine group could be found with p<.05.

In human-to-human communication, *nein* typically functions as an answer signal either supporting a negatively formulated proposal or as an answer to a clarifying question, for instance:

(8)   *ja nein <-> im Moment zeigt gar nichts zu mir irgendwie*
        'yes no <-> at the moment nothing is pointing to me somehow'

In the human-computer dialogues, however, *nein* fulfils very different functions: In 38.9% of the occurrences *nein* is used as a repair marker, marking problems in the formulation process:

(9)   *drehe die rechte Schraube nein <-> zurück*
        'turn the right screw no <-> undo'

In 61.1% of the cases, however, *nein* is uttered quietly to the speakers themselves, without displaying any interactive functions, for example:

(10)   *gegenüber <hum: atmen> <-> der fünfbohrigen Basisplatte <attrib> ah nein nein nein </attrib: leise>*
        'in front of <hum: breathing> <-> the bar with the five holes <attrib> oh no no no </attrib: quiet>'

Consequently, in the case of *nein*, not only does the quantitative distribution not correspond to the predictions of the register *computer-talk* (the analysis of variance shows no effect of the scenario), the functions also change considerably. However, it is this functional shift which supports the hypotheses of Hitzenberger and Womser-Hacker (1995).

Figure 5. nein

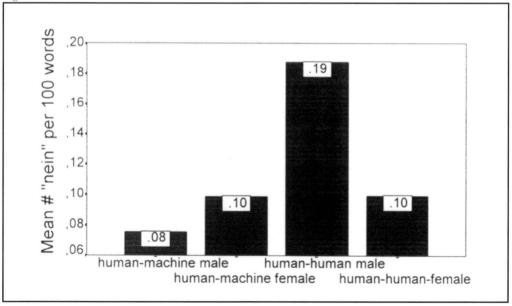

While *oh* usually serves as a turn-taking signal with additional emotional content to smooth possibly face-threatening acts such as requests to undo something or to combine parts, as in examples (11) and (12), two-thirds of the instances of *oh* occur in deliberations with expressive function without partner relation in human-to-computer communication (13). 25% function as repair markers (14):

(11)   *bitte? oh dann mußt Du es ja nochmal abmachen*
       'pardon me? oh then you'll have to undo it again'

(12)   *oh es ist echt schwierig*
       'oh it is really difficult'

(13)   *<attrib> oh das ist ja (ei)ne Siebenerleiste </attrib: leise>*
       '<attrib> oh this is a bar with seven holes </attrib: quiet>'

(14)   *das ganze ist jetzt <-> am gelben Kl/ <—> oh*
       'the whole thing is now <-> at the yellow cu/ <—> oh'

The functional shift in the occurrences of *oh* in the two corpora can explain why the prediction that the number of discourse particles will decrease in human-to-computer communication does not seem to be true of the distribution of *oh* for all speakers.

In spontaneous spoken-language dialogues among human communicators, the following are functions of hesitation markers such as *äh* and *ähm*:

- They mark important words, especially nouns. In communication with human speakers, these hesitation markers are typically employed in proposals, instructions or requests to smooth the force of the utterance. For instance, in the aeroplane dialogues, when signalling uncertainty about which term to use to refer to a part when combining two things, the speakers put the

Figure 6. oh

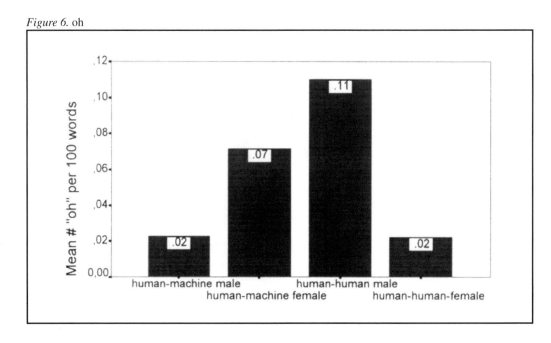

request in this way. The uncertainty about the terms cannot be motivated by a lack of knowledge since it also occurs if the subjects have referred to the item a number of times before in the dialogue, for instance:

(15)   *und in die Mitte setzt Du die ähm Schraube mit der Kerbe.*
        'and in the middle you put the um screw with the notch'

- They can be employed as turn-taking signals. Todt (1981) shows that initial hesitation markers occur after the same intervals as the first syllable would if the utterance began without hesitation. So initial discourse particles are turn-taking signals, but they also provide time for speech management if the utterance is not sufficiently planned after the usual interval between utterances:

(16)   *ähm jetzt hast das Teil was Du eben angeschraubt hast*
        'um now you have the part you have just connected'

- They function as repair markers, for example:

(17)   *und so zwar so daß sich ähm daß sie sich <-> in auf der gleichen Linie befinden*
        'and in a way so that they um that they <-> are on the same line'

- They mark boundaries between utterances, for instance:

(18)   *jetzt wird es ein bißchen schwieriger <-> ähm <-> darauf legst du jetzt mal <->*
        'now it'll be a little harder <-> um <-> on this you now put <->'

- They provide time for speech planning at any place in the utterance, for example:

(19)   *und jetzt ähm <->*
        'and now um <->'

As for *ähm*, in human-to-human communication, its functions are almost evenly distributed between male and female speakers, apart from its role as a *repair marker* for which it is used in only 10.4% of the cases by female and 6.2% by male participants.

In the interaction with the speech processing system, the number of instances of *ähm* which fulfil turn-taking functions increases to 52.9% for the men and to 42.0% for the women, while all other functions decrease; for women, for instance, the number of *repair markers* is reduced to 5.7%. For men, the number of fillers drops to 5.8% whereas it stays almost constant with the women.

It can be concluded that there are small differences in the functions *ähm* fulfils in the speech of male and female participants. However, concerning the quantitative distributions of *ähm*, considerable differences can be found. So although the general trend concerning the distribution of functions remains comparable between male and female speakers, in human-to-computer communication the total number of occurrences of *ähm* is almost four times higher for the women than for the men. The Mann-Whitney U test shows a significance of almost p<.01 between the male human-machine group and the female human-machine group.

The analyses of variances for *äh* provided a significance of p<.05 for the effect of the variable *scenario*. Looking at the functions *äh* fulfils in the two corpora, it turns out that in human-to-human communication, men use *äh* in all of the functions almost equally often (12.5%-16.6%), except when *äh* marks important words in order to smooth potentially offensive utterances

(42.7%). For female speakers, the distribution is similar, except that fillers only occur in 6.9% of cases, compared to repair markers in 21.8% of the cases.

For male participants talking to an artificial communicator, the function *äh* is employed in a completely different way: 49.2% are initial (turn-taking) occurrences and further 37.3% are repair markers. There are no instances of *äh* in which it segments utterances and only 1.4% in which it serves as a filler. The remaining 11.9% are markers of important information.

For women, the changes are much less dramatic: They use 38.5% of the instances of *äh* in connection with nouns. The number of fillers almost doubles to 12.8%.

That the number of markers of important information does not drop with female participants in human-to-computer communication is puzzling. In the human-to-human situation, these kinds of markers demonstrate which word has the highest information content and therefore contributes to the argument structure of the dialogues. Moreover, they smooth the force of an utterance. However, throughout the paper it became apparent that the interactive functions discourse particles fulfil in human-to-computer communication are reduced. Argument structuring and smoothing however have to be regarded as partner-oriented. So either women use *äh* in the interactive domain even when they are talking to a computer (in this case *äh* would constitute an exception to the tendency the other discourse particles display in the corpora) or their use of *äh* in this construction is motivated differently; for instance, female speakers may really display uncertainty before choosing a term. The high number of repair markings reported for *nein*, *äh* and *oh* provides further evidence that speakers are much more concerned about speech management than they are with human communication partners.

Figure 7. ähm

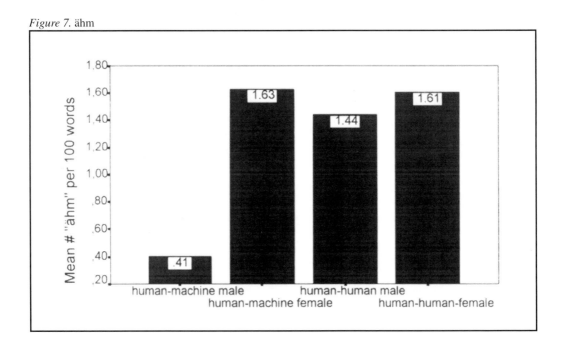

To sum up, it can be concluded that men and women behave differently in their use of discourse particles in human-to-computer communication. Generally, the quantitative distributions of discourse particles uttered by male speakers are in accordance with the postulation of a register *computer talk* while for female participants the quantitative distributions often contradict the predictions for the domain. It is therefore necessary to consider gender as an important variable in the investigation of 'computer talk'. Functional analyses have shed some light on the different distributions of the discourse particles in the two corpora. With respect to several of these discourse particles, severe functional shifts could be found. These may serve as a basis for the further investigation of differences between male and female speech in human-computer dialogues.

4. Conclusion

In distributional analyses it was found that although the total number of discourse particles decreases in the simulated human-to-computer scenario, only a restricted number of discourse particles is distributed according to the predictions of the computer-talk hypothesis. Most discourse particles display gender-related differences: for many of them the number of instances even increases instead of decreases in female speech in the interaction with an artificial communicator. Further functional analyses show that besides the distributional differences for men and women, a considerable functional shift for most discourse particles could be observed away from the interactive and towards the speech-management domain. Consequently, gender has to be regarded as an important socio-linguistic variable in the investigation of human-computer interaction.

Figure 8. äh

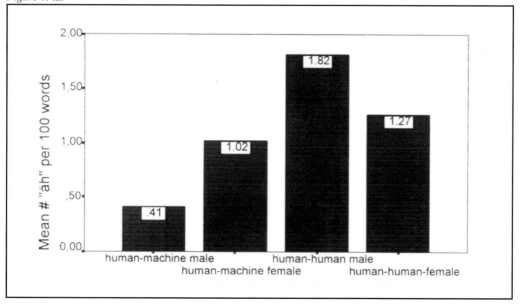

It can therefore be concluded that the computer-talk hypothesis has to be redefined; in particular, quantitative predictions have to be replaced by qualitative, functional assertions. So it is an oversimplification to postulate that the number of discourse particles simply decreases in human-to-computer communication. It has to be taken into account that discourse particles change their functions considerably: while in human-to-human communication they display functions with respect to discourse and argument structure, the turn-taking system, the speech management domain, but most importantly the interactive relationship between the communication partners; in human-to-computer communication they are mainly used to organize one's speech or have an expressive function in deliberations. In the corpora, female and male speakers seem to use discourse particles partly for different tasks (as in the case of *äh*) and partly in differing numbers (as in the case of *ähm*). Therefore, functional analyses with respect to female and male speech are necessary for assertions about human-to-computer communication.

References

Brindöpke, C., Johanntokrax, M., Pahde, A. & Wrede, B. (1995). *Darf ich Dich Marvin nennen? Instruktionsdialoge in einem Wizard-of-Oz Szenario: Materialband.* Report 1995/7, SFB 360 Situierte künstliche Kommunikatoren, University of Bielefeld.

Fink, G.A., Johanntokrax, M. and Schaffraniez, B. (1995). 'A Flexible Formal Language for the Orthographic Transcription of Spontaneous Spoken Dialogues', in *Proceedings of the Fourth European Conference on Speech Communication and Technology*, 871-74.

Fischer, K. and Johanntokrax, M. (1995). *Ein linguistisches Merkmalsmodell für die Lexikalisierung von diskurssteuernden Partikeln.* SFB 360 Situierte künstliche Kommunikatoren, Report 18, University of Bielefeld.

Fischer, K. and Drescher, M. (1996). 'Methods for the Description of Discourse Particles: Contrastive Analysis'. *Language Sciences* 18 (3-4), 853-61.

Fischer, K. (1996). 'Validating Analyses of Semantic Features in Interjections'. LAUD-Paper No. 276, University of Duisburg.

Hitzenberger, L. and Womser-Hacker, C. (1995). 'Experimentelle Untersuchungen zu multimodalen natürlichsprachigen Dialogen in der Mensch-Computer-Interaktion'. *Sprache und Datenverarbeitung* 19 (1).

Krause, J, and Hitzenberger, L. (eds.) (1992). 'Computertalk'. *Sprache und Computer* 12. Hildesheim et al..

Lindenfeld, J. (1996). 'Cognitive Aspects of Verbal Interaction', in Casad, Eugene H. (ed.). *Cognitive Linguistics in the Redwoods. The Expansion of a New Paradigm in Linguistics*. Mouton De Gruyter.

Marx, J. (1996). 'Die Computer-Talk-These in der Sprachgenerierung. Hinweise zur Gestaltung natürlichsprachlicher Zustandsanzeigen in multimodalen Informationssystemen', in Gibbon, D. (ed.). *Natural Language Processing and Speech Technology*. Results from the third Konvens Conference, October. Bielefeld: Mouton De Gruyter.

Sagerer, G., Eikmeyer, H.-J. and Rickheit, G. (1994). 'Wir bauen jetzt ein Flugzeug. Konstruieren im Dialog'. *Arbeitsmaterialien. Tech. Report*. SFB 360 Situierte künstliche Kommunikatoren, University of Bielefeld.

Schiffrin, D. (1987). *Discourse Markers.* Cambridge: Cambridge University Press.

Todt, D. (1981). 'Zum Auftreten von Füllauten in spontan gesprochenen Berichten'. *Nova Acta Leopoldina N.F.* 54 (245), 597-611.

Transcription Conventions

<attrib>	marks the beginning of a feature
</attrib: quiet>	marks the end of a feature, here: quiet
<hum>	marks the beginning of human noise
</hum: breathing>	marks the end of human noise, here: breathing
<hum: breathing>	marks an isolated breathing event
<noise>	marks the beginning of noise
</noise: micro>	marks the end of some noise from the microphone
<noise: micro>	marks an isolated instance of noise from the microphone
<->	marks a short pause
<—>	marks a longer pause
<sil: 2>	marks a pause of two seconds
()	mark parts of a word that are not realized
ri/	breaking off in the middle of a word
<par></par>	mark parallel speech

Exploring the Pipeline:

Towards an understanding of the male dominated computing culture and its influence on women

Christina Bjorkman and Ivan Christoff

Dept of Computer Systems, Uppsala University, P.O Box 325, S-751 05 Uppsala, Sweden

Fredrik Palm and Anna Vallin

Centre for Women's Studies, Uppsala University, St Johannesgatan 21, S-753 12 Uppsala, Sweden

Abstract

We present a project aimed at making the Computer Science Programme at Uppsala University in Sweden more attractive to women. The main goals of the project are to find explanations for the low number of female students attending the programme and to identify possible solutions to this problem. We focus on the prevailing culture of the programme. In the first phase of the project the programme is analysed from a gender perspective. A study, based on questionnaires and interviews, is carried out. The study will be completed during Spring 1997. The questionnaires have been analysed and the results from these are presented in this paper.

1. Introduction

The Computer Science Programme (CSP) at Uppsala University, Sweden, was initiated in 1981. It is a four-year programme, leading to an MSc degree. 60 students are admitted every year, the total number of students actively studying in the programme being approximately 240. During the 1980s the percentage of female students applying to the programme gradually decreased and levelled off at approximately 10%. It remained at this low level during the first half of the 1990s. This seems to be a common situation in many western countries. (In the autumn of 1996, the number of women beginners increased to 18%. It remains to be seen whether this is a trend or just a temporary fluctuation.)

In order to analyse thoroughly and improve the situation we initiated a project in Spring 1996, our goal being to make the CSP more attractive to female students. The goal is both *quantitative* (to increase the number of female students), and *qualitative* (to create a computing culture that is more 'female-friendly'). We believe that these are strongly connected, since a different computing culture could attract more women, while more women in computing would, we hope, lead to positive changes in the existing culture.

The main focus of the project is the culture, norms and attitudes among students and faculty. We seek to establish how the male dominated computing culture affects both male and female students. If we can understand what norms and attitudes dominate – and why – we believe we can find reasons for the imbalance between female and male students. We realise that these are complex issues, which most likely interact with issues such as curriculum design and teaching methods.

The project consists of several phases: the first phase is a study of the CSP from a gender perspective. The results from this study will provide a basis for the second phase, which will focus on determining the necessary changes that should be made to improve the situation. These changes will then be implemented and the results evaluated.

2. Obstacles for Women in Academia

There are many obstacles facing women both in the academic world as such, and in the field of computing.

Drawing on the work of Paula Caplan (1993), three main obstacles for women can be identified in the academic world. The *unwritten rules*, whose function is to conserve the traditional power structures, create difficulties for women (and other minorities) through blocking important information about how the system works, which individuals have the most influence (power) and what subjects have the highest status in the specific culture.

> The most powerful mechanism here is the wearing down of the individual woman through the dominant maleness of the environment, combined with the *paucity of clear, concrete rules* she could use to combat it (p. 45). (Our emphasis).

Furthermore, there exists a set of *myths* about the nature of the academic world. These myths contain views of academia as a democratic, objective, fair and open community, and about the role of women in this community. They also deal with the female essence: how a woman should act and how she should not act in order to be accepted, what women are like and what they are not. These myths are far from consistent but still determine how the behaviour of the individual woman is assessed by her male colleagues, and a woman often finds herself stuck because of them. This leads to the third obstacle, namely the presence of *Catch-22 situations*. These are closely interwoven with myths about the female nature. On the one hand, women are expected to behave in a warm, caring and essentially 'female' way to be socially accepted, while on the other hand, in order to reach success in their academic career, they have to behave in a way typical for prominent individuals in their environment. So, if a woman chooses a career instead of raising children, she risks being viewed as 'masculine' and not being socially accepted, but if she acts like a 'typical' woman, her chances of having a successful career are small (Caplan 1993, Hemenway 1995).

The negative effect of stereotypes in the computing culture (as in society in general) seems to be yet another critical obstacle for women. For extended discussions of the influence of gender stereotyping within the computing culture see Badagliacco (1990), Colley et al (1994), Pearl et al (1990), Shashaani (1994) and Turkle (1984).

Other problems facing women are: sexism (overt or not), lack of role models and mentors, and lack of support from parents and teachers in pursuing a career in computing. Equality in the field of computing cannot be viewed as an isolated problem.

3. Study of the CSP from a gender perspective

The first phase of the project is a study of the programme from a gender perspective. Here, we focus primarily on how students perceive the specific culture at the CSP, their own place in it and how they view problems of equality in computing. It seems relevant to examine how male and female students experience and relate to values of the dominant culture. Is it, for example, easier for male than for female students to accept and internalise these values? Are there differences in the identification with the role of 'the computer scientist'? In more general terms, do women's and men's different experiences and the promotion of male experience over female experience, serve the exclusion of women in computer science?

Taking a gender perspective, we acknowledge the power dominance of men in the field of computing. This power can partly be viewed as exercised through the overwhelming emphasis on male interests. Thus, skills and subjects considered most important in computer science today are closely linked to traditionally masculine interests in western society. At the same time as attracting men in large numbers to the field, this emphasis excludes traditional female fields of interest. Femininity is often equalled with technical and technological incompetence. But this power dominance is not to be seen as rigid in any deterministic sense. Rather, it is an ever on-going process where certain values and interests are constantly discredited in favour of others. It can be viewed as a perpetual struggle where the social constructions of computing, technology and masculinity are both resisted and defended. Computer science cannot be seen as an unquestioned and rigid male entity. Although the male domination seems almost completely stable, keeping it so is a process which demands a high amount of flexibility. This flexibility allows the dominant culture to resist competing interests in a much more local and effective way. Ignored and subjected values and perspectives can therefore both actively and indirectly be resisted.

Through analysing the discourse in which students express their views around equality and change towards equality we hope to be able to grasp the particular nature of the resistance in this specific social context.

4. Method

In order to survey the attitudes among the students attending the programme, a questionnaire was constructed. It consists of three main parts:

- *Background questions* , e.g. sex, years in the programme etc.
- *Open ended questions*, concerning the culture, which involves the study situation and social aspects of being a computer scientist.
- *Multiple choice questions*, in which students were to indicate to what degree they agreed with a statement. This part consists of statements regarding gender issues.
(See Appendix A for examples of questions.)

The questionnaire was distributed to students attending the programme in spring 1996. It was distributed to all the women (18 at that time) and to 100 men (randomly selected). Twelve women responded but only 30 of the men responded, in spite of being reminded several times. One reason for the poor response rate among the men is probably the length of the questionnaire (it took 30–60 minutes to fill out). However, this can also be interpreted as a lack of interest in these questions among the men.

Qualitative in-depth interviews have been conducted with nine female students, and six graduate women who are now active in either industry or academia. It is interesting to note that the latter were much more interested in participating than were the former. These interviews are presently being analysed and some indications are reported here. Similar interviews with male students are currently being conducted.

4.1 Analysis

In analysing the questionnaires and the interviews, the male and the female students were separated. Somewhat different methods have been used to analyse the two groups. The female minority is, as a group, probably both more aware of and affected by the existing problems than the male majority. Therefore it is important to get a picture of how the women view the current situation and if they have any personal experience of discrimination. It would also be interesting to determine whether this group internalises values, attitudes and norms as easily as the men. The male group would be interesting to study to find out what the dominating attitudes towards equality are. Since resistance to equality is seldom overt, we expect we would have to analyse this group's accounts carefully. Attention should not only be paid to the dominating norms and attitudes, but also to what variations in these mean. Reflections on behalf of the male students may reveal what parts of the culture they see as most loaded with status and prestige.

Deconstruction of the accounts is possible if we see language as a construction (Wetherell and Potter 1988). The language used in a specific context (e.g. computer science in the USA) is created out of a language that already exists (in this case English), from which the social culture chooses to take certain concepts, terminology, etc., while others are excluded. This use of language has consequences for the development of the culture, which individuals will be attracted to it, and what status society will attach to it. In the process of deconstruction the original text is broken down and analysed piece by piece until some kind of pattern emerges from the material. In this study, the accounts are made within the specific context of the CSP, and are probably affected by the fact that the study focuses on the low number of female students. This is important to consider when analysing the data.

The method used here is influenced by discourse analysis (DA) as developed by Jonathan Potter and Margaret Wetherell (Potter and Wetherell 1987). This fairly new branch in social psychology criticises traditional methods used in the field for being too focused on finding consistencies in data obtained. Although DA recognises the importance of consistencies, the main attention is here instead paid to variation and inconsistencies in the material. To understand how participants themselves experience their social context is to be able to explain why they contradict themselves and what function these variations have in the context. To strip participants' accounts of variation in order to reach some 'hard core' or 'real' beliefs is an approach discourse analysis firmly rejects. Instead, inconsistencies are there for some reason and they are central to account for in the analysis of how people use their discourses.

If an individual (or group) expresses different views on a phenomenon at different occasions all these should be considered. Depending on the situation or context within which a question is posed, the answers to it may be expected to vary. These variations reveal something about the individual's view of the phenomenon under study. One answer cannot be extracted as representing the view of the individual, while the others are regarded as irrelevant. For example, what the individual thinks he or she is expected to answer affects the account being made.

The accounts often maintain and profile the discourse specific to the culture, where the attitude or belief is expressed, thereby excluding other social contexts from one's own. Through revealing what functions certain expressions, norms and attitudes have for the culture, a more profound understanding of accounts made by members of the community can be achieved.

Influenced, among other things, by speech-act-theory, ethnomethodology and conversation analysis (Potter and Wetherell 1987), DA concentrates on language use. Descriptions or accounts of phenomena and events are never neutral; in fact, the firm conviction in DA is that they cannot be. All speech is in some way or another goal oriented – people do things with speech. Thus, it becomes important to examine the way people express themselves in different social texts or discourses. There is no search for underlying meanings beyond the material of which the analyst is trying to make sense. This does not mean taking it at face value. Rather it means looking at what is *actually* going on in the text. For example, if a participant in an interview responds to a question as if it were an accusation, it should be treated like an accusation in the analysis. Discourse analysis involves close readings of verbal and non-verbal transcripts and constant re-evaluations of the analyst's own interpretations and former readings of the text. In this process it is important to ask questions about, for example: What do participants try to accomplish with their speech? What consequences do certain ways of describing or accounting for particular phenomena or events have? And in what ways does speech (as well as other language use) shape, maintain or resist the current orders or situations? In the analysis of power and interest, the analytical tool is to look at what is at stake in the context.

The analysis of the questionnaires was inspired by DA. However, DA is better suited for analysis of longer, continuous discourses, such as, for example, discourses obtained in interviews. DA will mainly be used in analysing the interviews with the male students, in order to catch inconsistencies and contradictions in the discourses and thereby focus the complexity instead of simplifying. From the questionnaires we have noted that the male students often contradict themselves when it comes to questions concerning equality and gender issues.

5. Results and Discussion

We present the results from the analysis of the questionnaires together with a more general discussion of problems in the academic computing culture. The social impact on the female minority by this culture is illustrated through interpretations of the accounts given by the students.

Among the female students, two groups can clearly be distinguished. Approximately half of them (group A) seem to have adjusted themselves to the male-dominated culture. These women tend to have similar views on equality as the men. They accept the culture and do not feel that they experience any gender-related problems. The other half of the women view their own situation differently (group B). They are more interested in equality questions and are more positive towards changes in the environment. In addition, they seem to have experienced more problems as women in the computing culture. We could see that these women had a different background than the first group, e.g. they were not used to a male-dominated culture before starting their university studies, and had not adjusted to the culture in the same way as the first group.

Among the men, no such differences could be detected.

5.1 Non-sexism versus Anti-sexism

Linda Briskin (Briskin 1990) suggests that we should distinguish between *non-sexism* and *anti-sexism*. Non-sexism means seeing problems of equality as stemming from prejudice, and deals with this prejudice by making sex irrelevant. Anti-sexism 'highlights the function of structural inequality and empowers . . . through knowledge' (p. 3). While non-sexism focuses on personal moralities ('I am not sexist'), anti-sexism demands active actions against discrimination ('What can I do about sexism?'). To focus on morality means taking no responsibility for the existing problem, which leads to neutrality 'that can inadvertently serve to bolster the status quo' (p.3).

The non-sexist standpoint seems to be strongly represented among the male students. This is shown by a critical stance against affirmative action (see below) and attitudes avoiding the importance of gender, instead putting forward individuality and uniqueness.

There is a clear difference among the female students in the answers given in relation to non-sexism and anti-sexism. The women in group A seem to have a strong non-sexist view, when asked about equality. The rest of the women (group B) show a tendency towards an anti-sexist view.

A typical non-sexist viewpoint was expressed by one of the students, when asked if he believed that equality is important in order to promote the development of the field of computing:

> No! It is individuals who lead development. Whether the individual is male or female I believe is irrelevant.

Through non-sexist statements the importance of gender is played down. Taken at face value the motivation may seem quite sympathetic and liberal. However, looking at it more closely, it becomes just another way of saying that there is no need for equality. By pointing to the importance of individuals, instead of men and women, the obvious power imbalances in the field of computing are concealed. As we all know, being a man or a woman is an important aspect of our individuality and, in fact, shapes our lives. Agreeing with this, there is really no point in talking of individuality alone, when dealing with problems of equality. Individuals lead the development but the more important questions here are, for example: 'What individuals are engaged in the development?', 'What does this development look like?' and 'What development do we want?' If one has a non-sexist view, there is no need to discuss such issues. Silence about the existing problems is perfect for the dominant culture and its members. The path of development chosen becomes the only way of doing things. By creating a community of genderless 'computing people', where the function of gender and power is hidden, and indeed regarded as irrelevant, women are effectively excluded. In this community, where only ability and interest for computing counts, everybody is greeted. The strange thing is that almost only men come to this party. Half of the women in our study feel as if they were not invited, while the other half consider themselves invited and accept that the dress code is set by the men.

5.2 Affirmative action
There seems to be a fairly firm resistance to affirmative action among the students. When defining equality, many of the male students mentioned dislike for affirmative action at large and more specifically the use of fixed quotas for women. The women did not explicitly mention an aversion to affirmative action and only one woman mentioned quotas. However, some answers implied aversion to affirmative action. Affirmative action was seen as 'reverse discrimination', and no discrimination should be allowed.

5.3 Equality – A woman's problem
Many of the male students attribute the low percentage of women attending the programme to a general lack of interest for computing. Some of the men, however, are willing to see culture as a contributing effect. Among the women, we can see a clear difference between groups A and B. Women in the former group have answers similar to the men, while group B sees the reasons as more cultural.

With this dominating view, equality becomes primarily a woman´s problem. From this follows questions of the type: 'How do we change women's attitudes to computing?' Actions taken on the basis of this line of reasoning are bound to have short term effects. When the actions are withdrawn, these effects are lost.

Instead of concluding that the shortage of women depends on their lack of interest for computing, there is a need to go beyond this line of reasoning, asking questions that not only include the female minority but also the male majority. Through questions of the type: 'How do we change ourselves (and the dominant culture) in order to open up for individuals who today are more or less excluded?' more long-lasting effects are likely to be obtained. This requires that the dominant group be willing to let go of some of its power, which in turn requires that the existing problems and the responsibility for these, on the part of the dominant group, are recognised.

5.4 Qualitative versus quantitative change
The reasons for wanting to increase the number of women in computer science may differ between different groups of interest. Some may want the increase in order to get more qualified individuals into the field, some may want it to shift the power imbalances between men and women, and some may want it just because it would be nice with more women. Needless to say, there are also those who do not want, or do not see, any need for increasing the number of women at all (this group is left out of this discussion). We can identify two groups: those who are only interested in a *quantitative* change (i.e. an increase in the number of women), and those who are interested in more far-reaching and *qualitative* changes.

Qualitative changes aim at, for example, alterations in teaching methods (Frenkel 1990), and question the present order in the computing culture. An indirect effect of qualitative changes is an increase in the number of women. Quantitative changes focus primarily on what can be done to attract more women to computer science. The present order is not questioned; instead, the main strategy is to change the attitudes of women to the existing culture.

In the study the students were to take a stand with regard to three claims dealing with qualitative versus quantitative changes (Appendix A, statements 9-11). The two claims addressing quantitative aspects received many more positive responses than the claim addressing qualitative aspects. A majority of the students thought there was a need for more female role models in computer science (this was especially the case with the women, 75% of whom agreed with this statement), and that it was relevant to increase the number of women attending the programme in order to improve the education. Only a small minority of the men thought it would be relevant to introduce a course in the curriculum about the significance of gender in computing (statement 11). Among the women, those in group A tended to disagree strongly with this statement, while those in group B were positive to such a course.

This may indicate that while there may be a great deal of interest in quantitative changes, ideas for changes to the existing programme have little support. It is also interesting to note in this context that when comparing the three claims, it seems like the less concrete and more distanced from one's own environment a claim is, the more popular (or less threatening) it seems to the students. The definition or form of the programme seems to be little questioned, at least from the male students.

5.5 The belief that gender differences are relevant – being politically correct

Even though there was very little support among the male students for claims stating that men are more creative, efficient and ambitious when it comes to computers (Appendix A statements 14-16), comments with respect to these claims revealed some belief that gender differences are relevant. In these comments, men are characterised as more rational, focused, mathematically-minded and curious (when it comes to technical matters) than women, and women are seen as more creative, disciplined and socially able. This indicates that there might be a belief among some of the male students that the lack of women is due to the differences between the male and the female nature.

The women were more willing to agree to the statement that men are more efficient when working with computers. They explained this by the fact that men spend more time 'hacking' and are more interested in computers as such, while women like to use computers more as tools. On the other hand, the female students regard themselves as more creative with computers. Their comments also imply that, on the whole, women are more ambitious than men.

The high degree of 'political correctness' is at least in part, due to the context in which the study is conducted. As the purpose of the study is to examine the attitudes of students attending the programme, in order to improve the climate for women, the students were aware that their answers may have consequences for their education. Showing a liberal and free-from-prejudices mentality can in fact be important in maintaining the dominant culture. A non-sexist attitude (women are not less ambitious, creative, efficient, etc.) draws the focus to individual differences and the realm of morality – 'I am not sexist and there are no differences between men and women'. With such an attitude, there is no need for further equality work. Even among students showing a categorical dissociation from straightforward claims recognising relevant gender differences, beliefs in such differences are found in other answers made by the same students. These variations tell us not to see the answers given by the students as reflecting their real attitudes. Instead they mirror the picture of the current situation the students want to show us.

6. Conclusions and further work

The results of the study so far show that half of the women attending the programme seem to adjust to the dominant culture. Those who do not adjust experience more problems. Interviews with female graduates indicate that many of them have gone (or are going) through a process leading to re-evaluation of this adjustment and stressing their femininity. In this process, there can arise a conflict between one's identity as a woman and one's identity as a computer scientist.

We have found a contradictory view mainly among the men: sex is irrelevant (or at least it should be), *but* men and women are different, they think and function differently. This contradictory view is further explored in the interviews with the male students.

In this study we have concentrated on the culture of the computer science programme, in the sense of its social context. As Flis Henwood points out (Henwood 1993), in order to transform the gendered relations of technology, we also need to examine technology itself as culture. Technology and gender are not fixed and 'given' but cultural processes that interact with each other.

References

Badagliacco, J. M. (1990). 'Gender and race differences in Computing attitudes and experience'. *Social Science Computer Review* 8 (1) Spring.

Briskin, L. (1990). 'Gender in the classroom'. *Newsletter of the centre for support of teaching* 1(2–3), Sept.

Caplan, P. (1993). *Lifting a ton of feathers: a woman's guide for surviving in the academic world.* University of Toronto Press.

Colley, A. M. et al (1994). Effects of gender role identity and experience on computer attitude components. *Journal of Educational Research* 10(2), 129–137.

Frenkel, K. A. (1990). 'Women and computing'. *Comm. of the ACM* 33(11).

Hemenway (1995). 'Human nature and the glass ceiling in industry'. *Comm. of the ACM* 38(1), 55–62.

Henwood, F. (1993). 'Establishing Gender Perspectives on Information Technology: Problems, Issues and Opportunities', in Green, E., Owen, J. and Pain, D. *Gendered By Design.* London: Taylor and Francis.

Pearl, A. et al (1990). 'Becoming a computer scientist'. *Comm. of the ACM* 33(11), 47-57

Potter, J. and Wetherell, M. (1987). *Discourse and social psychology: beyond attitudes and behaviour.* London: Sage.

Shashaani, L. (1994). 'Gender-differences in Computer experience and its influence on computer attitudes'. *Journal of Educational Computing Research* 11(4), 347 - 367.

Turkle, S. (1984).*The second self.* New York: Simon and Schuster.

Wetherell, M. and Potter, J. (1988). 'Discourse analysis and the identification of interpretative repertoires', in Antaki, C. (ed.). *Analysing everyday explanation*, 168-83.

Appendix A - Examples from the questionnaire

The questionnaire was written in Swedish. Below are translated examples of questions. The examples are chosen (and numbered) to illustrate the discussion in the text.

Open-ended questions

1. What characterises a proficient computer scientist?
2. Do you believe you can become a proficient computer scientist?
3. What are the most important reasons for the low number of female students in the programme?
4. What do you mean by equality between men and women?
5. Is equality important to promote development in computing? (explain your answer)
6. What types of people study in the programme? How would you characterise them?

Multiple-choice questions

The students were asked to indicate to what degree they considered a statement to be correct. They were instructed to answer instinctively and to comment on the questions.

7. No women have contributed to the development of computer science
8. The social environment at the CSP benefits men more than women
9. It is valuable to increase the number of female students to improve the educational environment.
10. More female role models are needed in computing
11. It would be valuable to have an obligatory course about gender roles in computing
12. Women lack some basic qualities to become successful computer scientists
13. The number of women in the programme does not depend on the structure of the pro-gramme
14. Men are more efficient users of computers than women
15. Women are not as ambitious as men
16. Men work more creatively with computers than women
17. The low number of female students is largely due to women's lack of interest in computers
18. Women at the CSP must behave in a male way
19. There are no really competent female computer scientists in the faculty

How are We Seen? Images of Women in Computing Advertisements

Eva Turner

Middlesex University

Fiona Hovenden

The Open University

Abstract

This paper gives a brief introduction to the history of critique of advertising and the influence this critique has had on the advertising industry. We have applied this work to advertising in the field of computing. We give a detailed study of three years of advertisements in the *Personal Computer World* magazine, comparing many images of women and men. This is followed by a specific look at two advertisements from one computing company. Conclusions are drawn from the studies stating that women are portrayed mainly as decorative additions to advertisements, as performing relatively menial tasks when portrayed on their own, or in some form of subordinate position when portrayed in groups with men. Most of the advertisements still seem to be directed at men. The computing industry has not taken on board any of the above-mentioned critique.

1. Introduction

Apart from a brief period in the 1970s, the number of women employed in all levels of computing jobs has been substantially lower than the number of men. The 1991 statistics for the proportion of women occupying computing positions ranged from 3% of Data Processing Managers to 29% of Systems Analysts (Grundy 1996) and there is no indication that the situation has radically improved since. Though the use of computers in our work and everyday life has grown disproportionately to the use of any other new technological device, the proportion of women computing students and women university lecturers in computing remains in the region of 20% (Turner 1997). The research attempting to explain and rectify this has looked at many aspects of technology in our lives; the advertising of computer technology has not been researched and it may be one of the influences on women, when choosing their future careers.

If it is the case that information is power, then the distribution of the tools of information processing (i.e. computers) will influence the distribution of power. Currently, most of this power is still exclusively concentrated in men's hands. How does this influence the way people perceive society, social relationships and the position of women? (Beardon 1993, Voet 1993). Advertisements are one form of information dissemination, which begs the question, 'who is disseminating what to whom?' Computer technology advertisements represent the dissemination of information about the tools of information dissemination and as such need to be investigated. If it is shown that these advertisements are in any way excluding women from gaining access to computers, then women are being also excluded from gaining access to power.

Computer ownership from the gender point of view is difficult to establish. Some 40% of households have a computer and of course there are a very few companies without one. It seems that, from the prevalence of male pictures in the advertisements, the advertisers' assumption is that it is mainly men who survey the markets and the magazines and purchase the computer of their choice. As the overwhelming majority of Data Processing Managers are also men, then the assumption has to be that they are also the main purchasers of company computer equipment. Many women have joined the workforce and many of these women use computers in their jobs. However, what in the 1970s was a technical job became, with the development of computer technology, a stereotypical female position (glorified typist) with low social status attached to it. These workers do not have real purchasing or advisory powers and the advertisements do not address them.

2. Brief History of Advertising Critique

Kathy Myers (Myers 1986) gives a revealing political analysis of advertising. She analyses the use of advertisements as a political tool and concludes that the difference between advertisements and propaganda is at best blurred: the portrayal of women in advertising has always been used as a political tool to keep women in their place. Of course, advertising does not just influence our spending patterns; it also influences our perception of ourselves and of society. This has been the topic of many psychological and economic studies. It was the feminists in the early 1960s who first looked at the portrayal of women in advertisements and brought the whole question of their effect on social thinking into perspective. The literature, as well as direct action (defacing of adverts), tried to draw attention to the discrepancies between the advertisement portrayal and the real life of women. In the 1970s feminists effectively accused advertising and the media of producing misleading and dangerously subversive images of women, and by the early 1980s the movement became political and politicised.

In 1976 Pam Ings, account director at the Leo Burnett advertising agency defined advertising as 'a channel of communication which allows person or persons to make contact with a number of other persons for infinite variety of reasons but basically with the desire to inform, persuade and sell' (Women in Media 1976). The advertising industry saw itself as producing advertisements that needed to meet product criteria and 'emotional needs, because what we do, what we buy and what we wear are all statements about ourselves to ourselves and to the rest of the society'. Surely the aims of advertisers today have not changed. The question is whether they have taken on board the influence of advertisements on social thinking and whether there is a deliberate policy today to steer the thinking in any direction. If the primary function of advertising is to inform the public of the wide range of goods and services, then the secondary function is its involvement in the manipulation of social values and attitudes (Courtney and Whipple 1984). What an advertisement means depends on how it operates, not only in relation to production and consumption, but also in relation to technological, economic and social relationships. If the advertisement is treated as 'concentrated ideology reinforcing certain values, then the way we understand it and interpret it will inevitably influence our decisions'. In a number of studies, Courtney and Whipple document the ways in which both sexes are shown as stereotypes. Men are shown as working outside the home and involved in the purchase of more expensive goods and services, while women are more likely to be portrayed as non-active and in decorative roles.

The feminist interest in advertising has changed dramatically the way women are portrayed in advertisements these days. Few portray women as stereotypical sex objects. Some advertisers responded to feminist demands and acknowledged the changing image and role of women in society. One of the major effects of that movement, however, was the more exaggerated and stronger masculinity being championed in the commercial press (Mort 1996). Men began to create their own new images, publish their own magazines and their own advertisements which, in search of new markets, 'shifted the boundaries of masculinity' and defined new identities. This has prompted analysis of this new phenomenon as well as traditional images of men in advertising (Wernick 1994). However, no research of the 1990s deals with advertising in technology.

3. Decoding Advertisements

Judith Williamson (Williamson 1981) and Erving Goffmann (Goffmann 1987) were for us the two most influential authors on advertising. Williamson wrote her book at the height of feminist interest in advertising. She says she wanted an impersonal, structural approach to analysing advertisements so that a clear theory could be developed for their political understanding. She says, 'advertisements are selling something else besides consumer goods. In providing us with a structure in which we and the goods are interchangeable, they are selling us ourselves.' We found this statement and her approach to advertising analysis very useful. She also says that we need both social meaning and material goods. Advertising gives the material goods social meaning, so that the two needs cross. Material goods that we need are made to represent the other non-material things that we also need. The objects depicted in advertisements represent a sort of currency, i.e. something that represents a value. But the objects/products advertised are not themselves the currency; it is the images of feelings that become attached to the product, evoking the *promise* of that emotion. When the connection between the products and emotions is made, the emotions then gain the status of facts. The meaning is transferred. Williamson identifies several aspects/signs for deciphering advertisements in the text, pictures and camera angles.

Goffmann (Goffmann 1987) looks at advertisements and applies to them a theory of animal sexual behaviour. He defines behaviours as 'displays . . . under the pressure of natural selection, behaviours which become formalised – in the sense of becoming simplified, exaggerated and stereotyped'. Instead of having to play out an act, the animal provides a readily available expression of its situation, which allows for negotiation by those witnessing the ritual. Goffman includes human beings in the animal kingdom. Humans have a wide range of expressible attributes, for instance intent, feeling, relationship, social class, health, etc. The most deeply seated trait of humans is their gender – femininity and masculinity, which are the prototypes of essential expression. If advertisements are a form of expression, the receiver reads his/her own interpretation into these expressions.

Goffmann looks at pictures/photographs, private and public, as a medium of expression. Using a very large selection of pictures, he contrasts how we perceive the portrayal of models as opposed to a photographs of people in real situations. While portraits depict real individual characteristics, a scene in an advertisement depicts an activity recognisable in real life. Though there is a significant similarity, 'commercial realism' does not provide us with people portraying themselves. Advertisements are intentionally choreographed and provide us with something 'fuller and richer' than real-life glimpses, making use of our ability to switch from reality to participation in a make-believe life. Goffman examines what he calls 'small behaviours', where physical forms are well defined even if the social implications or meaning of the act are not clear. He categorises his pictures into groups – relative size of men and women, the feminine touch, the family, etc.

4. *Personal Computer World* Advertisement Analysis

On the basis of the above reading, we wanted to see whether the decoding criteria also apply to computing advertisements and whether there is any gender bias in computer advertising. We analysed advertisements from the magazine *Personal Computer World* between May 1993 and March 1996. In each issue there were between 161 and 176 advertisers. All the advertisements and the advertisers were concerned with computers: hardware manufacturers, retailers or software houses.

Late in 1996 we wrote to and telephoned the editor of *Personal Computer World* several times to enquire about its distribution numbers and patterns as well as its and its clients' policies on advertising and gender. Despite several promises, we have never received an answer to any of our questions. Our assumption about this magazine is that it is widely read by large and small corporate readers mainly to see what is on offer on the PC market. We guess that the main target readership are people who have, work with or understand computers and want to keep up with the latest reports on software, hardware and prices. The magazine contains some tutorials and articles which usually assume a fair amount of prior knowledge. Individuals who are thinking of buying new, or upgrading old, computers might consult *Personal Computer World*, but we do not think that the magazine would attract computing beginners. It is a glossy magazine, published monthly at a cost of £2.95. Each month it has between 630 and 700 pages, about 200 of which carry articles. All writers in the magazine are men. The vast majority of the pages carry advertisements. Many pages only show pictures of hardware and many advertisers list goods for sale. We have taken samples of all the advertisements which contained any pictures of people or parts of people and categorised them into groups of those showing women only, men only, groups of both sexes and hands only. The basic statistics in Table 4.1 emerged:

	men only	women only	mixed groups	men's hands	women's hands	mixed hands
1993	16	3	3	4	2	1
1994	20	3	8	8	1	0
1995	22	4	12	7	1	0
1996	40	10	19	5	1	0

Table 4.1: Average number of pages a month on which each category appeared

Many advertisements were repeated over the years, so we have selected one of each and divided them into what we call large and small; see Table 4.2 for statistics. Large advertisements are those with photographs half a page and larger; small are those with small pictures inserted into pages of text. For a 700-page magazine, the small pictures seem insignificant, usually appearing alongside long lists of goods and services. The multipaged A3- and A4-size advertisements with large pictures are more prominent, more visible, obviously more planned and thought through, often tied to a text telling a story.

	men only	women only	mixed groups	men's hands	women's hands
Total number	285	83	112	91	12
Large	113	22	46	37	2
Small	172	61	66	54	10

Table 4.2: Number of pictorial advertisements 1993-96 (repetitions excluded)

4.1 Women only

In the three years, only 83 different pictures of women were published, most of them very small, up to 5x6 cms. Most of the women photographed are very young, many with long hair. Only three black women appear among them.

4.1.1 Working Women

Of the small pictures only 17 show women with, or in front of, computer equipment. Only one advertisement shows a woman seriously engaged with a laptop computer on her lap, fully facing the camera, legs crossed, revealing a knee. A number of the women are obviously demonstrating a product to the viewer and the engagement with their work does not seem natural. It is clear from the text that most of the women are members of sales staff and help desk staff. The majority of the remaining pictures portray women as telephonists, not pictured in front of the computer.

4.1.2 Positive Images of Women

Only two large pictures can be classified as portraying real women. One is physically placed in front of a computer, where the woman is actively seeking to buy a computer to suit her needs. The picture is somewhat spoiled when on the next page a group of men offer to build one especially for her. The other A4-size photograph of a woman, it is suggested in the text, possesses computer skills and knowledge. She has successfully upgraded her machine. The other two A4-size advertisements use small pictures of women to promote modern and developing technology (sending a rocket into space).

4.1.3 Confused and Confusing Women

A woman small business owner is pictured praising a scanner. She gently strokes it and says 'It is so easy, I love it'. Confusing and confused is the woman pictured amongst flying equipment. The text suggests that she uses common sense to choose equipment but her picture suggests she is not up to it. A large paper lioness 'taken from the jungle of big business, pouncing out of her box, becoming quite domesticated and not needing any special diets' is being gently led by a beautiful woman. Is the woman like the cat, free pouncing lioness at first, who becomes domesticated, tamed and without special needs?

4.1.4 The Bitchy and the Difficult

Two women just had a fight over a printer (a large ad). Their faces are bruised around the eyes, their lips, bright red with fresh lipstick, twisted into victorious smile. The assumption here has to be that the printer built especially for them has been built by men to introduce peace where uncompromising chaos prevailed. In another large advertisement, Margaret, wearing glasses and looking sternly into the camera, is a 'difficult character' , she is older and therefore established, hence the name. She represents another male stereotype of a woman: pedantic, inflexible, to be viewed with a sigh.

4.1.5 The Defaced (all large advertisements)

Somehow the text associated with one of the advertisements says it all: 'you spend more time looking at your monitor than the one you love, so be choosy'. The picture shows a thick gold frame around a slim woman in an evening dress, her head substituted by a monitor. How important are women in men's lives, particularly when compared to the importance of their work, and what role do they play? In another two advertisements, one half of the women's faces have been replaced by a computer printout. The colour and the facial expressions in these advertisements are also indicative: the devilish purple and black makeup, the dark red lips and nails, the unnatural smile.

4.1.6 Sexual Objects

A number of small advertisements use photographs of women purely for decorative reasons to draw attention to equipment or services. Most of these women are portrayed as decorative or subservient objects. The large pictures depicting women as sexual objects are much more powerful. One shows an image of Marilyn Monroe with her skirt blown upwards, another a naked woman with leopard-like skin and a dreamy fuzzy face holding a mouse to her left breast. One shows a traditional Japanese woman as a symbol of the 'culture of service' and another a young blond dressed as Santa Claus, in high heels and a mini skirt, bending down to include a computer in her hamper of presents.

The advertisements described above are more or less the only images of women on their own that appeared, some more than once, in three years' issues of a very popular and widely read computing magazine: two large positive images of women, two promoting power and progress, the rest showing women as sex or decorative objects and good helpers. Women are also put in front of computers to demonstrate the equipment in the showrooms, somehow not looking very convincing as users with technical understanding.

4.2 Hands

Hands, together with the body leaning over the equipment, represent the confidence with which we handle technology. Of the many hands that appear in every issue of *Personal Computer World*, only 12 are female. Apart from being generally shown as smaller and having red finger nails, the most noticeable thing about them is how they handle the equipment. Their touch is gentle, stroking, delicate; 'the mouse you'll love to hold' is gently caressed. Only two of the female hands appear as large advertisements. About 90 different male hands appear in computing advertisements. Their touch is different more powerful and confident. Notable are the differences in holding equipment on fingertips, handling CD ROMs, mouse or a keyboard. Even the one male hand which is just gently touching the mouse is, in fact, electric and dark blue.

4.3 Mixed groups

The number of advertisements portraying men and women in the same picture may be a sign of changing times and of the industry accepting that women also use computers. We were therefore looking forward to sorting these out. Mostly, however, we were disappointed.

4.3.1 Representing real life

A number of advertisers have decided to show 'real life' using real employees or actors. The sales and help desk teams include men and women. However, with the realism of the scenes comes the stereotypical reality of the situations. Women in the offices are very much in the minority. Where the groups are standing upright, the women are always smaller than the men. The women are mostly portrayed as receptionists, data entry and word processing operators or secretaries. It is mostly men who handle the hardware, and where the reverse is the case, men are always positioned higher in the image.

There is also a positive image of women handling the hardware with confidence, teleconferencing with men, instructing men. However, the total of nine positive images is all we found in the almost 25000 pages we looked through, and even in these some of the men are positioned slightly higher than women.

4.3.2 Family

Nineteen advertisements in all were directed at families. Among those, only five disrupted the stereotypes. Mum using the computer at home and four little girls at school and home. None of the girls appears older than 6 (why?). The rest of the family advertisements have boys and dads or boys only as the focal point, with mums, dads and sisters looking on. Dads are positioned the highest in most cases and where there are sisters present, they are observing, not touching the hardware. The writing on one father's computer which the little boy is observing says, 'Dear Santa, I want a computer like my dad's'.

4.3.3 Users and Customers

Though advertisers now accept that women can also be users, advertisements portraying this are still in a minority. In one advertisement there is a boy but no girl in the crowd of users. While the one woman in a printer advertisement is practically encased in stacks of folders, the men around her are doing important jobs for which they need the occasional printout. In another, the man with the powerful Landrover has just purchased a powerful computer, the onlooking women are pleased. When the same women appear at work, they have very animated, almost gossipy conversations, while the men look very serious, seemingly engaged in some serious relationship.

4.3.4 Cartoons

Some advertisers chose to use cartoons for messages that could not be produced using real people. The feminists of the late 1970s would have loved to deface them. A fat woman bending over a filing cabinet, revealing her bottom to a thin man looking stunned and spilling his coffee over the computer, or a very chesty blond with a low décolleté, red long finger nails, drinking a glass of bubbly with a large male bear while a computer is being served to her by a waiter. We would also include an advertisement here in which a torso of a women is in effect also a cartoon. She has no face, but does have a low décolleté and an out-stretched hand along which little men are walking towards her cleavage.

4.4 Men Only

There are too many pictures in this category to describe them all so we have picked some that best represent the rest of them. These advertisements fit mainly into two further subgroups.

4.4.1 Real working men

It is noticeable that the men appear relaxed, confident and serious about their work, sometimes very excited. In comparison with the women they appear deeply engaged with their work rather than demonstrating a product to the viewer. As noted by both Williamson and Goffmann, the men almost never look into the camera. When men are used to advertise laptops, we do not see their legs. The large pictures of working men look even more convincing. A number of men just represent themselves. Their names and usually their status are indicated. They are confident, smartly dressed and young and appear enthusiastic and knowledgeable about the product which they advertise.

4.4.2 Power

A large number of advertisements use real and cartoon men as symbols of power. Sports appear often, performed by men, to demonstrate power, while the use of sports women is less clear. One woman tennis player is used to advertise a multimedia package and a series of pictures of one gymnast in various acrobatic positions illustrates lists of equipment. We found the following sports performed by men only: climbing, athletics, car racing, canoeing, football, parachuting, skiing, sailing, surfing, sumo, cycling, body building, ice hockey, cross country, American football, golf, speed skating and high diving. It is the aggressive and the fast face of sports that is most often depicted pictorially. The use of the male body and the associations with strength and aggression are most apparent; see the green Incredible Hulk bursting out of the picture, the Superman and the Batman. Famous revolutionaries, Bill Clinton with a clenched fist or Christ walking on water can also be associated with power.

5. Examples of Close Reading

From the broad survey of images presented above, this section considers two adverts in more detail, specifically looking at the relationship between the image and the text. The following advertisements all came from 1996 editions of *Computing*.

5.1 The Network Upgrade

The picture shows a man and a woman. The man is turned towards the viewer, but his gaze seems to be directed towards the woman's front. His right arm is around her waist, his left hand is palm open, mainly turned towards her, but part towards the viewer. This may be a directional gesture – 'let's go' – or a demonstrative, 'showing' gesture. The woman's left arm is around the back of his head, hovering above his shoulder, either being put around his shoulder, or being taken away from his shoulder. From the fact that they are smiling at one another, and the implication in the rest of the advert (see below), we assume that she is in the process of putting her arm around him.

The man is tanned, with a full head of thick, dark hair, and appears to be between 35 and 50 years old. He is wearing glasses. The woman has her face turned away from the viewer – she is looking at the man – so it is hard to tell her age. However, from the half-turned profile, she looks to be under 35. She is very slim, with smooth, tanned skin, and long fairish hair. Her hair is held back from her face by a pair of what seem to be sunglasses, rather than glasses, on top of her head. The man is wearing a light blue shirt, unbuttoned at the neck, and a navy blazer. The woman is wearing a black dress with white spots. It has a high neck, but is cut away sharply at the sides. If she wasn't so slim the curve of her breasts at the side would be clearly visible. Her arms are bare. From the way the material of her dress is ruffled by the pressure of his hand on her waist the material seems to be very lightweight.

Above the picture a heading claims: 'We'll really get you going . . .'. 'We'll' is in red, the rest of the text is in black. The word 'really' is enlarged. Underneath the picture, the sentence continues: '. . . with our Network Upgrade'.

Smaller text then goes on to say: 'If you've an important date with a network upgrade but find the prospect of spending time and money on installation is a real turn off, our Netware Server Upgrade will get you going fast. Our undeniably attractive combination of technologies is available at a tempting special price for a limited period. And at only £1,999 (exc. VAT) for hardware and software, it's a small price to pay for bringing users closer together and getting your business going.'

At the end a paragraph of slightly larger, italicized text says: 'So call us today – and let us show you a match made in heaven that won't feel like a ball and chain!'

The theme suggested by the picture is immediately picked by the mention of an important date. There is nothing else in the context of the picture, or the product, if we have looked this far already, to suggest that date means anything other than an assignation for the purposes of having sex at some point in the near, or distant, future. 'Upgrade', given this context, suggests a partner who is superior in every respect to those you are used to. However, it is also suggested that to have to spend time and money on 'installation' would dampen your ardour, so [the advertiser] offers you a solution that 'will get you going fast'. To 'get going' in this context then invokes the vernacular interpretation, to become excited, or sexually aroused. If we were in any doubt about the meaning of the main heading, the possibilities are now closing down rapidly. To get going fast, without an investment of time and money, also suggests a ready, willing and easily accessible sexual partner. This is further reinforced by the usage of 'undeniably attractive' and 'tempting' in the next paragraph.

This links to an earlier advert from the same advertiser which appeared in *Personal Computer World* in 1995, which starts with the claim 'You may get carried away!' It shows a young man, in a striped shirt, tie and smart trousers, carrying the advertised product. The accompanying text goes on to desribe the product, and then finishes: 'So, if you feel an uncontrollable urge coming on, why not just give in to it?'

This, again, seems to be 'buying in' to a notion of sexual urge. But the notion of an 'uncontrollable' urge accords more with the traditional notion of male sexuality. With the dual meaning of 'may' in the first line, the advert suggests that [the advertiser] is also giving approval to this kind of urge.

The final, italicized, paragraph reinforces the notion of the ideal sexual partnership, with 'match made in heaven'. However, up until this point a female reader could possibly have resisted the dominant codes suggested by the picture – older man, taking command of the situation, younger woman scantily dressed, gazing at him. It may have been possible to see either of them upgrading their partners, trading older models for new faster, more attractive versions. But, with the use of 'ball and chain' – traditional vernacular for the wife – a female reader is left with no illusions about her place in [the advertiser's] notion of the software market.

5.2 The Server

Approximately two-thirds of the advert space is taken up with a picture of a heavily pregnant woman, whilst the final third is a column on the right hand side containing the text and a picture of the product. The woman is standing with her right side turned towards us, and we can see her pregnant belly in profile. Her hands are clasped underneath her belly. Her face is fully turned towards us, and she is looking out at us, smiling. She looks kind and relaxed. The text begins in large red letters: 'she can't afford for the business to come crashing down while she's away.'

From this we may assume either that the business is her own or that she has considerable responsibility for it. Again there is an association here between women and concerns about affordability. Does the advertiser not want to offend men by suggesting that they cannot afford something, and so use the figure of a woman to convey the message instead?

The text continues, in smaller, black type: 'Servers are often at the heart of an organisation's IT operations and an ever-increasing dependence is being placed on their reliability. Whether they are used for applications, databases or networks, server reliability is essential.' From the red text we assume that 'she' refers to the woman in the picture. The referent of the black text is an organisation's server. So one reading may be that the woman in the picture has responsibility for her organisation's server. However, the change of referent is not introduced in any way – we switch directly from text about her to a description of servers. This leaves space for ambiguity between the identification of the woman and the server. But what the identity consists of is also ambiguous. The text may be suggesting that a server is at the heart of an organisation the way a mother is at the heart of a family (with an implicit message about motherhood as being about service and reliability). Or, it may be suggesting that women *are* servers, and should be placed in such positions – stressing, however, the importance of getting a reliable one.

We would suggest that the advert plays upon this ambiguity, and that all of the potential interpretations are engaged in order to project a certain message. This, in turn, suggests that the audience the advert is actually addressing may not be the one that it initially appears to be addressing.

In these examples we can see that the image and the text give messages, the overall message(s) of an advertisement may be modified by the relationship between the two. In the first example above, the text seemed to support the message of the image very clearly, and unsubtly. In the second, the message is more complex. This may occur for a variety of reasons. It may be that the organisation and its advertising agency were trying to advertise to women, but were not aware of how their message may be otherwise interpreted. Or that they were trying to advertise to men by presenting a comforting image of women. Or that they were implicitly making claims for their product by appealing to a specific image of women. Whatever the motives, what we are concerned with in this paper is the subtle effects such depictions have on women, the overall portrayal of the computing industry, and the ways that both may discourage women from making a career in the industry.

6. Conclusion

Individually and spread among long lists of products, most of these pictures appear harmless. However, systematically grouped together they suddenly become meaningful. It becomes apparent that women are not very favourably portrayed. The advertisements use lots of stereotypes and present pictures of women who do not appear very confident with the technology and do not have much status or power. When advertising, the computing industry is almost invariably addressing men. A detailed analysis of picture and text reveals hidden and ambiguous message.

There are other, more subtle, ways of suggesting that the world of computers is the world of men. Bony male legs, a man's feet in polished shoes relaxing on a keyboard, a neck with a shirt and a tie or a tie itself positioned next to a laptop, a cigar which does not represent happiness any more or a hand-written note on a screen from David to Paul.

Twenty years ago the feminist critique of the portrayal of women in advertisements reached its peak. Since then interest seems to have declined. The computer industry does not appear concerned with the portrayal of women in computing advertisements and the potential influence this has on the way women view themselves and are seen by men in relation to computer technology.

This paper is concerned with raising awareness among computing professionals about the subtle influences of media representation on images of themselves. Although there are some companies which have quite obviously understood the issues, there appear to be far too many that do not address these issues at all.

Acknowledgement

I would like to thank my friend Debbie Cowley for patient reading and re-reading this and all previous papers and for all her helpful suggestions.

Eva Turner

References

Bowlby, R. (1993). *Shopping With Freud*. London: Routledge.

Beardon, C. (1993). 'Social Citizenship and the Information Age', in Beardon, C. and Whitehouse, D.(eds.). *Computers and Society*. Exeter: Intellect.

Courtney, A. E. and Whipple, T. W .(1984). *Sex, Stereotyping in Advertising*. Lexington Books.

Goffmann, E. (1987). *Gender Advertisements*. Harper Torchbooks.

Grundy, F. (1996). *Women and Computers*. Exeter: Intellect.

Inglis, F. (1972).*The Imagery of Power, A Critique of Advertising*. London: Heinemann.

McCracken, E. (1993). *Decoding Women's Magazines, from* Mademoiselle *to* Ms. Macmillan.

Millum, T. (1975). *Images of Women, Advertising in Women's Magazines*. London: Chatto and Windus.

Mort, F. (1996). *Cultures of Consumption* London: Routledge.

Myers, K. (1986). *Under-Stains . . . the sense and seduction of advertising.* Comedia Publishing Group.

Turner, E. (1997). *What is Our Worth?,* IFIP Women, Work and Computerization 97 Conference Proceedings. Springer-Verlag.

Voet, R. (1993). 'Women as Citizens and the Role of Information Technology', in Beardon, C. and Whitehouse, D.(eds.).*Computers and Society.* Exeter: Intellect.

Wernick, A. (1994). *Promotional Culture, Advertising, Ideology and Symbolic Expression.* Sage.

Williamson, J. (1981). *Decoding Advertisements, Ideology and Meaning in Advertising.* Marion Boyars.

Women in Media (1976). *The Packaging of Women,* Seminar Report, London.

Women in Computing: A Cross-National Analysis

Rosemary Wright

Department of Social Sciences and History, Fairleigh Dickinson University

Abstract

This paper analyses cross-nationally the fall-off in women's participation in computer work since the middle of the 1980s. Using data from UNESCO, it presents the percentages of women graduating from mathematics and computer science programmes in 1990 in 71 countries, then follows the percentage trends from 1975 to 1985 to 1990 for 19 of the 71. From 1985 to 1990, the proportions of women completing such programmes were falling in 12 countries and rising in seven. The majority of the world's graduates completed their programmes in countries where the percentage of women was falling. Analyses of US data suggest that this fall-off may be partly due to computing's masculine occupational culture, which may be strengthening with the deployment of personal computers. This culture alienates women, causing many to decline to enter and those who do enter to leave more often than their male counterparts.

1. Introduction

This paper analyses on a cross-national basis the fall-off in women's participation in computer science programmes apparent in the United States since the middle of the 1980s (Leveson 1989). Using data from UNESCO (1995), it presents the percentages of women graduating from mathematics and computer science programmes in 1990 in 71 different countries. It then presents the trends from 1975 to 1985 and from 1985 to 1990 in the same percentages for the 19 countries for which data were available and whose programmes were significant in size.

While the combination of mathematics and computer science data is unfortunate, the UNESCO data set appears to be the only one to contain data from many countries. For the speculative purposes of this paper and based on an analysis of American data,[1] we may assume that, at least in the developed countries, the percentage of computer science graduates who are women is likely to rise and fall with the percentage of women in the combined figures.

With many more countries offering mathematics and computer science programmes in the 1990s than in the 1970s, the data in this paper about the common trends in the percentages of women in such programmes suggest that the international gender composition of computing may well be driven by the same cultural forces as the composition in the USA. A distinctly masculine occupational culture (Wright 1996) may be transcending national cultural differences to affect women's advance into the computer profession internationally.[2]

2. Cross-national data

Table 1 presents by country the percentages of women graduating from programmes in mathematics and computer science in 1990. Programmes at three International Standard Classification of Education (ISCED) levels are included in these statistics — Level 5, leading to an award not equivalent to a first university degree; Level 6, leading to a first university degree or equivalent qualification; and Level 7, leading to a post-graduate university degree or equivalent qualification (UNESCO 1995, Tables 3.14 and 5.4).

Interestingly, the 62,684 graduates from the USA, while comprising the largest entry in the table, do not form a majority of the world's graduates. In fact, they form only 37% of the graduates for whose countries these data were available. The country with the second highest number of graduates (22,163) is the Republic of Korea. The United Kingdom comes in third, with 17,733, followed by Canada with 9,410 and Germany (not including the former East Germany) with 7,389. Clearly, the US and the UK, which initiated the first computer science programmes following their development of computer hardware (Kraft 1979), no longer have a monopoly on such education.

Noticing the wide variation between different countries, we need to limit analysis to sizeable programmes to eliminate the effects of small sample size. Within the larger programmes just mentioned, however, we still see variation: Women were 36% of the graduates in the US and South Korea but only 28% of the graduates in the UK and 32% of those in Canada. This seems counter-intuitive in that, based on common culture and heritage, we would expect more commonality between the US, the UK, and Canada than between the US and Korea.

Table 2 attempts to unravel some of the mystery of Table 1. Delving further into the UNESCO data, we find that 19 of the 71 countries had data on the percentage of women graduates in 1975, 1985 and 1990, and were sizeable enough to have graduated at least 100 students in 1975. While the 19 represent only a quarter of the countries in Table 1, they include three of the four largest countries and three-quarters of the graduates. Data on the UK, the fourth country, were unfortunately missing from this data set.

At the bottom of the table, we see a net rise from 33% in 1975 to 38% in 1985, followed by a net fall in 1990 to 35%. By country, the relative sizes and patterns tell an important story: In eight countries, the percent of women graduates rose from 1975 to 1985, then fell back toward their 1975 levels. In four countries, the percent of such women fell over *both* periods, and in seven countries, the percent of women graduates *rose* over the two periods. The data from the first eight countries, especially the United States, are clearly driving the net rise and fall. The USA alone accounts for 64%, 69% and 50% of all graduates in the three years in Table 2.

As of 1990, we see that the American influence was still large but diminishing. The number of American graduates in 1990 had fallen to 80% of their numbers in 1985, while South Korean graduates had increased to 1028% of theirs. Using the totals on Table 1, the USA had fallen to only 37% of that table's graduates, while South Korea had risen to 13%. Given that data were missing from many countries in Table 2, this relative position is only suggestive but worth further investigation, given the rising proportions of women in computing in South Korea and Malaysia shown in Table 2, the movement of computer programming offshore (Yourdon 1992), and the low salaries afforded women in the developing world.

Countries	Total N	% Women	Countries	Total N	% Women
Africa			Europe		
Algeria	1025	34.5	Albania	7	42.9
Burundi	46	13.0	Austria	594	23.4
Egypt	1276	23.3	Belgium	904	27.0
Ethiopia	167	15.6	Bulgaria	531	69.5
Ghana	102	23.5	Croatia	95	31.6
Guinea	52	3.8	Czech Republic	263	26.2
Liberia	24	33.3	Denmark	232	27.6
Madagascar	201	15.4	Estonia	73	61.6
Mauritius	66	45.4	Finland	1682	20.9
Mozambique	9	66.7	Germany [2]	7389	20.7
Niger	19	10.5	Greece	1347	40.2
Rwanda	44	13.6	Hungary	289	20.1
Sudan	38	18.4	Ireland	1139	40.2
Tunisia	211	28.4	Italy	3364	51.2
Uganda	71	5.6	Netherlands	381	12.9
			Norway	245	26.5
North America			Poland	1321	62.0
Bahamas	18	77.8	Portugal	428	61.2
Canada	9410	31.5	Romania	630	62.5
Cuba	298	54.4	Slovakia	112	41.1
Nicaragua	101	68.3	Slovenia	33	48.5
St. Kitts & Nevis	28	64.3	Spain	4114	36.2
United States	62684	36.4	Sweden	1442	25.9
			Switzerland	376	13.0
South America			Macedonia	102	67.6
Brazil	6494	42.4	United Kingdom	17733	28.0
Colombia	1222	43.0			
			Oceania		
Asia			Guam	13	38.5
Cyprus	178	38.8	New Caledonia	237	27.0
Hong Kong	1641	26.6	New Zealand	502	26.1
Indonesia	1275	45.1			
Iran	670	30.7	Total	167887	35.1
Israel	818	36.9			
Japan	4370	23.9			
Jordan	1458	51.3	[1] Countries for which UNESCO data at		
Republic of Korea	22163	35.8	combined ISCED levels were available in		
Kuwait	130	52.3	roughly 1990. Data from 1989, 1991, or 1992		
Macau	57	26.3	were substituted when 1990 data were not		
Malaysia	1098	45.7	available.		
Mongolia	99	66.7			
Oman	7	28.6	[2] Not including the former German		
Philippines	1896	64.7	Democratic Republic.		
Qatar	38	73.7			
Syrian Arab Republic	23	30.4			
Thailand	295	17.6			
Turkey	2444	39.2			
United Arab Emirates	43	79.1			

Table 1. Cross-national Comparison of Women's Percentages of Graduates in Mathematics and Computer Science, 1990 [1].

Countries	1975 Total N	1975 % Women	1985 Total N	1985 % Women	1990 Total N	1990 % Women
Percentages Rising Then Falling						
United States	29196	32.3	78633	39.4 **	62684	36.4 **
Canada	2741	26.3	10983	33.3 **	9410	31.5 **
Japan	2802	23.3	3821	26.4 **	4370	23.9 **
Spain	269	33.5	1554	38.0	4114	36.2
Turkey	346	24.9	831	46.3 **	2444	39.2 **
Belgium	272	25.7	2378	30.3	904	27.0
Austria	156	7.7	372	27.4 **	594	23.4
Netherlands	111	9.9	229	14.0	381	12.9
Subtotal	35893	30.9	98801	37.9 **	84901	33.9 **
Percentages Falling Then Falling						
Italy	2832	59.6	2492	56.1 **	3364	51.2 **
Finland	764	32.3	1468	25.6 **	1682	20.9 **
Portugal	320	80.9	156	76.3	428	61.2 **
Hungary	310	52.3	310	43.9 *	289	20.1 **
Subtotal	4226	55.7	4426	45.8 **	5763	41.5 **
Percentages Rising Then Rising						
Republic of Korea	611	25.0	2155	25.9	22163	35.8 **
Germany [2]	1945	8.3	3296	17.4 **	7389	20.7 **
Jordan	111	30.6	1568	36.6	1458	51.3 **
Greece	954	22.1	1162	34.9 **	1347	40.2 **
Poland	1415	60.0	814	62.4	1321	62.0
Malaysia	123	29.3	468	43.8 **	1098	45.7
Bulgaria	472	62.5	638	63.6	531	69.5 *
Subtotal	5631	30.9	10101	32.0	35307	35.2 **
Net Rise and Fall	45750	33.2	113328	37.7 **	125971	34.6 **

Table 2. Cross-national Comparison of Women's Percentages of Graduates in Mathematics and Computer Science, 1975–1985–1990 [1].

[1] Countries for which UNESCO data at combined ISCED levels were available for all three time periods, limited to those with atleast 100 graduates in 1975. Data from 1976 or 1977 were substituted when 1975 data were not available. Data from 1989, 1991 or 1992 were substitute when 1990 data were not available.

[2] Not including the former German Democratic Republic.

Significance of difference to prior percentage: **p<.01 *p<.05

Also of interest, 54% of the 1990 graduates in Table 1 were in countries in which the percentages of women were falling in the late 1980s. At least 21% followed the opposite pattern, in that their percentages of women rose. While we don't know the situation of the missing 25%, the ratio of 54% to 21% and the past influence of the American pattern suggest that it is worth understanding that pattern in greater detail.

3. American data

Using American data from the National Science Foundation, Wright (1997) has analysed in depth this pattern of the rising, then falling percentage of women's participation in computer work. To summarise that analysis, we need to consider the relationship between graduating from programmes in computer science and working in the computer workplace.

Figure 1 does so by showing two related trends in the US: the change in women's percentage of those receiving bachelor's degrees (ISCED Level 6) in computer and information sciences,[3] and the change in women's percentage of those employed in computer work. These percentages are presented for 1971 to 1995, using data from the US Departments of Education and Labor As seen in the figure, women's representation among graduates of American programmes in computer and information science has risen from 14% in 1971 to 37% in 1984, from which it has fallen to 28% in 1994.[4] Women's proportion of American computer work has followed a similar, but later, pattern. In 1971 women were 15% of all such workers, which rose to a high of 36% in 1990 but fell back to 31% in 1995.

4. Women's choices not to enter and to leave computer work

To answer the question why women's progression has reversed, we must consider women's decisions at two points in time – entry and exit. At least in the USA, women are both choosing not to enter computer work and are also more likely than men to leave it. Regarding women's decisions not to enter, the programme and degree data in Table 1 and Figure 1 provide only one part of the entry picture. Both degree and worker data are presented in Figure 1 to show that the percentage of women receiving degrees is, in fact, related to the percentage of women employed in the computer workforce. One does not automatically follow from the other, however (Carey 1991/92, Wright 1997). Regarding women's decisions to leave, a separate analysis of 6,200 members of a National Science Foundation panel from the 1980s shows that after controlling for background, education, experience, period, specialty and industry, women are more likely to leave computer work in the USA than are men (Wright and Jacobs 1994).

The factors most frequently cited for women choosing not to enter computer work are their socialization away from mathematics and science; software being written mostly by and for men; the domination of computer training programmes by boys, men and male values; and a common perception that computer work is a field for men and anti-social individuals (Committee on Women 1991, Decker 1986, Hartman et al 1988, Newton 1991, Steering Committee 1993). Factors put forward for the *fall-off* in women's interest in computing include male backlash (Breene 1993, Faludi 1991) and women's attraction to alternative male-dominated fields such as business (Leveson 1989). Factors suggested for the fall-off in both men's *and* women's interest since the middle 1980s include an increasing misconception of the nature of the occupation (Cale et al

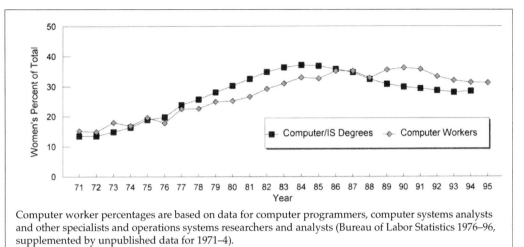

Computer worker percentages are based on data for computer programmers, computer systems analysts and other specialists and operations systems researchers and analysts (Bureau of Labor Statistics 1976–96, supplemented by unpublished data for 1971–4).

Computer/IS Degree percentages are based on data for Bachelors Degrees in Computer and Information Sciences (Department of Education 1995, supplemented by unpublished data for 1993–4). The data are for academic years, marking each by the calendar year in which the academic year ends.

Figure 1. Percentages of women in Computer/Information Science Bachelors' Degrees and working in computing, USA.

1991); an increase in the number of students taking programming in high school; and the personal computer having demystified, as well as given greater access to, computers (Committee to Assess 1992).

To investigate how these negative factors affect both entry and exit, let us turn to the occupational culture of computing, at least as it exists in the United States.

5. The American occupational culture of computing

Computers were first developed in the USA during World War II, when the first programmers of the Electronic Numerical Integrator and Computer (ENIAC) were women, called the 'ENIAC girls'. In the post-war years, computer work became a male preserve, viewed as requiring technical rather than mechanical skills (Kraft 1979). During the 1950s and early 1960s, computer systems were built and programmed by electrical engineers, primarily for military purposes and secondarily for business use. Through the late 1960s and 1970s, computer use grew exponentially in the business sector. Large mainframes became numerous throughout American corporations, joined by a host of mini-computers. Personal computers emerged in the 1980s. Accompanying the many hardware changes and reductions in size throughout these decades was a continual succession of operating systems, programming languages and applications (Tarallo 1987). By 1993, computers had become so widely deployed that almost half of all women and more than a third of all men in the US labour force use them in some form at work (US Bureau of the Census 1993).

Supporting users and computers throughout this period required a rapidly increasing population of computer professionals whose required knowledge changed constantly (Steering Committee 1993). Partly driven by the fluidity of the knowledge base, common interests and shared experiences have caused a distinct occupational culture to develop and evolve. The underpinnings of this culture were determined by the fact that electrical engineers built and maintained the first computers (Trice 1993).

Physically constructed by electrical engineers, the first computers embodied engineering values and norms (Hughes 1987). Electrical engineering — a strong, well-established occupation when electrical engineers developed computers — has therefore dominated and controlled the work content of computer work, one of its subordinate occupations (Simpson 1985). Because subordinate occupational cultures take on the ideologies and cultural forms of their dominant culture, the computer culture has assumed the occupational culture of electrical engineering (Trice 1993).

Women are more likely than men to find this culture alien because of its masculine nature (Kiesler et al. 1985, Turkle 1988, Wright 1996). We can understand the reasons by considering McIlwee and Robinson's (1992) cultural description,[5] which draws on Hacker's (1990), Cockburn's (1988), and Bailyn's (1987) arguments that technical work is socially defined as masculine.

In interviews with 30 male and 52 female engineering graduates of two public universities in Southern California, McIlwee and Robinson (1992) found two major components in the culture — an ideology and an interactional style. The ideology emphasises the dominance of technology, engineers / computer workers as producers of this technology, and organisational power as the basis of engineering/computer success. The interactional style requires looking, talking and acting like an engineer/computer worker, which in most workplaces means looking, talking and acting out a particular masculinity, which McIlwee and Robinson generalise to the 'male gender role'. The culture emphasises enactment of this masculinity, requiring aggressive displays of technical self-confidence and hands-on ability for success, defining professional competence in hegemonically masculine terms and devaluing the gender characteristics of women.

Women in this culture are particularly hurt by the obsession with technology and hands-on activities, because the gender socialization experienced by most women yields a distinct lack of experience in 'tinkering' with electronics. Even when they acquire the necessary skills, women do not seem to become as comfortable or as obsessed as their male counterparts. They are also hurt by the criterion for success being aggressive presentation of competence. Technical proficiency must be individualistic, displayed aggressively and competitively and concerned with physical technology rather than the social relationships that go with it. The display required is that of this masculinity, playing a role with which most women are uncomfortable, even when they are capable of its performance (McIlwee and Robinson 1992).

The evidence is strong that many computer workers in the 1990s still have an engineering-derived occupational culture, even with competition from a user-friendly 'culture of simulation' (Turkle 1995), the proliferation of MIS programmes in business schools, computer programming courses in two-year technical schools, and applications development for every conceivable business function. It is evident in the common practice of calling programmers software engineers (King 1994), the curricula of academic departments of computer science having a strong engineering content and approach, even where they are not in engineering schools

(ACM/IEEE-CS Joint Curriculum 1991), and a recent call for practitioners to obtain computer science and engineering credentials (Steering Committee 1993). Indeed, social scientists' descriptions of this culture notwithstanding, its engineering and masculine base is repeatedly cited and taken as given throughout a growing gender literature in computer science. See, for example, Shade (1993), Martin and Murchie-Beyma (1992) and Spertus (1991).

6. Conclusion

We began by noting how women's representation among the graduates of mathematics and computer science programmes in at least 12 countries has fallen since the middle 1980s. We reviewed earlier research on why at least American women choose not to enter computer work. The factors put forward for women's choosing not to enter the field are girls' socialization away from mathematics and science; software being written by and for men and boys; computer training programmes being dominated by boys, men and male values; and a common perception that computer work is a field for men and anti-social people. Factors suggested for the fall-off in both women's and men's interest include a misconception of the occupation, an increase in students taking programming in high school and the personal computer having demystified computers. Factors projected for the fall-off in women's interest include male backlash and women's attraction to alternative male-dominated fields such as business.

Viewing computing as having a distinctly masculine occupational culture is a way to unify most of these themes. Mathematics and science *are* at the core of the computing culture and proficiency in them is considered a masculine trait: certainly in the USA, software *is* written primarily by and for men (Huff and Cooper 1987). Computer training programmes *are* dominated by boys, men and male values, although there are signs of improvement, especially in women's training on and use of the Internet (Shade 1993). Women *continue* to perceive computer work as a field for men and anti-social people (Newton 1991, Shade 1993). All of these are compatible with computing having a distinctly masculine occupational culture, if not a distinct occupational masculinity (Wright 1996).

As to the fall-off in women's interest since the middle 1980s, more young women are indeed taking programming in high school but they may merely be getting turned off *earlier* when they enter the male-dominated computer rooms that many of them find alien (Sproull et al. 1987). Perhaps more women misconceive the nature of the occupation for the same reason – they encounter the masculinity *before* they find the portions of the work which might attract them to the field. And what of the personal computer having demystified and given greater access to the field? Well, again, young women may find they do not like it before they enter it. In the past, they had to go into it to find out they did not feel comfortable.

Putting aside the issue of male backlash, which cannot be proved one way or the other, there is a good case to be made for women's choosing alternative destinations, although not necessarily to alternative male-dominated occupations. Jacobs (1995) has shown that the decline of women's entry into computer science is part of a general stabilization in women's entry into male-dominated majors. Alternative destinations may, in fact, be computer-related: Turkle (1995) has argued that there is a growing culture of simulation accompanying the culture of computing, which she now calls the culture of calculation. Women are more likely than men to have soft programming styles — to program by trial and error instead of by careful planning (Turkle 1984). That this culture is more amenable to people with soft programming styles (Turkle 1995) suggests that the alternative destinations may well be *user* occupations in which women with soft programming styles may pursue their interest in computing without encountering its masculine occupational culture.

As for to women being more likely than men to leave computer work, analyses of American data show that while more men than women leave computer work on an absolute basis, the relationship reverses and women are more likely than men to leave after controlling for background, education, experience, specialty and industry (Wright and Jacobs 1994). In addition, more men than women in computer work are likely to be engineers. Consistent with the culture described above, being an engineer is a decided career advantage in this field, substantially increasing one's probability of moving to management (Wright 1997).

Once women enter computer work, at least in the USA, they face a culture in which engineers are rewarded more than non-engineers. Women in computer work do not fit the cultural mould. They are not male and, generally, they are not engineers. These findings suggest that the occupational masculinity may act as a deterrent to women *after* they're in the field, as well as before they enter. Indeed, it may be telling them through the occupational culture that they do not belong and should avail themselves of what Jacobs (1989) has called the 'revolving door' for women in male-dominated occupations.

Since the middle to late 1980s, computer downsizing and re-engineering have required many – if by now not most – individuals in computer work, at least in the United States, to work with personal computers (Anthes 1993, Horwitt 1990). Supporting others on PCs requires more knowledge of and tinkering with hardware. In a sense, computer work is returning to the 1950s, when hardware knowledge was essential. The occupational culture of computing glorifies such knowledge (McIlwee and Robinson 1992, Hacker 1990), and the departure of some women from the field may be due to this requirement increasing alongside the rapid diffusion of PCs: it would be interesting to track by country this diffusion against the trends in women's participation.

In summary, a good argument can be made that a major reason for both women's declining interest and their tenure in computer work in the USA is the masculinity of its occupational culture (Wright 1996). That a similar pattern of declining participation is occurring in a number of other countries suggests that at least some elements of this culture may transcend national boundaries. While the American situation is suggestive, additional research is needed to determine where and how this cultural transcendence may be affecting women in other countries, as well.

Endnotes

1. To verify that these two sets of data track closely in the USA, I compared data on the percentage of women who were computer science graduates, mathematics graduates and a combination of the two (US Department of Education 1996). The correlation between computer science and the combined was much higher than that between mathematics and the combined. At combined Levels 6 and 7 from 1975 to 1994, the first was .93, while the second was .50. At combined Levels 5, 6 and 7 from 1982 to 1994, the first was .98 and the second was -.41.

2. This paper uses the terms computer professional and computer worker interchangeably. For varying arguments whether computer work is a profession by sociological definition, see Abbott (1988), Denning (1991), and Orlikowski and Baroudi (1989).

3. The definition of computer worker used here is that of the Association for Computing in the United States (Denning 1991): a computer worker is someone who supports *other* people's usage of computer systems. In so doing, it includes computer programmers, systems analysts, data base administrators, and operations managers (see Orlikowski 1988). The many close ties between computer science and engineering (Steering Committee 1993) and the common practice in the 1990s of using the title software engineer for workers previously called programmer/analysts (King 1994), lead to the inclusion here of people with engineering titles such as systems and software engineer.

4. The apparent increase between the 1993 and 1994 percentages was an insignificant 0.3%. These percentages are consistent with the American data in Table 2, whose percentages are higher because the Table includes all ISCED levels.

5. McIlwee and Robinson draw extensively on research with electrical engineers to illustrate their general culture of engineering, arguing that the culture applies less well to their second case, mechanical engineers.

References

Abbott, A. (1988). *The System of Professions: An Essay on the Division of Expert Labor.* Chicago: University of Chicago Press.

ACM/IEEE-CS Joint Curriculum Task Force (1991). *Computing Curricula 1991.* New York: ACM and IEEE Computer Society Press.

Anthes, G. H. (1993). 'Not Made in the USA'. *Computerworld* December 6: 123.

Bailyn, L. (1987). 'Experiencing Technical Work: A Comparison of Male and Female Engineers'. *Human Relations* 40 (5): 299-312.

Breene, L. A. (1993). Women and Computer Science. *Initiatives* 55 (2): 39-44.

Cale, E. G., Jr., Mawhinney, C. H., and Callaghan, D. R. (1991). Student Perceptions of Information Systems Careers: Misconceptions and Declining Enrollments. *Journal of Research on Computing in Education* 23 (3): 434-43.

Carey, M. L. (1991/92). 'Occupational Advancement from Within'. *Occupational Outlook Quarterly*, Winter: 9-13.

Cockburn, C. (1988). *Machinery of Dominance: Women, Men, and Technical Know-How.* Boston: Northeastern University Press.

Committee on Women in Science and Engineering (1991). *Women in Science and Engineering: Increasing Their Numbers in the 1990s.* Washington DC: National Academy Press.

Committee to Assess the Scope and Direction of Computer Science and Technology (1992). *Computing the Future: A Broader Agenda for Computer Science and Engineering.* Washington DC: National Academy Press.

Decker, W. H. (1986). 'Occupation and Impressions: Stereotypes of Males and Females in Three Professions'. *Social Behavior and Personality* 14 (1): 69-75.

Denning, P. (1991). 'The Scope and Directions of Computer Science: Computing, Applications, and Computational Science'. *Communications of the ACM* 34 (10): 129-31.

Faludi, S. (1991). *Backlash: The Undeclared War against American Women*.New York: Doubleday.

Hacker. S. (1990). *'Doing It the Hard Way': Investigations of Gender and Technology*.Boston: Unwin Hyman.

Hartman, S. J., Griffeth, R. W., Miller, L. and Kinicki, A. J. (1988). 'The Impact of Occupation, Performance, and Sex on Sex Role Stereotyping'. *Journal of Social Psychology*. 128 (4): 451-63.

Horwitt, E. (1990). 'Downsizing Quandary for IS Pros'. *Computerworld* March 5: 1.

Huff, C. W. and Cooper, J. (1987). 'Sex Bias in Educational Software: The Effect of Designers' Stereotypes on the Software They Design'. *Journal of Applied Social Psychology* 17 (6): 519-32.

Hughes, T. P. (1987). 'The Evolution of Large Technological Systems', in Bijker, W. E., Hughes, T. P. and Pinch, T. (eds.). *The Social Construction of Technological Systems*. Cambridge, MA: MIT Press.

Jacobs, J. A. (1989). *Revolving Doors: Sex Segregation and Women's Careers*. Palo Alto: Stanford University Press.

Jacobs, J. A. (1995). 'Gender and Academic Specialties: Trends During the 1980s'. *Sociology of Education* 68 (2): April.

Kiesler, S., Sproull, L. and Eccles, J. S. (1985). 'Pool Halls, Chips, and War Games: Women in the Culture of Computing'. *Psychology of Women Quarterly* 9: 451- 62.

King, J. (1994). 'Engineers to IS: Drop that Title!' *Computerworld* May 30: 1.

Kraft, P. (1979). 'The Routinizing of Computer Programming'. *Sociology of Work and Occupations* 6 (2): 139-55.

Leveson, N. (1989). *Women in Computer Science: A Report for the NSF-CISE Cross Directorate Activities Committee*. Washington DC: National Science Foundation.

Martin, C. D. and Murchie-Beyma, E. (1992). *In Search of Gender Free Paradigms for Computer Science Education*. Eugene, OR: International Society for Technology in Education.

McIlwee, J. S. and Robinson, J. G. (1992). *Women in Engineering: Gender, Power, and Workplace Culture*. Albany, NY: SUNY Press.

Newton, P. (1991). 'Computing: An Ideal Occupation for Women?' in Firth-Cozens, J. and West, M.A. (eds.). *Women at Work: Psychological and Organizational Perspectives*, 143-53. Philadelphia: Open University Press.

Orlikowski, W. J. (1988). 'The Data Processing Occupation: Professionalization or Proletarianization?' *Research in the Sociology of Work* 4: 95-124.

Orlikowski, W. J. and Baroudi, J. J. (1989). 'The Information Systems Profession: Myth or Reality?' *Office: Technology and People* 4: 13-30.

Shade, L. R. (1993). 'Gender Issues in Computer Networking'. Paper presented at Community Networking: the International Free-Net Conference, Ottawa, August.

Silvestri, G. T. and Lukasiewicz, J. M. (1992). *Occupational Employment Projections. In Outlook 1990-2005* (BLS Bulletin 2402), 62-92. Washington DC: U. S. Government Printing Office.

Simpson, R. L. (1985). 'Social Control of Occupations and Work'. *Annual Review of Sociology* 11: 415-36.

Spertus, E. (1991). *Why Are There So Few Female Computer Scientists?* (MIT Artificial Intelligence Laboratory Technical Report). Cambridge, MA: MIT Artificial Intelligence Laboratory.

Sproull, L., Kiesler, S. and Zubrow, D. (1987). 'Encountering an Alien Culture', in Kiesler, S. and Sproull, L. (eds.). *Computing and Change on Campus*. Cambridge: Cambridge University Press.

Steering Committee on Human Resources in Computer Science and Technology (1993). *Computing Professionals: Changing Needs for the 1990s*. Washington DC: National Academy Press.

Tarallo, B. M. (1987). *The Production of Information: An Examination of the Employment Relations of Software Engineers and Computer Programmers*. Unpublished doctoral dissertation, University of California at Davis.

Trice, H. M. (1993). *Occupational Subcultures in the Workplace*. Ithaca, NY: ILR Press.

Turkle, S. (1984). *The Second Self: Computers and the Human Spirit*. New York: Simon and Schuster.

Turkle, S. (1988). 'Computational Reticence: Why Women Fear the Intimate Machine', in Kramarae, C. (ed.). *Technology and Women's Voices: Keeping in Touch,* 41-61. New York: Routledge and Kegan Paul.

Turkle, S. (1995). *Life on the Screen: Identity in the Age of the Internet*. New York: Simon and Schuster.

UNESCO (1995). *UNESCO Statistical Yearbook*. Paris: United Nations Educational, Scientific and Cultural Organization.

US Bureau of Labor Statistics (1976-96). *Employment and Earnings,* January. Washington DC: US Government Printing Office.

US Bureau of the Census (1993). *Computer Use in the United States: 1993* (Memorandum PPL-22). Washington DC: Education and Social Stratification Branch, Population Division.

US Department of Education (1995, 1996). *Digest of Educational statistics* Washington DC: U. S. Government Printing Office.

Wright, R. (1996). 'The Occupational Masculinity of Computing', in C. Cheng (ed.). *Masculinities in Organizations*. Thousand Oaks, CA: Sage Publications.

Wright, R. (1997). *Women Computer Professionals: Progress and Resistance*: Lewiston, NY: Edwin Mellen Press.

Wright, R. and Jacobs, J. A. (1994). 'Male Flight from Computer Work: A New Look at Occupational Resegregation and Ghettoization'. *American Sociological Review*, 59 (June), 511-36.

Yourdon, E. (1992). *Decline and Fall of the American Programmer*. Englewood Cliffs, NY: Yourdon Press.

Empowerment and Disempowerment: Active Agency, Structural Constraint and Women Computer Users

Harvie Ramsay
Strathclyde University

Androniki Panteli and Martin Beirne
University of Glasgow

Abstract

The analysis of gender in connection with information systems (IS) has tended to consider women as relatively passive victims of masculine power. In this paper we use case study material to present women as active agents, able to shape aspects of their situation and to challenge official power of decision-making in systems operation. However, the material also reveals contradictions and constraints which in the long run undermined the control women had gained reasserting gendered inequalities.

1. Introduction

Many of the established approaches to gender issues in work organisations have sought ways to unveil the systematic inequalities faced by women. Some of these focus on inequalities in external and internal labour markets (Reskin and Roos 1990; Gallie 1996); others on masculine organisational cultures which dominate and disadvantage women (Calas and Smircich 1992; Savage and Witz 1992); and still others on the gendered restructuring and degradation of the labour process in women's work. There is a tendency in all of these accounts, though, to consider women as the apparently passive victims of structural developments expressing male power and so to give little or no account of process or resistance, with few considering women as active agents (Wilson 1996). The most effective challenges to this have tended to come from detailed ethnographies of women workers, often in the labour process tradition but not confined by its narrower strictures (e.g. Pollert 1981; Cockburn 1983).

While most work on computing design or operative labour has tended to remain gender-blind, homogenising its workforce, there is a growing body of work which identifies the same kinds of inequality in this 'new' area of work as in more traditional areas, and the same methods as above have been applied to uncover inequality. This also reproduces the neglect of active agency of women designers and users (Webster 1996), though this has begun to be challenged by feminist writers (Green et al 1993). The methodologies most suited to this challenge are once again felt to be those which focus on the experiences and subjectivities of women IS workers, as well as the outcomes of their activities (Ormrod 1995). This suggests that case study research concentrating on the labour process is most likely to challenge the one-sided picture and give voice to women as active agents in a disadvantaged environment. Hence, case material provides the basis for our analysis.

The cases reported here fall into this broad tradition of ethnographic research, though they do not formalise this within such an approach as actor-network theory. Where structural factors are discussed, nonetheless, they are depicted through the patterning of eventual outcomes. These cases also have implications, e.g. for the problematical status of the conventional distinction between designers and users, for the question of empowerment in IS work, and for the orthodox approach to systems 'success' or 'failure'. These interweave with the gender dimension of the study in important ways. After all, it is hardly mere coincidence that while the majority of software engineers and IS managers are men, users – and especially users in routine, traditionally powerless non-manual grades – are overwhelmingly likely to be women.

2. Gender Inequalities in IS Work

First, we will consider the more 'orthodox' evidence of gendered inequality in computing occupations. Because this area of work is not heavy or 'technical' in traditional ways, there were hopes that it would not exhibit the same segregation and female disadvantage of occupations with a longer historical legacy. Ostensibly it could offer the potential for feminisation (a growing proportion of women in the labour force) without a parallel decline in economic or quality of work rewards previously associated with such a shift. Indeed, until at least the mid-1980s there were strong signs of feminisation (Wright and Jacobs 1995; Wright 1996), although the figures for women in computer-related occupations in the US levelled off and then began to decline into the early 1990s, as did those (at a much lower proportion of the IS workforce) in the UK and the rest of Europe.

Moreover, there is growing evidence of a segregation of male and female work in IS occupations. Women are still mostly found in the non-managerial group of IS personnel, such as operators or programmers, while men are predominant in managerial positions, such as project leaders or department managers (Baroudi and Igbaria 1995; Ordroyd 1996). There are also significant salary differences between male and female IS staff (Truman and Baroudi 1994). In Reskin and Roos' (1990) terms, there are signs of ghettoisation: women are increasingly concentrated in specialties that are becoming female-dominated but are, at the same time, of lower status than other IS jobs. In the process, the tasks allocated to these increasingly female roles become more routinised, providing less official scope for autonomy and creativity (Grundy 1996).

Meanwhile the emergence and progressive reinforcement of a masculine culture in the IS field (Tierney 1995; Wright 1996) is argued to compound the ghettoisation of the sub-professions and to make women more likely to leave computing jobs than men. An emphasis on 'hard' skills such as formal analytic logic, rather than interpersonal ones of teamworking, for instance, is said to further advantage the progression through the ranks of male entrants whilst discouraging women.

As we have argued already, the labour market and culture approaches can illuminate a great deal but they tend to leave women as passive in the face of inequity. They tell us little about the everyday experience of female IS staff, nor therefore do they elucidate the degree to which the process of male superordination is secure or fragile. It is to an exploration of these aspects of IS work that we now turn.

3. Starting With 'SADIS'

The case studies reported here are based on interviews with operators and managers in a number of Further Education colleges in Scotland. These colleges educate several thousand students each to a maximum of Higher National Diploma level (roughly equivalent to second year in a four-year Scottish degree course), mostly in vocational subjects, and also provide an opportunity for students to gain the Ordinary and Higher qualifications they did not get before leaving school. At the time of this research, the colleges were in transition from local authority to Scottish Office regulation, and tighter information flows were being planned to allow closer regulation and quasi-market incentives to operate. The information flows were also needed by the Accreditation and Awarding Council (AAC), which had to verify college certificates.

To this end, a new common information system (which we have fictionally dubbed 'SADIS') was requisitioned from Educational Administrative Systems Ltd (EAS). This was based on a program already written for a different setting, built on an Oracle platform. The new system was piloted in College A for a year in the early 1990s, and then deemed ready to roll out to a further 19 colleges. We visited five colleges to explore their experience of this system, though our most detailed interviews took place in College B.

SADIS was effectively imposed on the colleges, and the colleges' management initially and consistently underestimated both its importance and the difficulties to be overcome in rendering its functionality. For the most part, they recruited existing clerical and secretarial female staff to low-graded posts for a job expected to be primarily data collation and entry, assuming that the program would run straightforwardly and that project-managers (almost invariably male lecturers on part-time secondment) would undertake the responsibility to manage the system.

Thus in College A day-to-day control was increasingly exercised by Diane, a typist turned operator, who:

> . . . was basically seen as the SADIS person under Ben, and really, she controlled everything if you like . . . I think she just happened to be in the right place at the right time, and basically took control of the area and was available at the time and got used. (MIS Systems Manager)

In College C, Marcia reported: 'I was a secretary before I went in to the SADIS unit. I just had a PC, strictly a PC and never anything else.' Her greatest initial resources seem to have been her excellent college-wide connections and willingness to try something new. She had decided to embark on a computing qualification, though her IS knowledge and experience initially were almost non-existent. The training she received was brief and extremely narrow, as Kevin, the male lecturer allocated to the task of overseeing the system, was sent on what little was available. College B took a similar route initially, moving two female clerks to data entry and sending them on brief courses on SADIS, while the main training input, such as it was, went to Don, the lecturer seconded to manage the system. When it came to consolidating the data entry team shortly before registrations began, however, they recruited two students who had just completed a three-year qualification for Higher National Diplomas in Computer Studies in the college.

Maureen and Mary were employed as casual workers on short-term (six-week) contracts for data entry in the first instance. While their contracts were repeatedly renewed over the ensuing months, they remained on the bottom clerical grade, with no formal recognition of their qualifications or of their actual job content. They received almost no training initially (even internally), though later they were sent on a Structured Query Language (SQL) course. The gendered culture which surrounded their work location, and the ambivalent perception of their efforts by management, both described below, help to explain the persistence of this state of affairs.

3.1 Making SADIS Work

Despite official reassurances, it was soon becoming clear to the colleges that the SADIS pilot at College A had not ironed out the problems at all and that SADIS was still full of bugs and inappropriate functionality. In each location, as data were entered and the first reports and student registers were sought, chaos threatened. Initially those given the task of operating the system thus had to try and cope by themselves.

They did so in different ways and with varying degrees of success. In College E, for example, Sandra described how after two days' training, with no background in computing, she had been left to enter data with minimal support and with the system manager coming over only to do the daily data backup. She generated only the reports offered by the SADIS designers, never developing SQL skills. In College C, on the other hand, Marcia got management to fund her attendance at HNC and then HND evening classes in computing. She eventually learned SQL and so how to generate reports more in line with the demands of the college system. She attended the inter-college users' network meetings in the first two years and gradually found her way around the system.

The most ambitious interventions came from Maureen and Mary in College B, however. Their background made them particularly frustrated that the system could not produce forms and reports which matched the needs of the college. Moreover, they found that even simple (and constantly required) amendments to the data could not be made without a rerun of the entire system. They hesitated to act, given their low status, but: 'because there were the two of us we were much more blasé about it almost' (Maureen). In this they were tacitly encouraged by the 'hands-off' attitude of the systems manager, Don, who they realised knew little of SADIS, Oracle or SQL, and who was never there when things went wrong. More senior management, personified through the deputy principal, conveyed their preparedness to 'allow' the women to do whatever would produce results: 'He wanted this system to be a success, he wanted it up and running. The college itself had made no provision for that' (Mary).

First, Maureen and Mary took on the tasks of backing up the data and rebooting the system when it crashed. They began combing through the manuals, taking advice 'off-the record' from a lecturer (Philip) with whom they got on well, and started teaching themselves SQL. Fairly quickly they were able to instruct reports not catered for within SADIS. They kept written copies of the programming so they could restore it when EAS came in to do a system 'upgrade', which wiped their amendments. Eventually, they gathered their courage and also risked the more complex and dangerous task of changing fields and data, as a short-cut for amendments. Several times their hearts were in their mouths (a story we heard in the other colleges too, usually from systems managers) when they started an SQL sequence running, knowing that a system failure could wipe the data, at best requiring a long reboot from back-up and calling attention to their actions.

Despite their low status and rewards from College B, Maureen and Mary in effect undertook a significant amount of development activity – to label their efforts as just 'user' skills is to maintain the neat but artificial divide between designers and the rest. That division, moreover, may be seen as sustaining a largely gendered privileging of 'professional expertise', arguably a hegemonic masculine discourse (Collinson and Hearn 1996) which devalues and camouflages the agency of women 'users'. Masculine power exerted itself in other ways in these situations also, as we now discuss.

3.2 Power and Resistance

The seniority of certain key male figures in the colleges allowed them to exert power in a number of ways. Don in College B, for instance, would seek to present himself in a good light by intervening wherever possible between Maureen and Mary and other lecturers, and especially senior management, and by claiming credit when a problem was fixed by the women. Other male staff in particular would accept this, presuming that his authority and understanding of the system made this appropriate. His limited knowledge of the system was a handicap, but he sought to overcome this by referring questions on to Maureen and Mary, and then conveying their answers back as his own. When Keith was appointed systems manager a couple of years later, he used much the same technique. The senior administrator, meantime, would proclaim his own prowess:

> Once he announced, 'Actually I know all about computers, I did a six-week course'. We almost fell off our chairs - after all, he was talking to two people who had three years' training, yet if we said the system couldn't do something he would say, 'it must be able to, why can't you do it?' And at the same time he carried on taking his big salary and paying us a pittance. But we daren't laugh out loud.

Most unpleasantly, the women in College B reported a variety of tacit forms of more directly sexual harassment from Don, brushing past, leaning over them, making comments which were 'just jokes'. 'It was worse than outright blatant touching up, and yet you couldn't really challenge anything specific or complain without looking stupid.' Our research was not so detailed as to allow us to check on these matters in the other colleges.

There were other parallels elsewhere, though. In College C, Marcia found herself passed over for the systems manager post after two years of running the system. Graham, who got the job, exerted what she experienced as petty authority, forcing her to change her long-booked holidays to suit him, complaining about the chatter and loud radio played by the women to relieve stress and tedium in the various phases of their work, and freezing her out of the inter-college network.

However, the women did find ways of fighting back at times. This worked best when they responded collectively to a grievance. In College C, for instance, Marcia related how after the radio noise complaint (see above) Graham had come in at the end of the day to say something had come up which required a lot of work that night. 'He assumed they would work overtime, as they always had for me. But they just said, "Well, it looks like you'll be working very late, won't you", and went home'.

In College B, Mary and Maureen's commitment to efficient system operation limited their armoury. Yet, they responded to harassment with a barrage of mockery and punning humour. In addition, they were not above the skilful use of humiliation, which exploited Don's ignorance of the system and showed their own superior control:

'One time Don came down five minutes before he was due to hand over a job he'd promised the deputy principal. He asked if we'd done it and we said, "Oh, that's it printing now". So when the DP came in and asked for the report, he said, "Ah yes, I've just got it printing for you over here." And the DP went over and looked at it. And looked puzzled because it had nothing to do with what he'd asked for. Then Mary said, "No, that's not it. We did it earlier, it's over there." Don just ran out in a rage; but he couldn't say anything because he'd made a fool of himself.'

This resistance was not universal – in College E, for instance, we found a largely deferential response from Sandra, the long-serving administrator, to her male manager. Nor was there necessarily a female solidarity such as that which seems to have prevailed in College C. In College B, for instance, Maureen and Mary formed a tight-knit duo in exercising such control as they gained. Even Julie, who had been there before them and had received the initial training for data entry, and with whom they were friendly, does not seem to have joined in their assumption of tacit responsibilities. Moreover, the IS staff in College B were on a raised platform in the college office and so separated from the other women. A subcultural divide developed, it appeared, with little love lost between the two groups. We detected similar resentment, retrospectively, against Diane in College A; she was said by the other administrators we spoke to (all female) to have taken control and to have jealously guarded it.

3.3 Empowerment or Exploitation?

As 'involvement' has given way to 'empowerment' in the wider managerial vocabulary in recent years, so within the IS field 'user-involvement' has ceded to this term also. In some quarters this is uncritically acclaimed as the arrival of true participative systems, though others have more reservations about how far devolved decision-making is really substantial, secure and genuinely employee-centred.

Critical perspectives have been particularly slow to gain purchase in studies of IS work (Beirne and Ramsay 1988, 1992) but the recent contributions of Clement (1994) make progress in identifying the ambivalent nature of empowerment in this sphere. Clement distinguishes 'democratic' forms of empowerment, where employees exercise genuine control, from 'functional' versions, which are management-controlled and primarily pursue a managerial priority of work intensification. Clement recognises that there may be limitations to the extent of empowerment, but he seems relatively optimistic about the prospects for some genuine progress, especially where control is initially established through initiatives from below. The suggestion is that eventually management will give official recognition and status to such innovations and so also to their authors.

Meanwhile, the gendered aspects of the manifestations of involvement or empowerment have gone almost entirely unremarked. However, the multi-dimensional disadvantaging of women in the workplace, and the ways these impact on recognition of their 'skills' and capacity for decision-making, have an obvious and direct implication for a differentiated analysis of empowerment outcomes. This calls for an explicitly gendered analysis of empowerment in practice (Ramsay 1996). To Clement's credit, he does recognise that for work processes affected by software, the issue of user empowerment is gendered, since the vast majority of jobs under examination are performed by women and located in feminised occupations (Clement 1991).

Nonetheless, our observations, even in College B, lead us to part company with Clement, for reasons which invoke constraints arising partly in terms of general limitations on power devolution to employees, but with particular gender elements to the argument also. Maureen and Mary were able, through a combination of their unacknowledged training and the transitional nature of the situation in which they found themselves to assume a great deal of control over their situation. At the outset they found Don had disconnected the hardware and reconnected it themselves; thereafter they developed knowledge and skills which gave them an unusual capacity to make the system work. This also relieved the potential tedium of the job: 'It broke up the day. It also let us use some programming skills; it was a buzz to get things working.'

There was a price to pay for this 'buzz', however. Maureen and Mary bore the risk of being discovered by EAS (whose contract made intervention illicit), the strain of potential systems crashes and the knowledge that management's tacit approval for their efforts would not absolve them if things went wrong: ' "We don't want to know" was their line all the time, "we don't want to know what you're doing, just get it done, get the reports produced on time"' (Maureen). There was anger that neither of the women was given her place, but the saving grace was that this also minimised the cost of the risk: 'What's the worst that could happen? We get the sack. And really we weren't bothered, neither of us at the time really cared because we were only getting paid the lowest office job wages'. The nearest that either of these women came to recognition in the first year was when they were both sent on an SQL training course at a local university – the content of which they had already superseded with their own efforts. When Mary left, she had no other accredited experience and was unable to get the programming job she badly wanted.

Thus the control exerted by these women did not lead to emancipation, but rather to work intensification and, in effect, self-exploitation. We have developed the elaboration of Clements' analytical framework this implies elsewhere (Beirne et al 1996), but the important point here is to re-emphasise the interweaving of gender and empowerment outcomes in IS work that it reaffirms.

3.4 Re-enter Structure

For all the emphasis we have placed on women as active agents, the closing observation in the last section suggests the continuing power of structural factors to prevent equitable outcomes. This was most in evidence when we traced through the longer-run developments and discovered the parallel trajectories across the colleges. In each case, approximately two years after SADIS was put on release outside College A, management realised that the computerised system was becoming pivotal rather than peripheral to their administration. SADIS II was introduced and full-time systems managers were appointed. In every college we visited this was a male, usually with a degree and often a fair bit of systems experience.

In each college, the women on whom management had relied found themselves marginalised and their informal status declined. In College A, Diane left, being presented by her successor as 'unable to cope' with the loss of control. In College E and for Mary in College B, the result was actually a degree of recognition, with appointment to higher grades explicitly labelled as computing administration. However, this went along with less real control for those who had exerted it, though Mary found herself having to 'carry' a series of systems managers who stayed only short periods. Similarly, in College C, Marcia found Graham appointed as her boss, and then later was not even interviewed for a deputy post, with another man being brought in above her. Although her experience and knowledge was recognised, the frustration was evident. Two years later, shortly after speaking to us, Mary applied successfully for a systems manager's job at another college.

4. Conclusions

It would have been easy to write this as a gender-blind account of empowerment in IS. Many of these things could have happened to men, whether it be taking initiatives or being conveniently side-stepped when it suited management. Yet the fact that all our subjects in the colleges were women is hardly accidental. Many of the pressures and processes we observed had a clearly demarcated gendered texture. In each college, management, having benefited from the initiative and endeavour of these women, succeeded with relative ease in eliding much of their dependence and displacing their 'power', proving their own control to be far more substantial. Notwithstanding the importance we have attached to process and agency, the consistency of the pattern suggests to us the relevance of structural analysis.

Although each college exhibited distinctive local features, shaped by individual personalities, opportunities, networks and so forth, the amount of control the women operators assumed varied greatly. Yet the differences are variations around strong shared themes. We interpret what we found as evidence of a strong gendering of IS work, with a multi-dimensionality only visible to a combination of detailed multiple case analyses. The inequitable outcomes we have described certainly cannot be ascribed to feminine passivity. More abstractly, the dynamics of feminisation and ghettoisation proved to be far less simple, uncontested or unidirectional than is depicted in static accounts of work with computers.

Acknowledgements

We are grateful to the participants of this study who gave freely of their time to talk to us about their experience with SADIS and its successor systems. We would also like to thank the WiC reviewers for their supportive and helpful comments. Thanks are also due to the ESRC for funding the project from which this research material has been drawn.

References

Baroudi, J.J. and Igbaria, M. (1995). 'An Examination of Gender Effects on Career Success of Information Systems Employees'. *Journal of Management Information Systems* 11 (3): 181-201.

Beirne M. and Ramsay, H. (1988). 'Computer redesign and 'labour process' theory: towards a critical appraisal', in Knights, D. et al (eds.). *New Technology & the Labour Process*, London: Macmillan.

Beirne M. and Ramsay, H. (1992). 'Manna or monstrous regiment? Technology, control and democracy in the workplace', in Beirne and Ramsay (eds.). *Information Technology and Workplace Democracy*. London: Routledge.

Beirne, M., Ramsay, H. and Panteli, A. (1996). 'Participating Informally: Opportunities and Dilemmas in User-Driven Design', paper for the *Fourth Biennial Conference on Participatory Design (PDC'96)*. Cambridge, Massachusetts, November 13-15.

Brown, R. (1976). 'Women as employees: some comments on research in industrial sociology', in Barker, D.L. and Allen, S. (eds) *Dependence and Exploitation in Work and Marriage*. Harlow: Longman.

Calas, M.B. and Smircich, L. (1990). 'Rewriting gender into organisational theorising: directions from feminist perspectives', in Reed, M. and Hughes, M. (eds.). *Rethinking Organisation: New Directions in Organisation Theory and Analysis*. London: Sage.

Clement, A. (1991). 'Designing without designers: more hidden skill in office computerisation', in Eriksson, I. et al (eds.). *Women, Work and Computerization*. Amsterdam: North Holland.

Clement, A. (1994). 'Computing at work: empowering action by "low-level users"',*Communications of the ACM* 31 (11): 1268-87.

Cockburn, C. (1983). *Brothers: Male Dominance and Technological Change*. London: Pluto.

Collinson, D. and Hearn, J. (1996). 'Breaking the Silence: On Men, Masculinities and Management', in Collinson, D. and Hearn, J. (eds.). *Men As Managers, Managers As Men: Critical Perspectives On Men, Masculinities and Management*. London: Sage.

Gallie, D. (1996). 'Skill, gender and the quality of employment', in Crompton, R. et al (eds.). *Changing Forms of Employment*, London: Routledge.

Green, E., Owen, J. and Pain, D. (eds.) (1993). *Gendered By Design? Information Technology and Office Systems*. London: Taylor and Francis.

Grundy, F. (1996). *Women and Computers*, Exeter: Intellect Books.

Ordroyd, R. (1996). 'Is the IS industry a turn-off for women?' *Sunday Business* , 26 May.

Ormrod, S. (1995). 'Feminist sociology and methodology: leaky black boxes in gender/technology relations', in Grint, K. and Gill, R. (eds.). *The Gender-Technology Relation: Contemporary Theory and Research*. London: Taylor and Francis.

Pollert, A. (1981). *Girls, Wives, Factory Lives*. London: Macmillan.

Ramsay, H. (1996). *Engendering Participation*. Department of Human Resource Management, University of Strathclyde, Occasional Paper, no 8.

Reskin, B.F. and Roos, P.A. (1990). *Job Queues, Gender Queues: Explaining Women's Inroads into Male Occupations*. Philafelphia: Temple University Press.

Savage, M. and Witz, A. (1992). *Gender and Bureaucracy*. Oxford: Blackwell.

Tierney, M. (1995). 'Negotiating a software career: informal work practices and "the lads" in a software installation', in Grint, K. and Gill, R. (eds.). *The Gender-Technology Relation: Contemporary Theory and Research*. London: Taylor and Francis.

Truman, G.E. and Baroudi, J.J. (1994). 'Gender Differences in the Information Systems Managerial Ranks: An Assessment of Potential Discriminatory Practices'. *MIS Quarterly* June: 129-41.

Webster, J. (1996). *Shaping Women's Work: Gender, Employment and Information Technology*. London: Longman.

Wilson, F. (1996). 'Research Note: Organisational Theory: Blind and Deaf to Gender?' *Organisation Studies* 17 (5): 825-42.

Wright, R. (1996). 'The occupational masculinity of computing', in Cheng, C. (ed.). *Masculinities In Organisations*, London: Sage.

Wright, R. and Jacobs, J.A. (1995). 'Male Flight From Computer Work: A New Look at Occupational Resegregation and Ghettoisation', in Jacobs, J.A. (ed.). *Gender Inequality at Work*. London: Sage.

Women in the UK Software Industry - How Much do we Know?

Androniki Panteli, Janet Stack and Malcolm Atkinson

University of Glasgow

Harvie Ramsay

Strathclyde University

Abstract

The position of women in the UK software industry, relative to the position in other European countries and the United States gives real cause for concern. The need for and significance of empirical research to establish the underlying trends is becoming urgent. The paper identifies specific areas for research in this field and reports how the authors, who constitute an interdisciplinary team, plan to approach this issue.

1. Background

This research in progress study derives from the need to gain a comprehensive understanding of the gender composition and career patterns in the UK software industry. Given the explosive growth of the software field over the last decades, software employees constitute an increasingly important component of the labour force. It is therefore of significant importance for organisations in this industry to use all potential resources in the best possible way.

Software industry is a key sector within the UK and is the fastest growing sector in Europe. In 1995, the UK market for software and computing services increased by 18%, experiencing its fastest growth in real terms for a decade (1996 Holway Report, in *Financial Times*, 24 May 1996). Outsourcing was the most significant contributor to this exceptional growth. The UK market for information systems (IS) outsourcing grew by 45% and a further growth is expected by 24% between 1996 and 1999. Overall turnover of the companies in this sector has grown by about 22% and further growth is expected.

Within the growing sector of software development, however, there are strong grounds for thinking that there has been a failure to maximise talent and to utilise effectively potential human resources. There are three main reasons for this possible under-utilisation of resources in the software industry:

1. **Rationalisation.** The process of software development has been rationalised due to the increasing use of structured programming, design tools and methodologies. Such techniques not only formalise but also simplify and standardise software work. For instance, structured programming was criticised for imposing restrictions on the number and type of logical procedures a

programmer may use and restricting the ability of programmers to make independent decisions about the organisation of their programmes (Greenbaum 1979; Kraft 1977). Similarly, structured approaches to software development may prove restrictive to the experienced developers, particularly those who are capable enough to develop systems without a heavy reliance on methodologies (Avgerou and Cornford 1993). It has also been recognised that CASE tools appear to force 'a way of working which is controlled by the technology itself' (Fischer et al 1993) while they can also restrict the employment and career prospects of experienced, highly qualified IS staff.

2. **Lack of diversity.** Software development has been predominantly a white, middle-class and male-dominated occupation. Lack of diversity in work groups, however, reduces opportunities for creativity (e.g. Hoffman and Maier 1961; Watson, Kuman and Michaelsen 1993), while it also contributes to a failure to explore alternative ways of working and organising the development process away from the traditional masculine process (Wright 1996).

3. **Gender Segregation.** Although there has been an increase in the number of women entering IS occupations since the 1970s, women are under-represented in all member states of the European Union. In no member state of the EU, for example, is the share estimated to be above 30% and in most cases the share is closer to 20%. While all countries report an under-representation of women, some (i.e. Spain and France) consider that women are increasing their share of these jobs and will continue to do so in the future, while others (Germany, Italy, Belgium and UK) see a declining trend in the share of women among software developers. What is most significant for our study is that UK experiences the greatest downward trend in the representation of women in this sector of all member states of the EU (Social Europe 3/93).

Gender, diversity and rationalisation are not unrelated in software development. Clearly, gender is a crucial element of diversity. A *Computerworld* survey for instance, found that IS companies with a diverse workforce are more progressive in terms of innovative ideas and skills than those without. A diverse workforce introduces ideas and experiences into the workplace that may never be considered in a more traditional homogeneous environment (Bulkeley 1995). Furthermore, it was found that one of the benefits of a diverse workforce is that it broadens the skills of people who are not used to working in a diverse workplace. This will consequently enable developers to work more effectively within the user community.

Links have also been established between gender and rationalisation in the software industry. In the USA where there has been a higher and increasing representation of women in the information systems field, several researchers have suggested that software development is becoming feminised (Burris 1993; Donato 1990; Kraft 1977, 1979; Greenbaum 1979; Wright and Jacobs 1995). Based on Computerworld's Salary Survey (1995), women account for about 37% of IS professionals in the US, which although 7% below the national average of women in the total workforce in the country, is still higher than any EC member state. Several researchers have related feminisation to the rationalisation of the software development (Greenbaum 1979; Kraft 1977). They argued that the rationalised and routinised nature of the software development process provides opportunities to management to recruit inexperienced graduates, female and ethnic minority staff who are traditionally offered low monetary rewards. 'It is perhaps not surprising that contemporary rationalisation around computer systems is gendered' (Burris

1993:98), that 'automation and feminisation are proceeding as twin and highly interrelated' (Baran 1987:52).

Several researchers have claimed that there tends to be evidence for ghettoisation in the software industry. Ghettoisation occurs when women and men who work in the same field hold different job titles and ranks and as a result perform different tasks (Reskin and Roos 1990). Women are increasingly concentrated in a limited number of specialties (e.g. systems analysts, programmers, operators) and these specialties are becoming female-dominated and are of lower status than other specialties in the occupation, e.g. project leaders, IS managers. Empirical studies on gender careers in IS (Baroudi and Igbaria 1995) have shown that women are mostly found in the non-managerial group of IS personnel while men are predominantly in managerial positions. Men therefore are more likely than women to be project leaders, IS managers and consultants while women are more likely to be found in roles such as systems analysts, designers and programmers. Also, based on the *Computerworld*'s Salary Survey (1995), in the USA only 17% of chief information officers are women. In the UK, this percentage is much lower, with only 4% of the heads of IS departments being female. Significant salary differences were also found between male and female senior IS managers (Baroudi and Igbaria 1995; Computerworld Salary Survey 1995; Ordroyd 1996; Truman and Baroudi 1994).

Even when male and female employees have the same job title and formal role in their organisation, they might undertake different tasks and projects. In an exploratory study in the UK, Grundy (1994 1996) reported that men get intensively involved with the 'pure', abstract computing work which is challenging and prestigious and leave the 'messy' type of work to their female colleagues. This latter type of job involves tasks such as merging and tidying up databases and writing summary report programs which, although important for the effective functioning of every organisation, are nevertheless considered as monotonous and less glamorous. Sonnentag (1994), who examined the work situation of female and male team leaders in software development in German and Swiss organisations found that women in subteam and team leading positions experienced less complex work situations than did their male colleagues. Therefore, when a man was promoted to a team or subteam leader he was more likely to deal with an increased amount of complexity in his work and also to spend more time communicating with other people whereas for women, complexity and communication remained largely stable. Clearly then, the same job title does not imply the same job responsibilities and challenge.

2. The Current State of UK-based Research

Owing to the declining representation of women in IS occupations, the argument that this area is becoming feminised is weakly supported within the UK context. There has been, however, insufficient research on the level of rationalisation and ghettoisation in the UK software industry. As a result, little is known on the gendered work organisation of software development. In particular, we can identify three main areas where research is necessary in this country.

First, in the US, software development has been presented as a highly segregated occupation, making it easier to identify the ghettoisation phenomenon. The US-based Computerworld Salary Survey (1995), for instance, found that this is the most highly segregated specialty of all IS occupational groups (i.e. project manager, senior systems analysts, systems analyst, senior systems programmer, systems programmer, senior programmer/analysts, programmer/analyst, database manager, database analyst, data security administrator/analyst). This list presents segregation by hierarchy and specialty. It distinguishes between managerial and non-managerial occupations and also presents nine different specialties within software development alone. This reflects the increasing specialisation within the software development field and the emergent division of labour. In the UK, the studies available present this as a less segregated occupation, for they make reference broadly to systems managers, systems analysts and computer programmers and computer operators as the main groups involved in software development. We do not know whether this is an accurate representation.

Second, there is insufficient data as to the extent to which the fragmentation and rationalisation of software development influence the evolution of a ghettoised environment. Following from the discussion above that this occupation tends to be highly segregated, the rationalisation thesis is not satisfactory since the different specialties are not uniformly routinised nor formalised. Furthermore, the segregation of the software work could enable an increasing dispersion of women in more or less routinised specialties, an argument which either strengthens or weakens the ghettoisation thesis, depending on which of the two applies in practice. A US-based study (Wright and Jacobs 1995) suggests that there is lower ghettoisation but relied on insufficient categories or could be describing solely the US case and not UK. There is a lack of a detailed survey on these issues and there is a need for research that shows the degree of segregation within the UK software industry and its gender composition.

Third and most important, there is a need to investigate how the nature of software development influences and is being influenced by its gender composition. Several researchers have claimed that the entrance of women into the IS field fails to prevent the reproduction of a masculine culture (Knights and Murray 1994; Murray 1993). Software development often involves a tremendous amount of tension, requiring developers to work longer and unsociable hours. And it is often those who are able to cope with these demands and succeed that are promoted into the ranks of IS management (Knights and Murray 1994). The project-based, competitive nature of systems development is therefore an important means for the reproduction of the male-dominated IS environment, which also engenders and reproduces a 'particularly "gung-ho" form of "macho" masculinity' (Knights and Murray 1994:125). This is a type of masculinity that in turn values and elevates the linear-logical pursuit of project objectives that are deemed to provide a predictable, controllable and comparatively certain set of outcomes.

Arguably, this means that women are disadvantaged, especially if they are constrained by domestic responsibilities, and that the value of diversity is not realised owing to obstruction of more feminine and potentially constructive ways of working. Software process is a complex process linking areas of specialised expertise and knowledge requiring close co-operation and interactions within and between groups of IS developers (analysts, designers, programmers), IS managers and users. The masculine type of work may not therefore be to the best advantage of the industry, for it fails to use alternative ways of working and different ways of thinking about and organising the software development process.

At the same time, available research on gender and IS has been content to assume that female IS developers passively and unreflectively accept their disadvantaged position in the IS workplace. Management and male co-workers have been the central actors in shaping the nature and direction of software development while the efforts that women themselves make to gain occupational identity are overlooked. A study by Panteli, Ramsay and Beirne (1996) has shown the ability and willingness of female and [not only] male agents to construct and reconstruct the social reality within their workplace. Even though these people are not as visible as those who manage organisations, this does not mean that they are unimportant or without influence in the framing of their working practices. It is important to investigate the efforts that women themselves make to gain occupational identity and identify conditions that may contribute to this group of workers emerging as a privileged elite. It is therefore becoming extremely relevant for organisational efficiency and effectiveness to examine gender in workplaces and organisations concerned with software development.

3. Research Objectives

The research derives from a realisation that the amount of information on the gender dimension in the UK software industry is inadequate. With a market that is growing faster than in any other European member state, there is an urgency to investigate the process of career progression of female staff and the nature of their working practices inside software organisations. We therefore need to know:

1. What is happening? What are the factors that characterise the representation of women in this field? What is the distribution and role of women in software development occupations?
2. Why is it happening? For instance, how does the nature of the software development process (e.g. project-based, competitive, formalised and structured) influence the career progression of female IS staff?
3. What are the consequences? To what extent does the limited representation of women in this sector and their concentration on the lower ranks of the hierarchy affect the performance of the organisation and the outcome of the software development process?

4. Research Methods

This is an interdisciplinary research project between social scientists and computer scientists. The study will be carried out in three phases with a combination of quantitative and qualitative approaches. In Phase 1 we will obtain a nation-wide database that can provide information on the representation of women in the software industry, and the degree of industry segregation by both specialty and hierarchy. Although several surveys have been published on IS skills and other employment issues in the IS industry in the UK (such as the NCC Staff Issues in Computing, Computer Weekly Survey on IT skills and employment, IT survey by the Institute of Data Processing Management), these remained gender-neutral. Though men and women have participated in these surveys, researchers have not analysed the results by the sex of respondents. We believe it is important to give voice to gender-sensitive research so as to compare job roles and status of males and females in this industry. Findings of this phase can be invaluable for providing statistical answers to the 'what's happening' question.

Phase 2 of the research will look at what is happening within specific organisations. Between 20 and 30 software organisations, from various industry sectors and of different sizes, will be invited to participate in this phase. We will aim, through interviewing and documentation analysis, to get the organisations' account of why and how they view women's career development in software. More specifically, this phase will aim to provide an examination of at least the following organisational policies: recruitment processes, human resource management policies and training procedures.

Phase 3 of the research will involve a detailed examination of the gender composition of software development process in three organisations. The focus here will be on developing a context-based, process-oriented description and explanation of the phenomenon rather than a static description which could only identify causality. Data will be collected through a variety of methods: unstructured, semi-structured interviewing, documentation review and observation to cultivate understanding of our two research questions: 'why is it happening' and 'what are the consequences'.

Initially data collection will focus on the organisational level and seek information on, among other things: mission, structure and culture of the organisation and/or IS department. Traditions in software development, project team organisation, task allocation, use of tools and methodologies and user involvement will be sought. Part of these data will be collected from official organisational documents and supplemented by interviews with directors, managers and employees. Following from these, different projects will be studied to allow exposure to interactions between male and female peers, managers and users. The allocation of tasks during the major phases of software development (specification stage, systems design, programming/ analysis, coding, testing and implementation) will be closely examined in relation to gender. Along with the documentation review material, there will be observation of and interviews with team members during their daily work, on an individual and team basis. This is particularly beneficial in generating theory in case-study research. Previous gender studies that have identified distinct masculine and feminine cultures have been based on observation and interviewing of everyday routines (Gheraldi 1995; Dachler and Hosking 1995). Such triangulation of various data collection techniques (observation, interviewing and documentation) provides multiple perspectives on an issue, allows more information on emerging concepts and allows cross-checking whilst increasing the validity of the results (Glaser and Strauss 1967; Pettigrew 1990).

5. Further Research

The project is still in its early stages. At the time of writing the research framework has been developed and the methodology designed. By the time of the conference the authors hope to be able to present the findings from the first phase of the research.

Furthermore, the authors intend to report on the experience of the inter-disciplinary aspect of this research project. The study is directly concerned with the use of wealth and the promotion of increased efficiency of human and technical resources in the IS industry. An inter-disciplinary study is therefore important in effectively linking these resources, contributing to the production of work of immediate and lasting value. Moreover, we feel that close collaboration between computing scientists and social scientists is essential for methodology to be developed and results to be interpreted with understanding by both disciplines. The software development process needs examination and interpretation from a technical as well as an organisational aspect but these aspects are also interdependent and need collaborative analysis. If change is to occur in the gender composition and career patterns in the UK software industry, then findings from this research must inform the computing community through relevant publications and organisations. This process will be facilitated by a computing presence in the team. It is necessary for both disciplines to recognise the validity of this type of research and there is a need for the researchers to ensure that terminology employed is not mutually exclusive. It is our intention, by reporting on our team experience, to stimulate interest in the significance of inter-disciplinary studies in this field of research.

Acknowledgements:

We are grateful to the Principal of the University of Glasgow for funding the first phase of this research and to the WiC reviewers for their helpful and encouraging comments.

References

Avgerou, C. and Cornford, T. (1993). 'A review of the methodologies movement'. *Journal of Information Technology*, 5: 277-86.

Baran, B. (1987). 'The Technological Transformation of White-Collar Work: A Case study of the Insurance Industry', in Hartman (ed.). *Computer Chips and Paper Clips: Technology and Women's Employment.* Washington DC: National Academy Press.

Baroudi, J.J. and Igbaria, M. (1995). 'An Examination of Gender Effects on Career Success of Information Systems Employees'. *Journal of Management Information Systems* 11 (3): 181-201.

Bulkeley, D. (1995). 'PC Makes Sense'. *Computerworld*, June: 38-40.

Burris, B.H. (1993). *Technocracy at Work*. SUNY Series, The New Inequalities. Albany, NY: State University of New York.

Computerworld's 9th Annual Salary & Survey: 'Unequal Opportunities' *Computerworld*, September 4: 1/70-72,74,78.

Dachler, H.P and Hosking, D. (1995). 'The Primacy of relations in socially constructed organizational realities', in Hoskings D., Dachler, H.P. and Gergen, K.J. (eds.). *Management and Organization: Relational Alternatives to Individualism*. Aldershot: Avebury.

Donato, K.M. (1990). 'Programming for Change? The Growing Demand for Women Systems Analysts', in Reskin, B.F. and Roos, P.A. (eds.). *Job Queues, Gender Queues: Explaining Women's Inroads into Male Occupations*, Philadelphia: Temple University Press.

Gheraldi, S. (1995). *Gender, Symbolism and Organizational Cultures*. London: Sage.

Glaser, B.G. and Strauss, A.L. (1967). *The Discovery of Grounded Theory: Strategies for Qualitative Research.* New york: Aldine Publishing Company.

Financial Times, 24 May (1996). 'UK: Software Shows its Strength: The Holway Report has stressed the importance of outsourcing'.

Fischer, S., Doodeman, M., Vinig, T. and Achterberg, J. (1993). 'Boiling the Frog or Seducing the Fax: Organizational Aspects of Implementing CASE Technology', in Avison, D., Kendall, J.E., DeGross, J.I. (eds.). *Human, Organizational and Social Dimensions of information Systems Development*. Amsterdam: Elsevier Science Publishers, B.V. (North-Holland).

Greenbaum, J. (1979). *In the Name of Efficiency: Management Theory and Shopfloor Practice in Data-Processing Work.* Philadelphia: Temple University Press.

Grundy, F. (1994). 'Women in the Computing Workplace: Some Impressions', in Adam, A.; Emms, J.; Green, E. and Owen, J. (eds.). *Women, Work and Computerization - Breaking Old Boundaries Building New Forms* (IFIP Transactions A-57). Amsterdam: Elsevier Science, B.V. (North-Holland).

Grundy, F. (1996). *Women and Computers.* Exeter: Intellect Books.

Hoffman, L.R. and Maier, N.R.F. (1961). 'Quality and Acceptance of problem solutions by members of homogeneous and heterogenous groups'. *Journal of Abnormal and Social Psychology* 62: 401-07

Knights. D. and Murray, F. (1994). *Managers Divided –Organizational Politics and Information Technology Management.* London: Wiley Series in Information Systems.

Kraft, P. (1977). *Programmers and Managers: The Routinization of Computer Programming in the United States.* New York: Springer-Verlag.

Kraft, P. (1979). 'The Industrialization of Computer Programming: From Programming to Software Production', in Zimbalist, A. (ed.). *Case Studies on the Labour Process.* New York: Monthly Review Press.

Markus, M.L. and Robey, D. (1988). 'Information Technology and Organizational Change: Causal Structure in Theory and Research', *Management Science,* 34, (5): 583-98

Murray, F. (1993). 'A Separate Reality: Science, Technology and Masculinity', in Green, E., Owen, J. and Pain, D. (eds.). *Gendered by Design? Information Technology and Office Systems.* London: Taylor and Francis.

Ordroyd, R. (1996). 'Is the IS industry a turn-off for women?' *Sunday Business,* 26 May. 9

Panteli, A., Ramsay, H. and Beirne, M. (1997). 'Engendered Systems Development: Ghettoization and Agency'. Paper for the *Sixth IFIP-WWC97, Women, Work and Computerization Conference.* Bonn, Germany, 24–7 May 1997.

Pettigrew, A. (1990). 'Longitudinal Field Research on Change: Theory and Practice' *Organizational Science* 1 (3): 267-92.

Reskin, B.F. and Roos, P.A. (1990). *Job Queues, Gender Queues: Explaining Women's Inroads into Male Occupations.* Philadelphia: Temple University Press.

Social Europe (1993). 'Occupational Segregation of Women and Men in the European Community' Supplement 3/93: 70-6.

Sonnentag, S. (1994). 'Team Leading in Software Development: A Comparison Between Women and Men', in Adam, A.; Emms, J.; Green, E. and Owen, J. (eds.).*Women, Work and Computerization - Breaking Old Boundaries Building New Forms* (IFIP Transactions A 57). Amsterdam: Elsevier Science, B.V. (North-Holland).

Truman G.E. and Baroudi, J.J. (1994). 'Gender Differences in the Information Systems Managerial Ranks: An Assessment of Potential Discriminatory Practices' *MIS Quarterly,* June: 129-41

Watson, W.E., Kuman, K., and Michaelsen, L.K. (1993). 'Cultural Diversity's impact on interaction process and performance: Comparing Homogeneous and Diverse Groups' *Academy of Management Journal,* 36: 590-602

Wright R. (1996). 'The Occupational Masculinity of Computing', in Cheng, C. (ed.). *Masculinities in Organizations - Research on Men and Masculinities.* London: Sage.

Wright R. and Jacobs, J.A. (1995). 'Male Flight From Computer Work: A New Look at Occupational Resegregation and Ghettoization', in Jacobs, J.A. (ed.). *Gender Inequality at Work.* London: Sage.

Androgynous Women and Computing: A Perfect Match?

Paula Roberts

University of South Australia, St. Bernards's Road, Magill, SA 5072, Australia

Abstract

This paper describes a study of the life and work histories of 20 female executives who fulfil a variety of roles in the Australian computing industry. Amongst them are branch managers of national computer companies, senior systems analysts, engineers, and sales consultants, who are flourishing in the male-dominated information technology profession. The research reveals unique upbringings in homes and schools without prescribed sex roles. Of particular significance is the maternal influence and a pattern emerges of non-traditional mothers rearing non-traditional daughters. The women who are the product of these settings show a synthesis of traits previously ascribed to one or other gender. They display a natural rather than a learned confidence and leadership, together with both logical and intuitive thought. The research suggests a revisiting of the concept of androgyny (through ethnographic research instead of psychological testing) for its significance in the compatibility of women with computing.

Introduction

This story begins with a mystery and ends with a possible solution. In the middle are interrelated and interdisciplinary sections of research which help unravel the mystery and support its resolution.

The mystery is why so many women avoid careers in information technology (Roach 1993). Women are not inept in their use of technology, for they drive cars, use telephones and operate a variety of household appliances. But females avoid computers in primary and secondary schools, suffer their way through mandatory computer courses in universities, and then avoid the specialist computing studies which lead to careers in information technology.

In the business world few women use computers for purposes beyond basic administration and are under-represented at all levels of the information technology profession. Only a small proportion of women use the Internet, yet decades ago women hi-jacked that earlier business tool, the telephone, turned it into a communications medium and became its major users.

In two decades of studies into female avoidance of computers, researchers have suggested a variety of reasons for girls' lack of involvement. These include boys' dominance of computing resources (Hoyles 1988), the lack of female role models amongst computing teachers (Kramer and Lehman 1990), a female perception that computing is mathematics based (Perry and Greber 1990), failure to accommodate women's distinctive ways of working with computers (Turkle and Papert 1990), female anxiety with the male preoccupation with computers (Kiesler, Sproull and Eccles 1985) and so on.

A related body of research describes women alienated by the masculinity of the computer culture (Griffiths 1988), the military's impersonal driving of computer technology (Edwards 1990), an incompatible epistemological base (Jansen 1989) and the degradation of work brought about by computerization, (Zuboff 1988). Further female concerns relate to large-scale computer crime and the fallibility of computer systems entrusted to run high-risk systems in nuclear plants, aeroplanes and medical procedures (Forester and Morrison 1990).

Society has reason to be apprehensive of this new, pervasive technology, but women are absent from fora which might influence the limitation of computers to those things which machines can do more safely, faster and more easily than human beings. Also missing are women who might critically examine the utopianism of the global visionaries who would have us believe that libraries are dead, that digital information will supersede the collective wisdom of ages, that life will revolve around a computer screen, and that warnings of the spectre of a world population divided into 'information rich' and 'information poor' societies are the bleatings of neo-Luddites.

But fascinating contradictions exist in this seemingly universal female avoidance of computing, for while a majority of women choose other careers, certain women flourish in the information technology profession and bring benefit to it with their distinctive talents. In the short history of computing, the 19th-century Lady Ada Lovelace is honoured as the first computer programmer. In World War II, the 'ENIAC girls' were responsible for US military computer programming, and naval officer, Grace Hopper, is recognized as the developer of the COBOL programming language. From this historical evidence, it is obvious that certain women have chosen to be involved with computers and have made a significant contribution to the development of information technology. But the question remains: why are such women in the minority?

1. The Research Study

This paper describes recent research which has examined the life histories of 20 female computing executives. In personal interviews, reasons were sought for their choice of information technology as a career, and for their success in this non-traditional area for women.

The paper is in two parts. First, the research methodology and its outcomes are described. The paper then revisits the concept of androgyny, which, in the 1970s and early 1980s, excited social scientists and feminists, and then fell into disfavour. The paper discusses a current revitalization of androgyny research, which has moved beyond earlier models of self-reporting on a polarised scale of masculine and feminine attributes, to ethnographic studies which explore in individuals a synthesis of traits previously ascribed to one or other gender. Also discussed is the significance of the concept of androgyny for career choice.

1.1 Research Methodology

In 1996, 17 female members of the South Australian branch of the Australian Computer Society agreed to take part in a research study. With the exception of one programmer, the subjects were senior systems analysts, sales consultants or managers. Two were the State managers of prominent national computing companies.

Their ages ranged from the early twenties to the mid-fifties. Eight had adult children and three of these were female engineers; a remarkably high proportion in a country where only ten percent of engineers are female. The three daughter-engineers joined the research sample, bringing the total to 20.

In 90-minute interviews the subjects discussed facets of their family, school and work experiences, structured by 75 'open-ended' questions. The subjects were provided with the questions before the interview so there was an opportunity to recall earlier experiences and to reflect upon their impact on career choice.

1.2 Results

There was a surprising commonality in the experiences of the subjects, which a brief summary under the main themes will illustrate.

1.2.1 Home, school and societal influences on gender identity and career choice

1.2.1.1 Role of the mother in the family

Most subjects had mothers who had combined outside paid employment with traditional roles. Many mothers had had unusual life experiences. One, the wife of a senior officer, was herself a high-ranking officer in the British Army. Another was a wartime member of the Royal Airforce. Several had migrated with their families to Australia at the end of World War II, leaving an established career (such as teaching), and, in a new country, turned to manual work (fruit picking or other agricultural labour) to assist the family to re-establish itself.

One mother of six children did not engage in outside employment, but showed what her daughter described as 'courage and flexibility' in relocating her family, as her bank manager husband underwent continual career moves in South Australian country towns.

Another mother with two children (followed much later by an unexpected 'onset-of-menopause' baby), moved to London where her husband sought work, leaving the support of her family in Scotland. Her (subject) daughter noted, 'I was so sorry for her. She was so brave.'

What was significant in the subjects' narratives was that they described their mothers with pride, sympathy, amusement and affection. Only one of the 20 said that she had had an unsatisfactory relationship with her mother and was critical of her mother's seeming lack of direction in her life. Most described their mothers as 'strong' and 'independent' women.

The mothers were the heads of their households or occupied a joint leadership role. Most controlled the family's finances. One took in sewing at home to augment the family budget and worked long hours for little reward, but could not be persuaded to give up the work once the family finances had improved, expressing personal satisfaction with her performance in this challenging, paid work.

1.2.1.2 Role of the father in the family

The fathers in general were described by the subjects as 'non-traditional'. One father, whose own mother had died leaving a 'helpless' husband and young family, had deliberately set out to equip himself with household management skills, which he had applied in his own marriage. All except one of the subjects' parents' marriages were still intact.

In every case neither parent had exerted direct influence on the subject's career choice, but both parents encouraged their daughter to believe she could do 'anything she set her mind to'.

Of particular significance was parental support for studies in mathematics and science, in which all the women in this study excelled.

One subject recalled her 'privileged' upbringing as an only child, whose father treated her as a 'hoped-for' son. Her father was a constant companion, extending her pursuits to adventurous activities and sport, experiences possibly denied her had she a brother.

1.2.1.3 Family relationships

Most subjects recalled that the girls were more dominant. Order of birth appeared to have no significance in their choice of non-traditional career. Only two were first born and most came in the middle of the family order, while three were youngest. Most of their siblings had 'careers' rather than jobs but some had not worked, or could not work. One subject expressed her guilt that she was confident and successful but had failed to help her nervous, depressed brother, who had left his employment and had since lacked the confidence to work.

Many families had done out-of-the-ordinary things. One family had sailed and raced boats. This family's daughter (the research subject) and her husband took their own small daughters on a sailing boat around the world for five years. One of these girls later became an engineer (and another subject in this survey), while the other is presently serving in the merchant navy.

Most subjects classed their parents as adventurous or risk takers, while others described their parents as 'willing to take a chance' or 'quick to seize an opportunity'.

Only one of the subjects' parents' marriage had failed, and her father had spent his working life in a variety of situations, farming, then travelling Australia with his children to find work. He currently had a contract for removing sleepers from abandoned railway tracks in the Australian 'outback'. The daughter described her farm upbringing as a 'jill of all trades', amongst other things, driving tractors while quite young. She had moved interstate with her father and changed homes and schools without the stress and sense of disruption that others experienced. She commented that she had enjoyed and benefited from these many changes in her young life.

1.2.1.4 Self-identity

Nearly all subjects could not remember a distinct 'feminine identity' in their teenage years, nor their being influenced by 'prevailing images of femininity in the media or society'. Many used expressions like 'I wasn't "butch" though', or 'I liked boys', or 'I was conscious of fashion and bought the latest patterns to make my own clothes'. One remembered being cautioned by an aunt about her forthright and independent nature, saying 'You'll have to mend your ways or no one will want to marry you'. The subject commented with some amusement, 'I didn't change my ways and I did get married.' (Currently her husband works with her, in a similar role, in a large South Australian computing company.)

The subjects did not have groups of female friends in their adolescent years, nor in school or university. Most mentioned having only one or two special female friends, with whom they still have a strong relationship.

1.2.1.5 Effects of educational experiences on career choice

All subjects reported an easy interaction with males, with their brothers' friends and with male peers at school and university. All except two were educated in co-educational schools and none recalled feeling uncomfortable in advanced mathematics and science classes. Several reflected that because they had similar or more ability than the boys in these classes, they had no reason to feel different, nor were they treated differently.

Several remembered female teachers as 'strong women' but there were few female teachers of mathematics and science. Some recalled male teachers as helpful, but not influential in their career choice.

1.2.1.6 Personal epistemological position regarding technology

The subjects were asked a series of questions designed to gauge their compatibility or otherwise with the cognitive styles of computing, matters which have received attention in feminist critiques of information technology (Jansen 1989; Wacjman 1991; van Zoonen 1992 and Turkle 1996).

All subjects were bemused that computers might be described as reflecting male styles of thinking. They described their own thinking as logical and therefore compatible with computers.

They did not have well-formed views on either the positive or negative impacts of information technology on society, although some noted their defensive stance in social situations when describing their work and when faced with criticisms linking computers with job losses.

None displayed a special enthusiasm for mechanical and technical things in general, or computers in particular. They described computers as 'just tools', like motor cars and household appliances. Few of the younger subjects had home computers. The older ones who did have a home computer said their children were the prime users.

Almost without exception, the subjects had chosen their careers in information technology on economic considerations alone. When asked whether their career choice had been influenced by notions of 'service to others' or 'desire to work with people' (factors identified with female career choice by Ormerod 1971; Head 1980 and 1985; Smithers and Collings 1981), the subjects noted that these concerns had not influenced their choice, but had some influence on their current job satisfaction.

1.2.1.7 Perceptions of work cultures and women in non-traditional careers

None of the subjects regarded their work in computing as 'non-traditional', however most were active in attempts to attract women into the information technology profession through their service with the Women in Technology Special Interest Group of the South Australian branch of the Australian Computing Society.

Many subjects had long-standing careers in information technology ranging from 10 to 30 years. Most had held jobs of various designations, progressing from programmer to senior systems analyst, and some had moved to management. Two of the subjects were senior computing educators. The three engineers (who were amongst the youngest subjects) used computers as an integral part of their engineering activities and used sophisticated software for modelling mathematical processes and for design work.

The older subjects had taken career breaks of several years to raise their families but did not view this absence as a disadvantage when resuming their professional lives. Younger members of the group with children (including one who is a sole parent) made no comment on their dual role. Of the 15 married subjects in the study, only one had divorced.

Although most of the subjects commented on their organisations' formal equal opportunity policies, none had experienced the need to invoke these. Notable was the subjects' lack of experience of discrimination against them owing to their sex, and none had experienced difficulty in gaining acceptance of their professional capabilities.

All expressed pride and satisfaction in their professional role. When asked to describe typically 'good' and 'bad' days, most identified good days with tasks completed, and 'bad' as 'not much to show at the end of the day'. Some mentioned interaction with clients as an important part of job satisfaction. Two of the managers noted their pride in being female managers.

1.3 Summary

These narratives provide evidence of socialisation in homes without gendered roles and expectations, with strong mothers, who, by choice had moved outside the traditional female role. The subjects' fathers were, at most, nominal 'heads of households' and both parents were encouraging and supportive of their daughters' 'non-traditional' educational and career choices.

The female subjects emerge from these upbringings with confidence to tackle any career. Most came to computing by chance, selecting it for its attractive economic opportunities when they were first seeking employment.

All achieved well in mathematics and science throughout their schooling and enjoyed these studies. Most were good at competitive sport, and in sports not traditionally regarded as feminine.

It is tempting to describe the subjects as 'tom-boys' in their earlier years but their image now is that of attractive, accomplished, confident female leaders in information technology.

2. The Academic Literature

The academic literature is helpful in analysing the findings of this study, and for this purpose is summarised under headings of 'Social Construction of Gender', 'Concept of Androgyny', and 'The Effect of Maternal Employment on Career Choice'.

2.1 The Social Construction of Gender

Conway, Bourque and Scott (1987) note that as early as 1935 Margaret Mead advanced the idea that gender had a cultural, not a biological, base, which varied widely in different settings. However, Mead's ideas were swamped in the next two decades with biologically-based views which dominated the study of male and female behaviour.

Since the 1960s, a wider understanding of gender as a cultural phenomenon has developed through multi-disciplinary research. Gender scholars have analysed the family and other social, economic and political institutions which have been shaped by conventional views of male and female. It is now generally accepted that these gender stereotypes are characterised in society by a division of labour which has created a two-tiered labour market, remarkably resistant to change.

A significant body of research has examined the constraints which gender stereotypes have placed on the educational and vocational opportunities of females. Eccles (1987), for example, notes that, despite affirmative action and education programmes, few women pursue careers in the scientific, mathematical and technical fields, and women are less likely than men to enter professions which are mathematics-related. Eccles has developed a model of educational and occupational choice which suggests sex differences in choices are related to differential expectations for success, and differential values which result from gender-role socialisation.

The benefit for this current study is that, as a model of choice rather than avoidance, Eccles's model allows a focus on individual differences among women. Eccles argues these differences result from the influence of parents and teachers who value traditional gender-role prescriptions of appropriate activities, form different expectations for males and females, and provide different advice regarding students' future options. As a result of these experiences, and without accurate information on occupations, young women, in comparison with young men, develop less confidence in their mathematical abilities, less interest in studying mathematics and physical science, and less interest in pursuing careers in mathematics and science-related fields.

2.2 The Concept of Androgyny

The concept of androgyny has great significance for this current study. Androgyny preoccupied social scientists in the 1970s and early 1980s, then fell into disfavour, only to be revitalised in the 1990s for its utility in understanding how some females (and males) break free of gender stereotypes and live richer personal and professional lives.

Bem (1974, 1975, 1983) was foremost in revealing the promise of androgyny as a concept for understanding gender-free individuals and for raising gender-free children in a gender-laden society. Bem's 1974 Sex Role Inventory (the BSRI) required subjects to self-report by questionnaire on aspects of their personality that could be classified as feminine, masculine, androgynous (a combination of feminine and masculine) or undifferentiated.

A major criticism of the BSRI was its polarisation of feminine and masculine traits and uncertainty regarding their integration in self-identity. In current research involving open-ended self-descriptions, Vonk and Ashmore (1993) report their androgynous subjects as using situational qualifiers in describing their masculine, feminine and gender-neutral attributes, indicating that they enact masculine and feminine qualities on different occasions. This suggestion matches the findings in the current study, which shows females' displaying 'tomboyish' attitudes at times, yet in other settings wanting to be attractive to the opposite sex.

A comment on tomboyism is relevant here. Burn, O'Neil and Nederend (1996) found childhood tomboyism positively related to male instrumental qualities of assertiveness and self-reliance in androgynous females but noted tomboyism declined at puberty owing to social pressure.

Block, von der Lippe and Block (1973) conducted a rare longitudinal study of sex-role development in which 140 young children and their parents were interviewed; some 25 years later, these 'children', then in their thirties, were interviewed once more. Sedney (1987) summarises the study's outcomes as follows:

> Parents of androgynous offspring were stable and financially secure members of their communities, they generally were satisfied with their lives and their marriages, they agreed about discipline, and they emphasized values of fairness and responsibility to others. Parents in this group were judged to have good marital adjustment. ... In addition, the androgynous adults came from families in which the parents themselves exemplified androgynous personality styles and flexibility in their social-role definitions. ... Also, the parents' relationship was characterized by some form of unconventional sharing of responsibility (at a time when there was little social support for such a stance).

In a recent extension of Bem's work, Sedney has reported the extent to which parents are able to influence their children towards the development of non-stereotyped behaviours, noting that very young children actually resist gender-free behaviour, that is, girls want to play with dolls and boys want to play with trains; yet children appear to absorb a gender-free upbringing and reproduce it in adolescence, or later in life. As Sedney says, 'Although androgynous parents may not produce androgynous children, their children often do grow up to be androgynous adults.' Of particular value is her summation, 'What parents do in their own lives may be the most important lesson they hand down to their children in their psychological sex-role development.'

2.3 The Effect of Maternal Employment on Career Choice

A substantial literature provides evidence that maternal employment impacts on both the educational aspirations and career choices of females. Of value here is research which links maternal employment to daughters' choice of non-traditional occupations (for example, Almquist and Angrist 1970, Tangri 1972, Hansson, et al 1977, Hoffman 1980, Sholomskas and Axelrod 1986, Newton 1987, Smith 1990).

Hoffman provides a valuable summary of studies which examined the effect of maternal employment on the education of children. She notes 'daughters of employed mothers probably outperform daughters of unemployed mothers' and that 'both sons and daughters of working mothers hold a less stereotyped view of males and females'.

Smith (1990) applies the human capital approach to her study of some three thousand females. She contends a young woman's occupational choice is affected by her plans to allocate time between unpaid and paid work. If she intends to spend a large proportion of her life in paid employment, she is more likely to choose the better-paid traditional male occupations. A deciding factor in the choice of a life of paid work, and concomitant choice of a male occupation, is the female-headed household effect, and just as significant is the effect of the growing number of female-headed households on the wider community .

Perhaps Smith has identified here an accelerating social change and its impact on gender-based occupational choice, although if the female head of household is also a single parent, then economic distress will militate against equality of opportunity for women and girls, and also for increasing numbers of boys, as noted by Okin (1995).

3. Conclusion

This story began with the mystery of why a majority of women choose to avoid computer-related education and work, while others flourish in the male-dominated computing profession.

A likely solution to the mystery is that certain women escape the chains of gender both by their upbringing in homes where parents do not enact traditional sex roles, and in schools where teachers do not treat boys and girls differently, nor do they have differential expectations and aspirations for them.

It is now generally accepted that gender is a product of socialisation processes, and these processes will vary in particular cultures, as Mead brought to our attention as long ago as 1935. Such a view helps to explain the phenomenon of the differential participation of women in technology, such as in the old Soviet Union where as many women as men were engineers. Cultural influences may explain also the much higher level of acceptance of information technology as a career choice for women in Japan, China, India and Singapore.

Gender-free upbringings not only free up career choices in gender-laden communities such as western society, they also provide learning experiences for both sexes which may allow males and females to develop the 'multiple intelligences' of which they are capable (Gardner and Hatch 1988) instead of being consigned to think only in the ways of the dominant disciplines which they study, in styles of thinking which are differentially valued in their society.

It is tempting to think that if all girls were socialised in the way of the subjects in this current research study, then the problems of female participation in information technology would disappear. This is a dangerous over-simplification. Whilst these women have had the privilege of upbringings in gender-free environments, they did not choose gender-free studies. The sciences, mathematics and computing all bear the imprint of a distinct and limited masculine style of thought. Some might argue that the women in this study are nothing more than male clones.

If we are concerned that computer scientists continue to show as little concern for the social implications of computing as scientists have shown for the natural environment, then what does society gain by populating information technology with women trained as men?

By no stretch of the imagination could these women be classed as agents for change. This may disappoint those who would wish for a computer science more representative of women's values and accommodating of a wider range of thinking styles. The women in this study are excelling in a male world and it seems unlikely that they may have as a priority the changing of this privileged world, nor the ambition to make information technology more socially responsible.

So, the study may have provided just part of the solution for the complex problem of increasing the participation of women in computing. However, even this partial solution encourages hope for change, because socialisation processes can be changed. And increasingly it is understood how socialisation processes are as dangerous for men as they are for women.

For years, dietitians have warned us 'We are what we eat'. It would be wise for us to heed the strong message for women and for men which emerges from this research study (and coined by Whiting and Edwards 1988), 'We are the company we keep'.

References

Almquist, E.M. and Angrist, S. S. (1970). 'Career salience and atypicality of occupational choice among college women'. *Journal of Marriage and the Family* 32: 242-249.

Bem, S. (1974). 'The measurement of psychological androgyny'. *Journal of Consulting and Clinical Psychology* 42: 155-162.

Bem, S. (1975). 'Sex-role adaptability: One consequence of psychological androgyny'. *Journal of Personality and Social Psychology* 31: 634-43.

Bem, S. (1983). 'Gender Schema Theory and Its Implications for Child Development: Raising Gender-aschematic Children in a Gender-schematic Society' *Signs: Journal of Women in Culture and Society* 8 (4).

Block, J., von der Lippe, A. and Block, J. H. (1973). 'Sex-role and socialization patterns: some personality concomitants and environmental antecedents'. *Journal of Consulting and Clinical Psychology* 41: 321-41.

Burn, S.M., O'Neil, A. K. and Nederend, S. (1996). 'Childhood Tomboyism and Adult Androgyny'. *Sex Roles* 34 (5/6).

Conway, J.K., Bourque, S. C. and Scott , J. W. (1987). 'Introduction'. *Daedalus* Fall.

Eccles, J. (1987). 'Gender Roles and Women's Achievement-Related Decisions'. *Psychology of Women Quarterly* 11: 135-172.

Edwards, P. (1990). 'The Army and the Microworld: Computers and the Politics of Gender Identity'. *Signs: Journal of Women in Culture and Society* 16 (1).

Forester, T. and Morrison , P. (1990). *Computer Ethics: Cautionary Tales and Ethical Dilemmas in Computing*, Oxford: Basil Blackwell.

Gardner, H. and Hatch, T. (1988). 'Multiple Intelligences go to School: Educational Implications of the Theory of Multiple Intelligences'. *Educational Researcher* 18 (8): 4-10.

Griffiths, M.(1988).'Strong Feelings About Computers'. *Women's Studies International Forum* 11 (2).

Hansson, R.O., Chernovetz, M. and Jones, W. (1977). 'Maternal employment and androgyny'. *Psychology of Women Quarterly* 2: 76-78.

Head, J. (1980). 'A model to link personality characteristics to science}. *European Journal of Science Education*. 2: 295-300.

Head, J. (1985). *The Personal Response to Science*. Cambridge: Cambridge University Press.

Hoffman, L.W. (1980). 'The effects of maternal employment on the academic attitudes and performance of school-aged children'. *School Psychology Review* 9: 319-335.

Hoyles, C. (1988). *Girls and Computers*, Institute of Education, University of London.

Jansen, S. C. (1989). 'Gender and the Information Society: A Socially Structured Science'. *Journal of Communication* 39 (3).

Kiesler, S., Sproull, L. and Eccles, J. (1985). 'Poolhalls, chips and war games: women in the culture of computing'. *Psychology of Women Quarterly* 9 (4).

Kramer, P and Lehman, S. (1990). 'Mismeasuring Women: A Critique on Research on Computer Ability and Avoidance'. *Signs: Journal of Women in Culture and Society* 16 (1).

Mead, M. (1935). *Sex and Temperament in Three Primitive Societies*.

Newton, P. (1987). 'Who Becomes an Engineer? Social Psychological Antecedents of a Non-traditional Career Choice', in Spencer, A. and Podmore, D. (eds.). *In a Man's World*, London: Tavistock.

Okin, S. (1995). 'Inequalities between the sexes in different cultural contexts', in Nussbaum, M. and Glover, J. (eds.)*Women, Culture and Development*, Oxford: Clarendon Press.

Ormerod, M.B. (1971). 'The Social Implications Factor in Attitudes to Science'. *British Journal of Educational Psychology* 41 (3): 335-8.

Perry, R. and Greber, L. (1990). 'Women and Computers: An Introduction'. *Signs: Journal of Women in Culture and Society* 16 (1): 74-101.

Roach, J. (1993). 'The Glass Ceiling - is it a Mirage?' *Computerworld* 16: 8.

Sholomskas, D. and Axelrod, R. (1986). The Influence of Mother-Daughter Relationships on Women's Sense of Self and Current Role Choices. *Psychology of Women Quarterly* 10: 171-182.

Sedney, M.A. (1987). 'Development of Androgyny: Parental Influences'. *Psychology of Women Quarterly* 11: 311-26.

Smith, P.A. (1990). 'The Choice of a Sex-Nontraditional Occupation: The Female-Headed Household Effect'. *Youth & Society* 21 (3): 399-406.

Smithers, A. and Collings, J. (1981). 'Girls studying science in the sixth form', in Kelly, A. (ed.). *The Missing Half*, Manchester: Manchester University Press.

Spence, J.T. and Helmreich, R.L. (1978). *Masculinity and Femininity: Their Psychological Dimensions, Correlates and Antecedents.* Austin: University of Texas Press.

Tangri, S.S. (1972). 'Determinants of occupational role innovation among college women'. *Journal of Social Issues.* 28: 177-99

Turkle, S. (1996). *Life on the Screen: Identity in the Age of the Internet*, New York: Simon and Schuster.

Turkle, S. and Papert, S. (1990). 'Epistemological Pluralism: Styles and Voices within the Computer Culture'. *Signs: Journal of Women in Culture and Society* 16 (1): 129-57.

Van Zoonen, L. (1992). 'Feminist theory and information technology'. *Media, Culture & Society*, 14.

Vonk, R. and Ashmore, R.D. (1993). 'The multifaceted self: androgyny reassessed by open-ended self-descriptions'. *Social Psychology Quarterly* 56 (4): 278-87.

Wajcman, J. (1991). *Feminism Confronts Technology.* Sydney: Allen & Unwin.

Whiting, B.B. and Edwards, C.P. (1988). *Children of Different Worlds: The Formation of Social Behavior.* Cambridge, MA: Harvard University Press.

Zuboff, S. (1988). *In the Age of the Smart Machine.* New York: Basic.

We Can, We Don't Want to: Factors Influencing Women's Participation in Computing

Gerda Siann

University of Dundee

Abstract

This paper presents a series of analyses derived from the most recent HESA (Higher Education Statistics Agency) figures of the gender balance in entry to courses with computer science either as the sole major or as a secondary subject. The conclusion that is drawn from these analyses is that the proportion of female students on computer science courses, at the undergraduate level, tends to approach parity when computer science is studied in combination with other subjects. This conclusion is discussed with reference to the social and psychological factors underpinning the relative reluctance of high flying students of both sexes to enter Science, Engineering and Information Technology courses. It is suggested that it is preference rather than structural barriers which is the major factor in the relatively low participation of women in university courses with computer science as the sole major.

1. Introduction

By the year 2000 it is estimated that over 80% of the jobs within the UK will involve the use of Information Technology. Concern has been expressed by academia and industry regarding the decrease in the number of women entering IT-related courses and subsequently the software engineering profession – a phenomenon which has occurred since the early 1980s. Britain is falling well behind other countries. (Whitehouse et al, 1996)

Remarks like these permeate the literature on Women in Computing and in this paper I want to look critically at the concerns expressed. Initially, I would like to look at the claim that there has been a decrease in women entering IT-related courses. Following this, I want to look at the related issue of the relative reluctance of both sexes, but especially women, to enter computer and SET courses in general. Finally, I want to examine some of the reasons that have been offered for these trends.

2. Gender Differences in Entry to Computing Courses

I have recently commissioned HESA (the Higher Education Statistical Agency) to provide a break-down by gender of their most recent data set (July and December 1995).

In this section I want to discuss three tables I derived from this. The first relates to undergraduate courses with Computer Science as a major, the second to undergraduate courses with Computer Science as a secondary subject, the third to masters courses in Computer Science.

The first table, Table 1, indicates the numbers of students by gender studying Computer Science on its own or with various secondary subjects. The first entry in the Table is for students majoring in Computer Science only (females, 19%). The next two entries show students majoring in Computer Science with secondary subjects in a computer science speciality (females, 12%) and Engineering and Technology (females, 6%). These three entries clearly show major under-representation of women.

However, if we look at the three biggest of the remaining categories we see that the proportion of students who are women on courses combining Computer Science with a secondary subject in Business and Administrative Studies is 32%, with Mathematical Sciences 28% and Social, Economic and Political Studies 40%. In the next largest category, Computer Science combined with Languages, women actually outnumber men.

Table 2 shows undergraduate courses with Computer Science as a secondary subject. The actual numbers studying on these courses, relative to the Computer Science majors, are, of course, small but nevertheless it can be seen that women tend to be over-represented or represented at near parity on a number of courses where Computer Science is taken as a secondary subject.

Table 3 shows the gender representation on Masters' courses in computer science and indicates similar trends in that, in general, Computer Science seems to attract more females in combination than on its own.

I think the trends revealed by these figures do give cause for more optimism than is revealed in the quotation which appears at the beginning of the paper in that there seems to be a clear indication that more women could be attracted to the academic study of computing if more stress were laid on courses which offer it in combination with other disciplines. While I have no comparative figures for previous years, I would be most surprised if there has not been an increase over time in women studying computing, on those courses which offer it in combination with other disciplines.

3. Computing, Science, Engineering and Technology

The concern over the under-representation of women on academic courses in computing is frequently linked to similar concerns in the related areas of science, engineering and technology. Similar trends to those outlined above are clear, from the HESA figures, in these areas as well. For example, while women are under-represented on courses with a sole major in Physical Sciences (35%), their participation when Physical Sciences is studied in combination with secondary subjects increases markedly in many cases. For instance, in the case of Agriculture and Related Subjects it is 54%, with Subjects Allied to Medicine it is 48%, with Architecture, Building and Planning it is 42% and with Creative Arts and Design it is 48%.

Secondary Subject	Female	Male	Total	% Female
No secondary subject	7110	29819	36929	19.3
Computer Science (speciality)	52	385	437	11.9
Engineering & Technology	48	785	833	5.8
Business & Administrative Studies	575	1236	1811	31.8
Mathematical Sciences	199	502	701	28.4
Social, Economic & Political Studies	226	336	562	40.2
Languages	270	218	488	55.3
Biological Sciences	60	109	169	35.5
Physical Sciences	39	118	157	24.8
Education	57	51	108	52.8
Humanities	39	68	107	36.4
Librarianship & Information Science	30	68	98	30.6
Creative Arts & Design	19	62	81	23.5
Combined	17	61	78	21.8
Law	14	24	38	36.8
Subjects Allied to Medicine	2	1	3	66.7
Architecture, Building & Planning	0	2	2	0

Table 1. Gender participation in undergraduate course with Computer Science as a major.

Secondary Subject	Female	Male	Total	% Female
Education	138	85	223	61.9
Librarianship & Information Science	45	36	81	55.6
Humanities	29	29	58	50.0
Languages	61	67	128	47.7
Creative Arts & Design	32	45	77	41.6
Law	2	3	5	40.0
Business & Administrative Studies	334	537	871	38.3
Social, Economic & Political Studies	44	72	116	37.9
Mathematical Sciences	378	1048	1426	26.5
Engineering & Technology	47	552	599	7.8

Table 2. Gender participation in undergraduate course with Computer Science as a secondary subject.

Secondary Subject	Female	Male	Total	% Female
Mathematical Sciences	14	43	57	24.6
Engineering & Technology	10	73	83	12.0
Business & Administrative Studies	20	95	115	17.4
Librarianship & Information Science	1	1	2	50.0
Languages	1	3	4	25.0
Humanities	2	0	2	100.0
Creative Arts & Design	6	11	17	35.3
No secondary subject	1657	6019	7676	21.6
Grand Total	1711	6245	7956	21.5

Table 3. Gender participation in Masters' courses with Computer Science as a secondary subject.

In much the same way, if we turn to Engineering and Technology, the HESA figures show that while women are only 14% of those majoring in it alone, they form 45% of those combining it with Biological Sciences as a secondary subject and 51% of those combining it with Creative Arts and Design as a secondary subject. This indicates that, as with computing, studying science and engineering in combination with other disciplines is more attractive to women than studying them on their own.

4. The Flight from Science and Engineering Courses

The past decade has seen female participation in what might be termed the 'elite' professions at parity or higher (for example, veterinary medicine, law, medicine, accountancy) but despite the considerable input into strategies such as the WISE initiatives for drawing women into engineering and computing (and, to a lesser degree, into science), female participation has risen far less than in other professions.

I have always argued that, in general, it is a minority of students, of both sexes, who are keen to study SET subjects, but that of that relatively small number, the majority are males. What many other analysts have tended to do, however, is to see the problem as lying in women's reluctance to enter these fields, rather than as part of an overall tendency for young people of both sexes to reject these areas. My belief that what we should be looking at is a general, rather than a specifically female trend, is illustrated in the last round of the clearing house. I cite, for example, a quotation from the *Guardian* of 20 August 1996:

> But there are still vacancies on more than 20,000 courses, according to UCAS, with some universities finding engineering and science places hard to fill. Cut-throat competition between colleges and universities for engineering students has prompted Tony Higgins, the chief executive of UCAS, to warn admissions tutors against poaching. Further education college principals had complained they were losing thousands of students accepted on diploma courses but then offered degree places at universities. (p. 8).

These trends were also referred to in a recent article in the *Times Higher Educational Supplement*. It was suggested that not only was the calibre of students taking up science in the 'old' universities lower than in other disciplines but that in the 'new' universities the ratio of applications to places ranged from 13 to one for creative arts to between 5 and 7 to one for science and engineering (Patel 1996). This relative reluctance to study science and engineering extends to computing as well and similar trends are seen in the USA where there has been a fall off in both sexes' interest in careers in computing since the 1980s (Wright 1996).

Later in this paper, I look at this tendency from a psychological perspective but at this stage I want to stress some of the pragmatic reasons that might lie behind this trend. The first is the fact that, particularly with the decline in British industry, there has been a marked reduction in job opportunities for science, engineering and computing graduates (except, perhaps, in school teaching in the last decade). For example, Figure 1 shows that despite the applied nature of Computer Science and Engineering degrees, graduates are not in markedly different positions from their contemporaries in Languages or Humanities, six months after graduation.

However, even where jobs are available for people in these areas, their pay is seldom as high as that of other professionals. Further, their salaries are also poor in relation to other European countries (Patel ibid). Science and engineering graduates in Britain are also held in lower esteem than their peers in other professions (Patel ibid). This relative lack of status is also perceived by undergraduates. For example, when Fiona Wilson, Graeme Findlay and I asked 226 second year science and engineering students how the general public rates the social status of scientists compared to other professions such as law and medicine, 60% responded with 'less', 16% with 'equal', 5% with 'higher' and 18% with 'don't know' (Findlay et al 1997).

Perhaps related to this perception of relative lack of prestige is the study by John Wilkes of the reactions to a career in computing with 155 A-level students in three markedly academic schools in Cambridge. Not one of these academically gifted students was contemplating a career in computing. He found that there was a perceptible feeling of something between aversion and indifference to computing, particularly amongst the female students, which did not stem from ignorance of computers or lack of experience in computing. Rather, he ascribed it to the effects of cultural and occupational media stereotyping which portrays computer professionals as 'nerds' and 'tekkies'.

5. Why the Flight is More Marked in Women

The findings by Wilkes, in common with much anecdotal evidence that has been cited, suggest that computer science is not particularly attractive to academic high flyers, particularly in the case of females. I have suggested above that this reluctance probably owes a great deal to pragmatic aspects such as employment prospects, status and pay, but there clearly are

Figure 1. Percentages of UK students in work or further study six months after graduation (adapted from the *Guardian Higher Education Supplement*, 7 January 1997, p i)

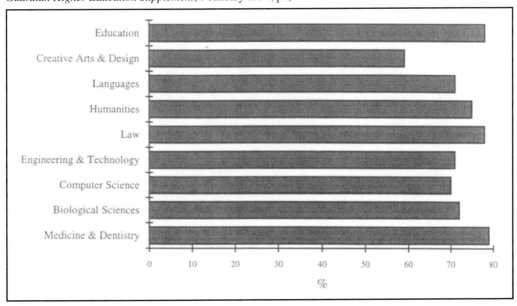

psychological forces at work as well. In this section I want to present an overview of those factors that have been suggested in the literature and the empirical evidence appertaining to each factor.

5.1. Sex stereotyping of subject choice at school

We have recently carried out a study of over 1000 English secondary school children which confirmed that, in general, girls certainly enjoy arts and humanities subjects more and boys prefer science and technology (Lightbody et al 1996). Nevertheless, there is ample evidence that when females are aiming to study medicine, veterinary science or dentistry they have no difficulty in choosing and doing well at the requisite science subjects such as Physics and Chemistry. Further, Durndell's repeated surveys in 1989, 1992 and 1995 (see Durndell and Thomson, 1997) indicate that a number of women who choose not to study computing nevertheless have the requisite entry requirements. Particularly in Scotland, with its normal school leaving objective of five or more Highers, rather than three or more A-levels, there seems little evidence that girls are precluded from studying computer science because schools have steered them into stereotyped choices which deny them the requisite entry qualifications. Indeed, in a recent large scale study we carried out in Strathclyde, many girls in the focus group discussions assured us that school staff were very keen to encourage them to choose science options (Lightbody et al 1995).

5.2. The academic/occupational masculinity of computing

There is an impressive amount of literature (Wright 1996) arguing that in its early years, because of the non-hierarchical and non-structured nature of the early computer industry, computer science provided a very user-friendly environment for women. It is further suggested that as the computer industry became more powerful and more hierarchical, the climate which had favoured women changed. Hence, as the industry grew, women withdrew. Currently, it is argued, computer culture emphasises 'masculinity, requiring aggressive displays of technical self-confidence and hands-on ability for success, defining professional competence in hegemonically masculine terms and devaluing the general characteristics of women' (Wright ibid, p 86).

There is, of course, no denying that this macho bias exists in large swathes of the industry, but I would argue that a similar occupational masculinity has been very characteristic of a number of 'elite' professions which women now enter at parity or near parity. These include medicine and veterinary medicine, both of which rest to a large extent on a background in science and a mastery of technological equipment. Nevertheless, despite formidable opposition, particularly in medicine with its emphasis on public school and sporting values, women have persisted heroically in their attempts to overcome entrenched patriarchal values. Thus, if computer science is a male dominated culture, it is not alone in this respect and consequently the relatively low level of females in it cannot be unreservedly ascribed to its masculine culture.

Of relevance to the issue of the masculinity of computer science are the repeated surveys carried out by Alan Durndell and his colleagues (Durndell and Thomson ibid). Their samples have been cohorts of students who have had the requisite qualifications but have chosen not to study computing. When the students were asked to allocate importance for suggested items in their choice not to study computing, Durndell and his co-workers found that, for both sexes, all the items that overtly referred to gender such as 'Males can be hostile to females with abilities in computing' were rated as 'very unimportant' by both sexes. Factors that were rated as more important included items such as 'The subject matter would not be interesting' and 'I am more interested in people than objects'.

My own research tends to confirm these findings. In a set of interviews with female software engineers, I found that they were unlikely to cite factors pertaining to the occupational culture/masculinity of computing as inimical to their progress. But they did focus on factors which impeded them that are common to women in other occupational groups. The first of these was the lack of 'family friendly' policies which they saw as affecting men as well as women. Second, they referred to being disadvantaged by being excluded from what Atkinson and Delamont (1990) have termed 'indeterminate' knowledge. (This term refers to knowledge that is not explicitly discussed in formal settings.) They reported that because men had friendship, social and 'locker room' networks that excluded them, they were often not privy to gossip and informal information. But I should stress that this was not seen by my sample of 17 as a major problem.

I am not, of course, arguing that the progress of women is not being impeded by these factors but I am suggesting that they are not unique to computing.

5.3. Lack of role models

It has also been argued that women choose not to enter computing because of the lack of female role models. This lack has, of course at some stage, applied to women entering almost all occupations that are not service related and has certainly applied to all the elite professions. Furthermore, our own study of 226 students on SET courses provided little evidence to support lack of role models as an important factor in women's perception of their progress. We asked our sample whether a low number of female teachers was likely to affect students. The 99 female students responded as follows to the three response choices: 'disadvantages females', 11%; 'disadvantages males', 0%; 'makes no difference', 89%. In response to the question 'Does the gender balance of staff matter to you?' the responses to the three options by the female students were as follows: 'a lot', 1%; 'a bit', 21%; 'not at all', 78%.

These findings do not suggest that most women, at an explicit level at any rate, find the lack of role models on university SET courses disadvantageous. However, it is also clear from my interviews with women software engineers, as well as from research conducted in areas other than SET, that most career women appreciate the assistance of networks of other women as well as the assistance of more senior staff (male as well as female) as mentors (Wilson 1995).

5.4. Lack of confidence/experience with computers

There is no doubt that, as a number of research projects (including some of my own – e.g. Siann and Macleod 1986) demonstrated in the late 1980s and early 1990s, females have tended to have less experience of computer use, be marginalised by males at school in access to computers and in general to have less confidence in their computing ability. But in the latter half of the 1990s computers used as word processors, in retailing, in controlling stock, in libraries, in design, in travel agents, etc., have become so ubiquitous that in almost every occupation young people of both sexes make use of them. Gender differences in use at school are also diminishing but one abiding gender difference remains. This is that boys are far more likely to make use of computers for games than girls. As Alan Durndell, Peter Glissov and I (Durndell et al 1995) showed in a survey of 429 secondary school pupils in Scotland, while it was possible to identify a substantial number of heavy computer users amongst the males, none were found amongst the females. Our conclusion was that girls did not lack confidence in using computers at home but were not interested in computer games. In general, they tended to use them for pragmatic – e.g., word processing – purposes. We suggested that Sanders' maxim about women computer users 'We can, I can't' should be amended to 'I can but I don't want to'.

5.5. Computer Science is seen as lacking social involvement and social commitment

Following from a number of studies I have recently undertaken, I have concluded, as have Pauline Lightbody and Alan Durndell, that females are rejecting SET courses for positive rather than negative reasons. By this I mean that it is not barriers which exclude women but women who exclude themselves. For example, as part of the study I carried out with Pauline Lightbody and others in Strathclyde (Lightbody et al 1997), we asked students on SET courses and students on courses such as medicine and law how important they rated a number of work-oriented issues. We found that those enrolled on SET courses were significantly less likely to rate as important the chances of working closely with other people and the public and the opportunity to 'help society'.

In general, I conclude that female school leavers know what they want, and, at the moment, what they want does not, in the main, include careers where the major focus is on SET. This orientation leads them to reject computer science as a major or exclusive choice but, as I hope the beginning of this paper demonstrates, it is also likely to lead them to study computer science when it is allied with subjects that appear to offer more human contact and/or social responsibility. Furthermore, I believe that today's generation of young women, as well as being socially motivated, are also pragmatic. Hence, while computer science appears to lag behind the 'elite professions' in job opportunities, status and pay, it will continue not to attract the most gifted students, male as well as female.

Acknowledgement
I would like to thank Steve Oatey of HESA for assistance with the statistics quoted in this paper.

References

Atkinson, P. and Delamont, S. (1990). 'Professions and powerlessness: female marginality in learned professions'. *Sociological Review* 38 (1): 90-110.

Durndell, A. and Thomson, K. (1997). 'Gender and computing: decade of change'. *Computers and Education* 28 (1): 1-9.

Durndell, A., Glissov, P. and Siann, G. (1995). 'Gender and computing: persisting differences'. *Educational Research* 37 (3): 219-227.

Findlay, G., Siann, G. and Wilson, F. (in preparation). 'Motivational factors on SET courses at University'.

Lightbody, P., Siann G., Stocks, R. and Walsh, D. (1997). 'Factors which influence women's choice of career'. *Educational Studies* 23 (1).

Lightbody, P. and Durndell, A. (1996). 'Gendered career choice: is sex stereotyping the cause or the consequence?' *Educational Studies* 22 (2): 133-146.

Lightbody, P., Siann, G., Stocks, R. and Walsh, D. (1996). 'Motivation and attribution at secondary school: the role of gender'. *Educational Studies* 22: 13-25.

Lightbody, P., Siann, G., Walsh, D. and Tait, L. (1995). 'Gendered career paths: channelled or chosen?', in Lloyd, G. (ed.) *Knitting Progress Unsatisfactory: gender and special issues in education*. Edinburgh: Moray House Institute of Education.

Patel, K. (1996). 'Talent leak due to low pay'. *Times Higher Educational Supplement*, 22-3-96: 4.

Powell, G. N. (1993). *Women & Men in Management, 2nd ed.* London: Sage.

Sanders, J. (1987). 'Closing the computer gap in schools', in Daniels, J. Z. and Kuhle, J. B. (eds.). *Proceedings of the 4th GASAT Conference*. Lansing: National Sciences Foundation.

Siann, G. and MacLeod, H. (1986). 'Computers and children of primary school age: issues and questions'. *British Journal of Educational Technology* 2 (17): 133-44.

Whitehouse, C., Lovegrove, G. and Williams, S. (1996). 'But isn't computing boring?', in *Proceedings of PASE: The first Westminster Conference on Professional Awareness in Engineering. 1-2 February, 1996*. London: The Royal Society.

Wilkes, J. (1996). 'Nerds, Suits, Tekkies and wary teenagers', in *Proceedings of PASE: The first Westminster Conference on Professional Awareness in Engineering. 1-2 February, 1996*. London: The Royal Society.

Wilson, F. (1995). *Gender and Organisational Behaviour,* London: McGraw Hill.

Wright, R. (1996). 'The occupational masculinity of computing', in Cheng, C. (ed.). *Masculinities in Organisation*, London: Sage.

Computing, Computer Science and Computer Scientists: how they are perceived

Fiona Wilson

Department of Management, University of St Andrews

Abstract

This paper is designed to enlarge our understanding of how computing is perceived. It will examine attitudes towards and attributes of computing, computer science and computer scientists in the research literature and use initial findings from a quantitative and qualitative study of Computer Science. The aim is to look in much more depth at the thought processes which lead to women's lack of participation in Computer Science. The paper shows how students believe they have an equal chance in Computer Science and are failing to acknowledge inequality in the subject area. The arguments men and women use to defend their views of a just world are documented.

Introduction

The thorny issue of women, computing and equity is very much alive (Grundy 1996). The daily practice concerning the use of computers in education does not reflect the principle of equity (Janssen Reinen and Plomp 1996). Females do not lack ability. Girls have been shown superior to boys in several specific areas of programming, for example (Anderson 1987; Kiesler et al. 1985) but they lack encouragement. Males have an advantage over females in their experience of computing before university entrance (Durndell et al 1987; Shashaani 1994), although this may now be less so (see Roberts 1995 and Whitley 1996). More boys than girls own computers at home (Shotton 1989; Janssen Reinan and Plomp 1996). Having a computer at home can increase confidence or liking for computers (Colley et al 1994). Recently there has been news that few women use the World Wide Web; 70% of users are male (*The Guardian*, Saturday 21 December 1996, p.6).

Perhaps as a result of greater use and knowledge of computing, boys see computers as being more enjoyable, special, important, friendly and cheaper than girls do (Levin and Gordon 1989) In contrast, females show more negative attitudes towards computers (Collis 1987; Colley 1994; Shashaani 1994; Durndell et al. 1995; Janssen Reinan and Plomp 1996) They report less comfort and skill with computers (Wilder et al 1985). and are, in general, rather less interested in computers than their male peers (Durndell et al. 1987; Shashaani 1993) although girls from single sex schools and from Asian origin enjoy computing more than most girls (Culley 1986). Females score lower in computer aptitude tests and have less prerequisite math ability (Dambrot et al 1985). While women and men have not been found to differ in cognitive abilities (Linn and Hyde 1989) they have different standpoints (Harding 1991). Women doctoral students are found to show comparable performance quality but women feel less comfortable, confident and successful than men (Pearl et al 1990).

The anti-female bias is strongest in traditionally male fields (Spertus 1991) and Information Technology is seen as a male world. Educational software and computer games target adolescents – and provides a male culture where predominant themes are war, battles, crimes, destruction and male-oriented sports and hobbies. Alan Durndell claims that by the time girls are 15 or 16 they have been turned off career choices involving computers owing to 'violent and immature' computer games (*The Guardian*, Saturday 21 December 1996, p.6). The personal qualities required for computer scientists are those usually associated with men – hard-headedness, single-mindedness, ambition, toughness (Leeming 1996). Females feel that taking too much interest in technology threatens their image of themselves as women (Lage 1991).

This then might be one explanation why women appear to have less enjoyment from computers. Another explanation comes from Collis's (1985) paradox 'We can, but I can't'. Women are personally unable to work effectively with computers. Females might feel the need to stress equality between both gender groups (we can enjoy computers) but when asked about their own individual attitudes say they personally feel less enjoyment in using computers (see also Janssen Reunion and Plomp 1996). Perhaps a more accurate representation of this attitude is 'We can but we won't'. We feel ambivalent about the technology so count ourselves out. Technology is male and threatens our image as females. Feminine women have to behave in what are deemed socially appropriate ways (Nicolson 1996:11).

A further explanation for women's lack of enthusiasm for computers comes from the socialisation experience. Yeloushan (1989) found that a major social barrier for females is the attitudes of parents and teachers who believe that computers are learning tools predominately for males. The ratio of computers to pupils in schools, the location of computing in science and maths classes and the emphasis on experience gained in computer clubs, all have benefited boys rather than girls (Newton 1991; Culley 1996; Hoyles 1988).

There may be a less bleak picture to paint. Siann et al (1988) showed how the negative stereotyping of female computer scientists is becoming increasingly less likely. Francis (1994) and Colley et al (1995) support this finding by showing how only a small number of students held gender stereotyping views of computer use, but Colley et al, (1995) say that this is not encouraging them to participate more. Stockdale (1987) claims that when women students are introduced to computers in such a way that computers are presented as non-threatening, not linked with mathematics and as instrumentally useful, motivation and interest in computers increases markedly. If the amount of computer experience is controlled, males and females respond with similar levels of interest (see Chen 1986). Female teachers can create a participatory climate for all students which creates a better classroom environment for female students (Crawford and MacLeod 1990).

In the light of the more pessimistic findings, a number of university computing teachers since 1987 have been formally addressing the problem of the lack of women in computing, but the figures are do not yet show a significant increase (see Lovegrove and Hall 1987; Lovegrove et al 1994; Lovegrove and Segal 1991; Williams et al 1996; Whitehouse 1996). Most recent evidence shows that just 12% of full time undergraduates on British computing science courses are women (*Education News* 1996). A similar situation exists in the USA (Wright 1996).

This research was designed to see whether more optimistic findings about perceptions of computing could be found among computer science students and to examine why so few females wished to be involved in Computer Science.

2. Research Methodology

Two main methods were used:

a) Questionnaires were distributed to all students on first year Computer module. There are 63 males and 14 females registered for the Computer Science module (52 of whom returned questionnaires - 14 females and 38 males). One hundred and seventy questionnaires also distributed to a Psychology course of which 130 were returned but these results are not reported here.

b) Semi structured interviews. Twenty of the Computer Science students (16 male and 4 female) were interviewed individually after they completed practical classes.

3. Context of the Research - Computer Science

The research data was collected in November 1996. In the Computer Science Division there are few women amongst both staff and students. There are currently ten females, including two secretaries, out of a staff of 41. The Computer Science module requires an 'A' level or Higher Mathematics. It may be that this contributes to the lack of female participants if females have less maths ability (Dambrot et al 1985). It has been found, however, that at 'A' level the gap between boys and girls is gradually closing (Elwood and Comber 1996) so as many females as males should have the qualification, even if they receive fewer A and B results than males. There are gender differences in choice at 'A' level; once choice is introduced, higher proportions of males choose science and maths while females choose arts and humanities (Elwood and Comber 1996). Those females who do choose a subject which is less traditional for their gender comprise a small, select group who do well in relation to the majority of the group. It might be expected, then, that the females on this course were a small select group who might be expected to do well and should express the attitude 'we can, and we will!'

4. Findings from questionnaires

The findings show three significant differences between men and women students:

• When asked if they read computer magazines, a significant difference was found between men and women across the whole study and within groups. Significantly more females than males said they did not read computer magazines. In Computer Science while no women 'sometimes, regularly or often' read computer magazines, 57.9% men did.

• Significantly more males that females, both across the study and within groups, said that they were good with computers. In Computer Science over half the men (68.4%) strongly agreed or agreed with the statement 'I am good with computers' where as only 14.3% of women could agree. This may, in part, be due to prior qualification where 44.5% male and 35% of females had an A level, CSYS or Higher grade Computing

- Across both groups, significantly more females than males agreed with the statement 'Computers make me feel nervous'.
- Other findings - not statistically significant
- In Computer Science, while almost equal numbers had a computer they could use at home, when asked if they had their own computer more males (52.6%) than females (28.6%) had their own computers and more males had their own computer with them at university. More males (55.3%) than females (28.6%) used a computer on a daily basis outside the module. It may be, though, that the males are WWW surfing or playing games rather than working on the module. This finding would require further research to investigate total productive time spent before definite conclusions could be reached.

In Computer Science, 42.8% of women and only 15.8% of men said they either agreed or strongly agreed with the statement 'I have less prior computer experience than other St Andrews' students in this module'. The lack of experience was then reflected in their confidence.

The more welcome finding is that Computer Science women were confident in their ability in Mathematics. More women (92.9%) than men (78.9%) felt they had an aptitude for Maths and more (57.1% f; 47.4% m) had 'A' level Maths.

5. Findings from Semi-Structured Interviews with Computer Science students

How do you feel about the fact that women were very much a minority in the division? Is this an issue for you?

Computer Science students are reluctant to acknowledge the issue that there are so few women in Computing. Of the 20, ten students said this was not an issue or not really an issue. Two believed that there was a change happening and more women would be found in computing in the future. (Each individual has been assigned a number and their gender: M or F).

One male student went as far as to deny the fact that there were so few women. 'It's just an opinion. Jobs are a matter of choice.' He was asked why it was just an opinion when the fact was that there were only ten females out of 41 staff. 'If you look into it, there is probably a degree of sexism. There is not sexism in the course but it is thought of as a male subject – this is the stereotype' (M15).

The women want to believe they live in a just world. A female student said, 'More women could do it if they wanted to. Women have an equal chance' (F1). One, however, acknowledged the difficulty: 'It is more noticeable in Computing than in other departments. It does make it more difficult at the beginning. You are aware very much of being in a minority.' (F3)

Are men or women afraid of computers?

Eight students said that they did not think that there were gender differences. One male said 'Everyone's equal' but went on to say 'Having said that, my mother is afraid. People are afraid of deleting files that are important, doing something wrong when computers are expensive' (M4).

Two students (M4, M9) said that their mothers were afraid while another mother (of M7) was 'unsure'. Only one father was mentioned as afraid.

Some thought it had more to do with familiarity of background. 'My mates just don't know how to use them. It's complicated. They are not afraid but just not comfortable working with computers' (M5). One female student said it depended on your background while another thought it was to do with experience. 'I think some people are. I know people who won't do a module because they don't understand computers and will feel others can do but they can't, both men and women. Some have done computing already. It is mainly lack of experience. Those who haven't the experience feel disadvantaged. It is more girls that feel this way but some lads as well' (F3).

A number thought 'afraid' was too strong and 'intimidated', 'hesitant', 'unsure' or 'apprehensive' might better describe how men or women felt. Very few thought women were more afraid than men. One male thought females may be a little more technophobic, less interested in the way things work, more interested in what it can do for them (How did he know this?). 'I know this from personal experience. When you talk to males they are often more interested in how a piece of equipment or technology works' (M10). One thought that men tend to be more confident anyway (M15), while another thought 'More so women afraid than men' (M16).

What about other technology, for example domestic technology like video recorders or washing machines? This may be dependent on the complexity of the technology, who is used to them, your age, confidence or your lifestyle.

Here are some quotes which illustrate that there may be differences in behaviour but not necessarily ability :

> In the home you expect men to be more dominant, even if they do break what they are trying to fix! (M7)

> TVs and videos are more male - they are expected to tune them and stuff when things go wrong (M9)

> Possibly the stereotype holds true with men working the video and the women working washing machines (F2)

> Men are meant to be technically better but I do not agree with this. Men get the instruction book first. Given the chance, women can do just as well (F1).

Few would say that women and men are different in terms of their ability but one said:

> My Mum can't use a video, she hasn't a clue (M16).

Do you think there are differences in the way men and women students feel about Computer Science (e.g. enjoyment/ motivation)?

The students were clearly divided on this issue. Seven thought there was no difference here while one said that it varied by individual and another said 'probably not'. Those who thought there were differences made the following points:

I suspect there is. Boys seem to enjoy computers more and spend more time in computer departments (M7).

A minority actually enjoy the subject. Out of those, more men enjoy it. Almost everyone is motivated as all are conscientious and that's the type of student who comes here – everyone would like to do well (M10).

Most of my male friends spend about three hours a day on the Internet and e-mail. None of my female friends do. Women are more motivated if they have problems, motivated to do something about it (M11).

I would say most women are not intending to carry on with it (CS); it is a basis for others subjects. People outside the module want to do e-mailing and that's all really (F3).

The girls I've met are not so interested in computers. I don't know why it is but it's just natural to me. Girls like more in Arts – views. Boys don't care so much about this. (60/40% boys and girls) – they are not all like this (F4).

Only in so much as I'd imagine females work up a perception of Computer Science being a male based subject, a male stronghold, all boys together in the computer room. It's a misperception (M13).

Yes, for sure. I'd say fewer females tend to take the subject let alone continue with it. It is assumed to be an option for a male (M15).

How would you describe the personality of a Computer Scientist?
The majority (12) thought that there was no particular personality, that computer scientists were 'normal' or everyone was different. Some were aware of the stereotypes:

Stereotypically – they probably have glazed eyes and don't have much of a life as they spend so much time talking to computers. It's not like the stereotype though. I am sure there are one or two around (M7).

The stereotype that came through in three of the answers, however, was a technical person who liked to see how things worked:

They like puzzles, how things unfold, like seeing what something can do, like an engineer (M1)

Quite technical, it requires technical knowledge. Pretty much the same as any other student (M13)

'I think they look to see things work rather than use them – want to take, for example, a video recorder apart. They are fun people, not shy' (M14)

Does the way Computer Science is taught here accommodate or suit the needs of both men and women students?

Almost all thought it did. There were some interesting qualifying remarks though:

I think it does unless women are put off by all the male lecturers that have had so far (M7).

Yes. They seem to be aware of the problems (F3).

Again the issue of thinking there were more female students now came up:

Fair in this respect as there are more women now (M10)

What changes would be needed to encourage women and men students? Many of the students had some ideas about what might be tried, though they had not had the opportunity to think through this issue. Here is what was suggested:

Change of attitudes - people thinking there are stereotypes. There is no attitude problem in here (M2).

I'm not sure how women would feel. They might find it preferable to have more women though I am happy. It is mainly male dominated in the sciences. Women are more in the Arts departments (M7).

Perhaps if there were more women staff and it wasn't so male dominated (F3).

There is then a sex-based view, held by a few, that women are a bit more afraid of computing or technology and that women prefer or are attracted by the Arts (4) despite the fact that they have equal opportunity.

There is much denial of the female/male stereotype to be found but not always very consistently. This is seen by examining the interviews individually, rather than under question headings, as has been done above. For example one female (F1) argued in her interview that men and women hold the skills needed for computing equally and that 'more women could do it if they wanted to; women have an equal chance' yet concedes that whether or not you are afraid depends on your background knowledge and whether you have been brought up with a computer. Similarly, another female (F4) said that whether or not you have computing skills depends on your background (she and her brother had been treated the same) but she thought that girls were not so interested in computers. A male (M10) said, 'Everyone had equal opportunity to be on the course so it is personal preference' but 'women may be a little more technophobic, less interested in the way things work, more interested in what it can do for them'. More men enjoyed Computer Science than women, he thought. Another male (M15) denied the fact that there are less women in Computer Science but conceded later that fewer females take the subject and it is assumed to be an option for a male.

It is clear that women are less involved – there are far less of them on the course and the four that were interviewed do not plan to continue. There are various explanations from the men on the lack of women's involvement.

The first is that the situation is changing therefore there is no problem or issue to address:

There are more women than there used to be (M5 + M10) and there are more in Maths (M11). The second is that women do not enjoy computing or have more sense than enjoy it:

I don't think women like machines (M11)

Women have more sense than guys and that that's why they stay away from the stupid machines (M11)

Both these explanations require no action. A third is that females feel less experienced and men are more confident:

Those who haven't the experience feel disadvantaged. It is more girls that feel this way but some lads as well (F3).

Men tend to be more confident anyway (M15).

An associated reason is that women are guided by misperception:

I'd imagine females work up a perception of Computer Science being a male based subject, a male stronghold, all boys together in the computer room. It's a misperception' (M13).

6. Discussion of Results

The women Computer Science students in this study showed that they were less experienced with computing and less integrated into a computing culture. Fewer owned computers or had them at university and their usage of them was lower. They also did not read computer magazines.

The magazines contain minimal higher level technical information which would develop cognitive skills or abilities. One newly launched magazine is called *T3: Tomorrow's Technology Today* and is advertised as 'a men's mag about home cinema, computers, hi-fi . . after all it's blokes for whom this stuff is designed: we like big TVs and new computers and good looking hi-fi and expensive gadgets that we don't really need'. The newly launched *Escape* magazine is described as the magazine for 'boys behaving badly rather than techno nerds'. 'And it has everything a self-respecting bloke wants: horny babes, boobs, booze, loads of laughs, oh and bundles of information on electronic entertainment' (*The Guardian*, Monday 28 October 1996).

These magazines are unlikely to help directly with technical skills but they may help increase levels of familiarity and experience with computers and therefore male confidence. The magazines and games may help men feel part of the computing culture, its shared values and norms, which requires both social knowledge of that culture and technical knowledge of computers as machines (Kiesler et al. 1985). Men are more likely to assume that they are naturally 'good at computers' (Newton 1991).

Not surprisingly women feel less prepared for and less confident about Computer Science. Early research has shown that while women are equal to men in academic ability and self esteem, they are lower in self confidence (Maccoby and Jacklin 1974; Borge et al. 1986). While these women felt lower in their computing experience, they were more confident in their mathematical ability.

7. Conclusions

While most would like to believe that men and women have an equal chance and there are equal opportunities, there are some relatively unconscious processes here which help militate against women choosing Computer Science. These students may wish to believe that they live in a world where there is justice and equality of opportunity (for a similar attitude, see Nicolson and Welsh's 1992 study of medical students where students were indignant when potential gender inequalities were suggested to them) but some fail to see, or acknowledge the inequity and injustice which exists. Some fail to take account of the male dominance of technology.

An alternative explanation of the findings is that women do not want to be seen as different or 'other' so emphasise that equality exists; they resist the perpetual re-inscription of women as 'other' (Ermath 1989), particularly if this means women are constructed as 'other' to the 'technologically gifted' male (Wajcman 1991). In emphasising 'we are not different' they emphasise similarity of abilities and so avoid being segregated or excluded from scientific/technological work (Fox-Keller 1986:168). Women are certainly not less able and we must be wary of psychological research which shows differences between men and women; the differences shown here are due to what is expected of women, socialisation and previous learning experience of computing. But as Fox-Keller notes, women will not gain equality by demanding to be treated the same as men; they will be 'negated in the quest for assimilation' (1986:169).

In order to defend their views of a just world and equality, a number of strategies can be adopted. Three strategies have been adopted here:

a. The situation is changing (the men seem to believe this).
b. Men and women are seen as equal but different – women do not enjoy computing as much. This would be supported by the data from both the questionnaires and interviews where women use computers less often, have less confidence in their abilities and are more attracted to the Arts.
c. There is a misperception that computing and technology are for males.

Those who believe there are already equal opportunities will see no reason for action or change. Those who believe there is misperception or that women feel less confident (perhaps owing to family background or socialisation) may be tolerant of changes being made to encourage more women into Computer Science but may be more likely to be content to see the status quo maintained. The women do not want to be singled out for special treatment (we know this from informal discussion) but do lack belief in their equal abilities. As a result, they might just count themselves out and express ambivalence towards Computing.

There is then, a much more complex argument here than simply 'women can compute but won't'. While issues of equity are not seen as such, then little change is going to happen. For change to occur women are going to have to acknowledge the masculine culture of technology and wish to see that change.

References

Anderson, R.E. (1987). 'Females surpass males in computer problem solving: findings from the Minnesota Computer Literacy Assessment'. *Journal of Educational Computing Research* 31 (1): 39-51.

Borge, M.A., Roth, A., Nichols, G.T. and Nichols, B.S. (1980). 'Effects of Gender, Age, Locus of Control and Self Esteem on Estimates of College Grades'. *Psychological Reports* 47: 831-837.

Chen, M. (1986). 'Gender and Computers: The beneficial effects of experience on attitudes'. *Journal of Educational Computing Research* 2 (3): 265-282.

Collis, B (1985). 'Psychosocial implications of sex differences in attitudes towards computers: results of a survey'. *International Journal of Women's Studies* 8 (3): 207-213.

Collis, B. (1987). 'Sex Differences in the Association Between Secondary School Students' Attitudes Towards Mathematics and Towards Computers'. *Journal for Research in Mathematics Education* 18 (5): 349-402.

Colley, A. (1994). 'Gender and Educational Computing', NIBPS Newsletter 4: 4-8.

Colley, A., Hill, F., Hill, J. and Jones, A (1995). 'Gender Effects in the Stereotyping of Those with Different Kinds of Computing Experience'. *Journal of Educational Computing Research* 12 (1): 19-27.

Crawford, M. and MacLeod, M. (1990). 'Gender in the College Classroom: An assessment of the 'Chilly Climate' for Women'. *Sex Roles* 23 (3/4): 101-122.

Culley, L (1986). *Gender Differences and Computing in Secondary Schools*, Loughborough: Department of Education.

Dambrot, F.H., Watkins-Malek, M.A., Silling, S.M., Marshall, R.S. and Garver, J.A. (1985). 'Correlates of Sex Differences in Attitudes towards and Involvement with Computers'. *Journal of Vocational Behavior* 27: 71-86.

Durndell, A., Macleod, H. and Siann, G. (1987). 'A Survey of Attitudes to, Knowledge about and Experience of Computers'. *Computer Education* 11 (3): 167-175.

Durndell, A., Glissov, P. and Siann, G. (1995). 'Gender and Computing: Persisting differences'. *Educational Research* 37 (3): 219-227.

Education News (1996) Summer p.4

Elwood, J. and Comber, C. (1996). *Gender Differences in Examinations at 18+*, Final Report, Institute of Education, University of London.

Ermath, E.D. (1989). 'The solitude of women and social time'. In Forman, F.J. and Sowton, C. (eds.) *Taking our time: feminist perspectives on temporality*, 37-46. Oxford: Pergamon.

Fox-Keller, E. (1986). 'How Gender Matters, or Why its' so hard for us to count past two'. In Harding, J. (ed.) *Perspectives on Gender and Science*, London: Falmer Press:.

Francis, L.J. (1994). 'The Relationship Between Computer-Related Attitudes and Gender Stereotyping of Computer Use'. *Computers and Education* 22 (4): 283-289.

Grundy, F. (1996). *Women and Computers*, Exeter: Intellect Books.

Harding, S. (1991). *Whose Science? Whose Knowledge? Thinking from women's lives*, New York: Cornell.

Henwood, F. (1993). 'Establishing Gender Perspectives on Information Technology: Problems, issues and opportunities'. In Green, E., Owen, J., and Pain, D. (eds.) *Gendered by Design? Information Technology and Office Systems*, London: Taylor and Francis.

Hoyles, C. (1988). *Girls and Computers*, London: Bedford Way Papers.

Janssen Reinan, I. and Plomp, T (1996). 'Gender and Computers: Another area of inequality in education?' In Pelgrum, W.J., Janssen Reinen, I.A.M., and Plomp, T. (eds.) *Schools, Teachers, Students and Computers: a Cross-National Perspective*. IEA.

Keisler, S., Sproull, L. and Eccles, J.S. (1985). 'Pool halls, chips and war games: Women in the culture of computing'. *Psychology of Women Quarterly* 9 (4): 451-462.

Linn, M.C. and Hyde, J.S. (1989). 'Gender, Mathematics and Science'. *Educational Researcher* 18: 17-27.

Lage, E. (1991). 'Boys, Girls and Microcomputing'. *European Journal of Psychology of Education* 1: 29-44.

Leeming, A. (1996). 'Professionalism and IT - the contribution that could be made by women if they were there'. *PASE 1996 - Professional Awareness in Software Engineering, Conference Proceedings*, University of Westminster, 1-2nd Feb.

Levin, T. and Gordon, C. (1989). 'Effect of Gender and Computer Experience on Attitudes Towards Computers'. *Journal of Educational Computing Research* 5 (1): 69-88.

Lovegrove, G. and Hall, W. (1987). 'Where have all the girls gone?' *University Computing* 9: 207-210.

Lovegrove, G., Whitehouse, C. and Williams, S. (1994). 'Women and Computing: IT EQUATE, Staffordshire University and Schools, Development and Role of Women in Technology'. *International Conference in Beijing, China*, September.

Lovegrove, G. and Segal, B. (1991). *Women into Computing, Selected Papers 1988-1990*, Springer-Verlag.

Maccoby, E.E. and Jacklin, C.N. (1974). *The Psychology of Difference*, Palo Alto: Stanford University Press.

Newton, P. (1991). 'Computing: An ideal occupation for women?' In Firth-Cozens, J and West, M.A. (eds.) *Women at Work: Psychological and Organizational Perspectives*, Buckingham: Open University Press.

Nicolson, P. (1996). *Gender, Power and Organization*, London: Routledge.

Nicolson, P. and Welsh, C.L. (1992). *Gender Inequality in Medical Education*, Preliminary Report to Trent Regional Health Authority, cited in Nicolson (1996).

Pearl, A., Pollack, M., Riskin, E., Thomas, B., Wolf, E. and Wu, A. (1990). 'Becoming a Computer Scientist, A Report by the ACM Committee on the Status of Women in Computing Science'. *Communications of the ACM* 33 (11).

Roberts, E. (1995). *Women into Computer Science: Barriers to academic success*, Jing Lyman lecturer series, Stanford University (see Leeming).

Shashaani, L. (1993). 'Gender-Based Differences in Attitudes Toward Computers'. *Computers and Education* 20 (2): 169-181.

Shashaani, L. (1994). 'Gender Differences in Computer Experience and Its Influence on Computer Attitudes'. *Journal of Educational Computing Research* 11 (4): 347-367.

Shotton, M. (1989). *Computer Addiction*, London: Taylor and Francis.

Siann, G., Durndell, A. , Macleod, H and Glissov, P. (1988). 'Stereotyping in Relation to the Gender Gap in Participation in Computing'. *Educational Research* 30 (2): 98-103.

Siann, G., Macleod, H., Glissov, P. and Durndell, A., (1990). 'The Effect of Computer Use on Differences in Attitudes to Computers'. *Computers Education* 14 (2): 183-191.

Spertus, E. (1991). *Why are there so few female computer scientists?* MIT report.

Stockdale, J.E. (1987). 'Desexing Computers. In Proceedings of the *4th GASAT Conference*, University of Michigan, cited in Siann et al, 1988.

Wajcman, J. (1991). *Feminism Confronts Technology*, Cambridge: Polity.

Whitehouse, C., Lovegrove, G. and Williams, S. (1996). 'But Isn't Computing Boring' *PASE 1996 (International Conference on Professional Awareness in Software Engineering)* London, Feb.

Whitley, B.E. (1996). 'Gender Differences in Computer-Related Attitudes - It depends on what you ask'. *Computers in Human Behavior* 12 (2): 275-289.

Wilder, G., Mackie, D. and Cooper, J. (1985). 'Gender and Computers: Two surveys of computer-related attitudes'. *Sex Roles* 13 (3/4): 215-228.

Williams, S., Lovegrove, G. and Whitehouse, C. (1996). 'Working Towards Equality in IT in the Year 2000', *GASAT- 8 International Conference on Gender and Science and Technology*, India, January.

Wright, R. (1996). 'The Occupational Masculinity of Computing'. In Cheng, C. (ed.) *Masculinities in Organizations*, Thousand Oaks: Sage.

Yeloushan (1989). See Janssen Reinan, I. and Plomp, T (1996).

Women, Computing and Moral Responsibility

Paula Roberts

University of South Australia, St. Bernard's Road, Magill, South Australia

Abstract

The transparency of information technology makes it invisible in assessments of moral responsibility for the unanticipated outcomes of its use, such as computer crime and the human and environmental disasters caused by its malfunction. Women have a vital role to play in developing standards for the ethical use of information technology beyond the restricted views of the codes of practice of the professional associations. This role must encompass an influence on decisions regarding the digitalization of information and its global distribution, ethical, self-regulation in the community of users of the Internet, the macro issues of social change attributable to computerization, and the exacerbation of social inequities brought about by the distribution of computing resources. But women, at the moment, are under-represented in computer-related work and education, particularly at levels where their influence might bring about change. Education for the ethical use of computers is neglected in the information technology courses of most Australian universities. This paper describes a programme in computer ethics at the University of South Australia which is undertaken in a compulsory computing subject in an Arts degree (where the majority of students are female) and discusses the programme's philosophical base, its content, methodology and outcomes.

1. Introduction

This paper discusses the ethical dimensions of the use of information technology and suggests a role for women in computing which is compatible with the ideology which shapes women's lives and which has profound influence on female educational and career choice. These and other concerns have underpinned the design of a programme in the social and ethical implications of computing which has brought a new dimension to the study of information technology and has significantly increased the retention of women in computing studies in an Australian university.

2. Women, computers and ideology

Feminist critiques of the under-representation of women in information technology mostly have neglected a consideration of the role that ideology plays in shaping women's education and career choice, despite a varied and significant body of research which has examined this phenomenon (such as Bem and Bem 1970, Ormerod 1971 and 1981; Lipman-Blumen 1972; Head 1980 and 1985; Unger, et al 1986).

In 1970, Sandra and Daryl Bem identified the concept of a 'nonconscious ideology', based on a set of values and beliefs, which are the outcome of socialization, and which shape the career and life paths of women and men. Likewise, Lipman-Blumen (1972) in her survey of female undergraduates noted how an ideology related to sex-role affected these young women's career choices.

Despite significant changes in society, including the feminist movement, over the past twenty years, Yoder and Schliecher (1996) found that 'while overt attitudes (towards occupational gender stereotypes) may have changed, more subtle indicators of gender stereotyping have persisted across the past two decades'.

The 'subtle indicators' noted by Yoder and Schliecher relate in no small part to a female ideology which leads women to undertake 'people-centred' occupations, a phenomenon identified by Ormerod (1971 and 1981) who examined the under-participation of girls in science and found a 'social implications' factor to be significant in female choice of science studies. Head (1980 and 1985) noted the need for science to 'be presented in the context of the needs of society and individuals' if science was to attract girls. And Unger, et al, (1986), noted a dissonance between the ideological assumptions of faculty and those of female undergraduates whose 'personal epistemologies may reflect early experience, and may relate to sociocultural positions seemingly distinct from theoretical orientation'.

More recent Australian evidence is pertinent. In 1995 a Federal government sponsored study into the participation of women in science, engineering and technology revealed that in 1975, female enrolments in veterinary science in Australian universities were a mere 5%. In the 20 years to 1995 enrolments had shown a remarkable increase to 55%. A survey of university veterinary science course managers (who had interviewed their students on entrance) attributed this turn-around in female participation to the screening in Australia over several years of the British television series *All Creatures Great and Small*. This television programme showed the working lives of veterinarians as intimately involved with people and community as with animals and veterinary science, thereby changing the perception of the veterinary profession and encouraging female participation.

An anecdote, more recent still, supports this notion of the 'people factor' in female career choice. After the thrilling air and sea rescue of the British and French yachtsmen in the Vendée round-the-world yacht race from the Southern Ocean in January 1997, an Australian recruitment officer (in a television interview) reported a large increase in applicants wanting to join the Air Force. The reason given most often by male intending aviators was 'wanting to fly'; the reason given by females was 'wanting to save people's lives'.

Whilst a masculine ideology in respect of technology has been well documented (for example, Hacker 1990; Wacjman 1990; van Zoonen 1992) and has served to explain the masculine, seemingly uncritical acceptance of technology in general, and computerization in particular, women's ideological position in respect to information technology has largely gone unexplored. The work of Breakwell and Fife-Schaw, (1987) and Breakwell, et al, (1986, 1987), which builds on Cotgrove (1982), is important in making good this omission.

Cotgrove (1982) found a stable relationship between sociopolitical and economic beliefs and attitudes to science and technology. In an extension of his research, Breakwell and Fife-Schaw (1987) surveyed 1751 British schoolchildren in the 14- to 18-year age group and found their attitudes towards information technology to be uni-dimensional and largely 'pragmatic rather than evaluative'.

In related research, Breakwell et al (1986 and 1987), surveyed over five hundred university undergraduates (247 females and 287 males), to test Cotgrove's hypothesis that pro-technology attitudes are associated with desiring technological work. Breakwell and her colleagues found that aspiring technologists (predominantly male) were 'convinced of the importance of industrial training, and persuaded that technological innovation besides being inevitable will bring general benefit'; while women, although acknowledging the employment potential, were unconvinced of the benefits of information technology.

In replication studies of Breakwell et al's research almost a decade later, and at a time of much higher levels of computerization in society, Roberts (1995) found similarly, that female Arts undergraduates who aspired to human-centred careers, acknowledged the inevitability of the uptake of technology, but were doubtful of its positive outcomes for society.

Breakwell and Fife-Schaw (1987), on the basis of their findings, suggest that policy-makers who aim to encourage more young people to work in information technology should understand that:

> modifying views of new technology and subsequent occupational aspirations may not be so simple because such modification may impinge on socio-economic beliefs that are central to the individual's core concept of social identity and to his or her world view.

Teachers should also take heed of these research findings, for categorizing female reticence in respect to participation in computing as 'avoidance' instead of 'choice' puts a uni-dimensional label on a multi-dimensional problem. It ignores also the matrix of social and personal beliefs which constitute the ideological basis of people's lives. Increasingly, as researchers identify differences between the value systems of women and men, then ideology is accepted as yet another facet of human personality which develops from the different socialization experiences of the sexes.

3. Ethical Issues and Computing

The teaching of the social and ethical dimensions of a technical discipline such as computing brings benefits for the participation of women by revealing its 'other face'. In so doing, a more compatible ideological base for women's study of computing is established, which balances the 'technology for technology's sake' ideology which invariably underpins the teaching and practice of computing.

It is relatively easy to depict computing as a people-centred subject; for the ethical dimensions of computing provide a rich and interesting field of study in areas which most students have not previously explored.

Apart from humanizing a technical subject, there is also the considerable benefit for society as a whole of a more informed citizenry which has an understanding of the dangers as well as the benefits of computerization, and an ethical base for the conduct of human affairs when using computers.

Many of the social and ethical issues of computing which have special attraction and interest for female students (as well as a significant proportion of male students) are covered in the topics detailed below.

3.1 The unreliability of computer systems

Unlike other pervasive technologies such as electricity, television and the motor vehicle, computers are much less reliable and much less predictable, yet despite their instability, they are used for critical applications in medicine, aviation, nuclear power and missile systems, sometimes with disastrous results, as has been documented (Wray 1988, Mellor 1989, Forester and Morrison 1990, Leveson and Turner 1993, Roush 1993, among others).

As Ladd (1989) contends computing professionals must assume moral responsibility for preventing disastrous outcomes from computer mistakes, and for what people unintentionally do to harm other people through the use of computers. He argues that the premise that the moral acceptability or unacceptability of a particular technology depends on what it is used for and who uses it, is a 'moral cop out'. There are at least two kinds of things that we, as responsible human beings, need to watch out for; first not giving the computer control over jobs that it is unequipped to handle, and second, providing some way to decouple the computer if things go wrong.

3.2 Computer crime

Computerized systems are also at the mercy of misuse by human operators. They are vulnerable to the violation of the privacy of information, to large-scale computer crime, software theft, the creation of viruses and the corruption of data, as noted by Denning (1991 and 1995), Johnson and Nissenbaum (1995), Roush (1995), Behar (1997) and many others.

While governments, in recent times, have enacted legislation to punish the perpetrators of these so-called 'victimless' crimes, recent estimates in the United States put the cost at billions of dollars a year, with the true extent unknown, for very few 'white collar' computer criminals are detected, while those that are discovered go unpunished because organisations are reluctant to prosecute for fear of revealing breaches of security.

More significant still for the interest and involvement of women is the recent extension of ethical interest from a business to a societal level in that unfolding and fascinating area for sociological examination, the Internet.

3.3 The Sociology of the Internet

The Internet is a composite of reality, vision and propaganda, which from the 1980s worked as a communications network without exciting much attention; but the last few years have brought a rapid expansion of its technological capabilities and the number of its users. And how might women influence the development of this new society? A simple answer is that they might promote and participate in critical debate which may shape this society for the common good.

Areas which immediately present themselves for ethical examination and informed debate are:

- technological utopianism,
- the commodification of information,
- the digitalization of information, and

- the rise of a global civil society.

3.3.1 Technological Utopianism

The Internet with its promise of unfettered access to information and communication between the peoples of the earth (processes which, it is claimed, will enable the creation of harmony and democracy as the norms of a new global society), is a utopian vision. Its supporters parade its computer-based gifts without providing blueprints for how this new vision might be achieved and without considering what might be the unanticipated consequences of this technological magic.

As Young (1987) points out:

> The Gutenberg press, the wireless telegraph, the telephone, the radio, microwave transmission, microchip technology have not, objectively, reduced hunger, murderous warfare, the concentration of wealth, or the number of despotic governments. Such a careless reading of history serves to promote the pecuniary interests of (the) communications industry.

3.3.2 Information as commodity

It is generally accepted that information has replaced industrial goods as the principal commodity of the information age, yet, traditionally, information exchange has been a central element in the economy of most societies. What is different in this new form of information as commodity is the methods of its capture and exchange and the supremacy of digital information, with the corresponding devaluing of analogue information, that is, traditional forms of information. This new hierarchy discourages the valuing of alternative information, for example, oral information, in our own and other societies.

The information age is not emerging simply as a result of technological innovations, it is being driven by the information industry The media provides only positive images of the new information society, making its negative aspects more difficult to see. For example, statements that billions of new pieces of information are created every year, and that three-quarters of all existing information was created in the past two decades, reflect the uncontested belief that continual growth in information is synonymous with the growth of knowledge. Klapp (1982) argues:

> Information accumulating at an exponential rate is outstripping meaning formation, so that we have more and more knowledge of which we do not know what to make—a growing gap of which awareness produces symptoms so many writers have described as a crisis of meaning.

3.3.3 The Digitalization of Information

Roszak (1994), a self-confessed 'neo-Luddite', warns of the 'heedless and premature application of technology' in the information industry and unwarranted claims that libraries are in their death throes (for example, Swan 1988; Holderness 1992). Roszak notes the computer enthusiasts who appear not to consider how everything they want to have on their machines is going to get there, supported by librarians who promise 'virtual libraries' without considering the costs involved. No search can find what has not been scanned or keystroked into a database but recognition of the cost of scanning and keystroking is pushed aside in the enthusiasm for digitalization.

Mann (1993) is sceptical about support for the digitalization of libraries, not only because of the cost, but for the loss of unorthodox materials which could not be made electronically accessible.

A formidable practical problem is the ageing of high tech equipment (Homer 1992; Lerner 1993; Norman 1993). Age takes a heavier toll on computer disks and tapes than it does on paper, for old books and paper files (especially if the paper has been deacidified) can still be consulted decades, or even centuries later; but not so computer materials, which have an estimated lifespan of about 20 years. Not only do computer materials grow old but so do their languages, logic and the mechanisms that can communicate with older storage devices, as both hardware and software drift towards obsolescence.

3.3.4 The rise of a global civil society

While the utopian dreams that the world's information store will become freely available to all its citizens face formidable practical problems, the dreams for a global network of communication hold more promise.

Frederick (1994) describes a new phenomenon being nurtured by the communication technologies - a global civil society, best represented by the non-governmental organisations which are active in human rights, consumer protection, peace, gender equality, racial justice, and environmental protection. The growth and influence of the global civil society faces two fundamental problems: increasing monopolization of global information and communication by transnational corporations, and the widening disparities between the 'info-rich' and 'info-poor'. Frederick believes the Internet may provide a solution to these problems.

Bagdikian (1989) is less optimistic, predicting that by the end of the century five to ten corporate giants will control most of the world's media as well as data networks and telecommunications infrastructures. He points to the disparities between the world's info-rich and info-poor populations in virtually every communications medium, as print illiteracy is now being replaced by computer illiteracy.

4. Computerization and the Influence of Women

Dunlop and Kling (1991) emphasize society's need for an informed citizenry which understands both the opportunities and challenges of computerization, and as Ladd (1989) suggests, assumes moral responsibility for the way information technology 'shapes our conduct, our attitudes and our institutions'.

An essential part of this moral responsibility is the development and use of predictive knowledge, that is, an informed anticipation of the effects (good and bad) of the use of information technology.

As Jonas (1981, p.8) warns,

The fact that . . . predictive knowledge falls behind the technical knowledge that nourishes our power to act, itself assumes ethical importance. The gap between the power to foretell and the power to act creates a novel moral problem. . . . No previous ethics had to consider the global condition of human life and the far-off future, even existence, of the race. These now being an issue demands, in brief a new conception of duties and rights, for which previous ethics and metaphysics provide not even the principles, let alone a ready doctrine.

How might Ladd's concept of moral responsibility apply to the global citizens of the Internet? In any frontier society which is beyond legal jurisdiction, the education of its citizens for self-directing, moral behaviour is of prime importance. It is the new information society's best chance for fulfilling its utopian promise if, by the sheer weight of numbers, it can exert influence on the democratization of information provision as successfully as it has on the democratization of communication.

And here is an important role for women in information technology which is compatible with a female ideology of 'people-centredness', in which an ethic of responsibility is implicit.

5. Ethics and Computing at the University of South Australia

At the University of South Australia the teaching of ethics is integrated within the mainstream computing curriculum. The ethics programme is a component of a compulsory computing subject which is the first in a computing major for some students but, for most, is the only computing subject in their university studies. The significance here is that this programme may provide a once-only chance for a consideration of the ethical dimensions of computer use by practitioners who most likely will use computers for all of their working (and personal) lives.

The introductory computing subject consists of three strands:
- the technical properties of computers;
- practical experience with applications software;
- the social and ethical implications of computer use

The *social and ethical implications of computer use* strand is a weekly, semester long, programme which examines the effects of computers in the workplace, and in government, the military, medicine, law, academia and in communications, with a special focus on the Internet.

A major consideration in teaching the ethics programme is how to avoid the resistance of students to what they might construe as didacticism or moralising. The programme centres on the belief that an ethical stance cannot be imposed on others but develops instead through a personal choice from alternatives. On the basis of this belief the programme aims to increase the students':
- understanding of personal ethical behaviour and decision-making
- ability to recognize ethical issues and alternative resolutions
- awareness of corporate ethics and possible conflict with personal values
- awareness of the ethical dimensions of the role of computer users.

A successful approach that has satisfied these considerations is the use of values clarification exercises which have sparked the students' interest in examining their own value systems, thereby personalizing ethical issues and moving away from the view of ethics as an abstract subject.

Personal values are explored through clarification exercises (for example, Raths et al 1966) in which students examine beliefs which constitute a personal ideology, implicit in their life and career aspirations. The students become deeply involved in this exploration of self, as has been noted by Kohlberg and Gilligan (1971). Discussions extend to how a business organization, government department, or professional body might establish a values base for its modus operandi, and formalize and make this public in a code of practice, by which its personnel or members are bound.

The programme moves from values clarification to an examination of the stages of moral reasoning identified by Kohlberg (1981) as a schema for the analysis of ethical decisions:

Stage one: A person is primarily motivated by the desire to avoid punishment from a superior power

Stage two: A person is primarily motivated by the desire to satisfy his own quasi physical needs

Stage three: A person is primarily motivated by the desire to be accepted by another individual

Stage four: A person is primarily motivated by the desire to be accepted by the institutions which others approve, by fulfilling institutional expectations and roles

Stage five: A person is primarily motivated by the variable and conditioned contracts and conventions which he has deliberately entered into for his own benefit and the benefit of others

Stage six: A person, primarily motivated by his own conscience and judgement, seeks to apply that with consistency and respect for others.

The students relate the Kohlberg schema to everyday situations, often with rueful self-disclosures and much amusement. For example, they debate whether driving more slowly in a speed zone is an example of a moral decision at the highest level of 'respect for others', or is at the lowest of Kohlberg's levels, 'the desire to avoid punishment from a superior power'. Other situations may involve, for example 'wanting to help others, because it makes you feel good', as one student suggested (stage two or stage three?) or trying to impress a lecturer to get a higher grade by writing an essay which reflects the lecturer's views, rather than the student's own views (stage two or stage four?), engaging in less than ethical practice in order to keep their part-time employment (stage four?) or, in fighting to keep a university campus from closing, enjoying the 'rare opportunity' (as one student described it) of operating at stage 6.

These honest, lively discussions are spiced with brave declarations of what 'bugs' students in unjust and powerless situations, as well as the challenges they experience in their personal, working and academic lives.

These early sessions represent opportunities for ethical decision-making based on personal choice, while later sessions examine ethical decision-making in corporate settings where there may be conflict between personal ethical standards and organisational norms. The phenomena of 'group think' and 'whistle blowing' (Gellerman 1986, Jackall 1988, Andrews 1989) provoke lively debate when they are related to contemporary examples of these happenings which are ever-present in the media.

In another session, students discuss their prepared responses to two 'moral dilemma' scenarios from Parker et al (1990). Of significance is the divergence of student response to these scenarios, a difference, which appears to be related to gender.

Gilligan (1982, and in her other studies which have spanned two decades) has identified a 'different voice', represented by a moral stance which appears to be distinctly feminine. Gilligan defines this as a feminine-gendered 'ethic of responsibility' which relies on thinking which is both contextual and relational. In the experience in this ethics programme, when female students work with the ethical dilemma scenarios, they have seemed reluctant to assume a particular stance and they take more time than male students to form an opinion. Males are more likely to see problems in what they describe as 'black and white' terms – 'it's either right or it's wrong' – while female students spend time in teasing out the various nuances of the situation before arriving at a conclusion. One suspects that what is being observed is a contrast between a rights-based and a people-based approach to ethical dilemmas. This raises interesting speculations and suggestions for further research.

At the beginning of the social and ethical implications of computer use strand, the students consider a short, 'moral dilemma' from the Parker et al collection and make an individual, written response for personal review at the end of the programme. In the final ethics session the students re-examine this first response, write another and then compare their two opinions. Many students identify a change in their reasoning from what some describe as moving from 'an intellectual response to a moral response'.

5.1 Outcomes

While it is unrealistic to consider that a short programme in computer ethics might bring about lasting attitudinal change (and obviously this outcome could be measured only over an extended period of time), there is evidence in many of the students of an increased sensitivity to the ethical and social implications of the use of computers.

Noteworthy is the reaction of female students, not only to the computer ethics programme, but to the wider study of the social implications of computer use. In their evaluation of this subject, many record their concern about important issues like the commercialisation of information and the polarisation of the global community into those who have ready access to the Internet, and those who are so far behind even in print literacy. Most students state they knew nothing of these issues before undertaking the programme.

Many female students signify their intention to enrol in further studies in computing. This female interest in what they term the 'people aspects' of computing is significant and needs to be encouraged, for the participation and retention of women in computer education in this university, consistent with Australian and world-wide experience, is declining.

More important still, is the indication of a female desire for involvement in the practice of computing, within the wider community and as part of the 'global community'. One senses that such involvement may be compatible with a feminine ideology that looks beyond the technology to the people who use it and whose lives and institutions are shaped by it.

References

Andrews, K.R. (1989). 'Ethics in Practice'. *Harvard Business Review*: Sept-Oct.

Bagdikian, B. (1989). 'The lords of the global village'.*The Nation* : June 12.

Behar, R. (1997). 'Who's reading your e-mail?' *Time* Feb. 3: 64-67.

Bern, S.L. and Bern, D.J. (1970). 'Case study of a nonconscious ideology: training the woman to know her place'. In D.J. Bern (ed.) *Beliefs, Attitudes and Human Affairs*, Belmont, CA: Brooks/Cole Publishing.

Breakwell, G.M. and Fife-Schaw, C. (1987). 'Young People's Attitudes Toward New Technology: Source and Structure'. In J.H. Lewko (ed.) *How Children and Adolescents View the World of Work*, San Francisco, Jossey-Bass, Inc.

Breakwell, G.M., Fife-Schaw, Lee, C.T. and Spencer, J. (1986). 'Attitudes to New Technology in Relation to Social Beliefs and Group Memberships: a Preliminary Investigation'. *Current Psychological Research and Reviews*, Spring, 5 (1): 34-47.

Breakwell, G.M., Fife-Schaw, Lee, C.T. and Spencer, J. (1987). 'Occupational Aspirations and Attitudes to New Technology'. *Journal of Occupational Psychology* 60: 169-172.

Commonwealth of Australia, Office of the Chief Scientist, Dept. of the Prime Minister and Cabinet (1995).*Women in Science, Engineering and Technology*, Canberra, Australian Government Publishing Service.

Cotgrove, S. (1982). *Catastrophe or Cornucopia?* Chichester: Wiley.

Denning, D.E. (1991). 'The United States vs Craig Niedorf'. *Communications of the ACM* 34 (3): 24-32.

Denning, D. (1995). 'Encryption: the case for Clipper' *Technology Review* July: 49-55

Dunlop, C. and R. Kling (1991). 'The Dreams of Technological Utopianism'. In Dunlop, C. and R. Kling, R. (eds) *Computerization and Controversy*. Boston: Academic Press.

Forester, T. and P. Morrison. (1990). *Computer Ethics: Cautionary Tales and Ethical Dilemmas in Computing*. Oxford: Blackwell.

Frederick, H. (1994). 'Computer Networks and the Emergence of Global Civil Society'. In Harasim, L.M. (ed.) *Global Networks: Computers and International Communication*. Cambridge, MA: MIT Press.

Gellerman, S.W. (1986). 'Why "good" managers make bad ethical choices'. *Harvard Business Review* July-August.

Gilligan, C. (1982). *In a Different Voice*. Cambridge, MA: Harvard University Press.

Hacker, S. (1990). in D.E. Smith and S.M.Turner (Eds.) *'Doing It the Hard Way': Investigations of Gender and Technology*, Boston: Unwin Hyman.

Head, J. (1980). 'A model to link personality characteristics to science'.*European Journal of Science Education*. 2: 295-300.

Head, J. (1985). *The Personal Response to Science*, Cambridge: Cambridge University Press.

Holderness, M. (1992). 'Time to shelve the library?'.*New Scientist* Dec.5: 22.

Homer, S. (1992). 'Battling on with veteran computers'. *New Scientist* Nov.14: 32.

Jackall, R. (1988). *Moral Mazes: The World of Corporate Managers.* New York: Oxford University Press.

Johnson, D. G. and J.W. Snapper. (1985). *Ethical Issues in the Use of Computers.* Belmont, CA:Wadsworth.

Johnson, D. G and Nissenbaum, H.G. (1995). *Computers, Ethics and Social Values.* Englewood Cliffs: Prentice-Hall.

Jonas, H. (1984).*The Imperative of Responsibility: In Search of an Ethics for the Technological Age.* Chicago: University of Chicago Press.

Kohlberg, L. (1981).*The Philosophy of Moral Development: Moral Stages and the Idea of Justice.* San Francisco: Harper & Row.

Kohlberg, L. and Gilligan, C. (1971). 'The Adolescent as a Philosopher: The Discovery of the Self in a Post-conventional World'. *Daedalus* 100: 1051-1086.

Klapp, O. E. (1982). 'Meaning Lag in the Information Society'. *Journal of Communication* 32(2): 56-66.

Ladd, J. (1989). 'Computers and Moral Responsibility: A Framework for an Ethical Analysis'. In Gould, C. (ed.)*The Information Web: Ethical and Social Implications of Computer Networking*. Boulder: Westview Press.

Lerner, F. (1993). 'Arsenals into Data Stores'. *New Scientist* January 9: 47-48.

Leveson, N.G. and Turner, C.S. (1993). 'An investigation of the Therac-25 accidents' *Computer* 26 (7): 18-41.

Lipman-Blumen, J. (1972). 'How Ideology Shapes Women's Lives' *Scientific American* 226: 34-42.

Mann, T. (1993). *Library Research Models: A Guide to Classification, Cataloguing and Computers.* New York: Oxford University Press.

Mellor, P. (1989). 'Can you count on computers?' *New Scientist* 11 Feb.: 52-55.

Norman, D. (1993). 'Will tomorrow's computer be able to read today's files?' *Apple Directions* Oct: 14.

Ormerod, M.B. (1971). 'The Social Implications Factor in Attitudes to Science'. *British Journal of Educational Psychology* 41 (3): 335-8.

Ormerod, M.B. (1981). 'Factors differentially affecting the science subject preferences, choices and attitudes of girls and boys'. In Kelly, A. (ed.) *The Missing Half: Girls and Science Education..* Manchester: Manchester University Press.

Parker, D.B., Swope, S. and Baker, B.N. (1990). *Ethical Conflicts in Information and Computer Science, Technology and Business.* QED Wellesley, MA: Information Sciences.

Raths, L.E.,Harmin, M. and Simon, S.. (1966). *Values and Teaching*, Colubus: Merrill.

Roberts, P. (1994). 'The Place and Pedagogy of Ethics in the Computing Curriculum'. *Australian Educational Computing* 9 (1).

Roberts, P. (1995). 'Ethics, the Neglected Factor in Computing Education'. In Tinsley, J.D. and van Weert, T.J. (eds)*WCCE '95 Liberating the Learner.* London: Chapman and Hall.

Roberts, P. (1995). *Women, Computing and Ideology: a Study of the Entry Attitudes of Female Arts Undergraduates.* (unpublished report).

Roush, W. (1993). 'Learning from Technological Disasters'.*Technology Review* Aug/Sept: 50-57.

Roush, W. (1995). 'Hackers: Taking a byte out of computer crime' .*Technology Review* April: 32-40.

Roszak, T. (1994). *The Cult of Information.*, Berkeley, CA: Univ. of California Press.

Swan, J. (1988). 'Information and Madness'. *Library Journal.* February 1: 28.

Toffler, A. (1980). *The Third Wave*, New York: Bantam Books.

Unger, R.K., Draper, R.D. and Pendergrass, M.L. (1986). 'Personal Epistemology and Personal Experience'. *Journal of Social Issues* 42: 67-79.

van Zoonen, L. (1992). 'Feminist theory and information technology'. *Media, Culture & Society* 14.

Wajcman, J. (1991). *Feminism Confronts Technology*, Sydney: Allen & Unwin.

Wray, T. (1988). 'The everyday risks of playing safe'. *New Scientist* 11 Feb.:61-65.

Yoder, J.D. and Schleicher, T.L. (1996). 'Undergraduates regard deviation from occupational gender stereotypes as costly for women'. *Sex Roles* 34 (3/4): 171-188.

Young, T.R. (1987). In Slack, J. and Fejes, F. *The Ideology of the Information Age.* Norwood, NJ: Ablex: 118-132.

A Survey of Local Demand for IT/ Computing Skills Relevant to Women Returners

Anne Davidson

The Women and Work Programme, Coventry University

Abstract

This paper describes a 'snapshot' survey of IT skills demand expressed in job advertisements in a local and in a national newspaper, and examines the implications for women's IT training and job prospects.

39% of local jobs advertised required computing/IT skill(s). Demand was highest for word-processing skills (34%), followed by spreadsheets (19%) and database (11%). There was a smaller demand for networking, DTP/graphics, accounting software, programming, technical/hardware, CAD, UNIX and Internet/multimedia skills.

Demand for word-processing skills was inversely related to salary. Demand for other user skills peaked in intermediate salary bands. Demand for computing *infrastructure* skills (e.g. programming, networking, database design/administration) peaked in the highest salary band. The proportion of jobs asking multiple IT skills rose with salary, but 40% of secretarial jobs also requested two or more IT skills

8% of the local jobs required a degree (or similar). The only other IT qualification specified was RSA word-processing – requested in 9% of local 'IT' jobs – but almost exclusively for posts in the lowest two salary bands.

1. Introduction

The Women and Work Programme, based at Coventry University, has a long history in offering courses designed to help women re-enter the labour market after unemployment or a career break. In the past two years, the Women and Work Programme has been a partner, with other local training providers and Coventry City Council, in a European-funded project whose express aim is to facilitate progression routes for the training of unemployed women and their re-entry into the labour market. Information technology training is a key feature of this project, and one of the challenges has been to provide training which not only leads to progression in terms of recognised qualifications *but* also addresses contemporary local skills shortages and emerging needs.

Women returners face many obstacles in their efforts to re-enter work but the acquisition of key, contemporary IT skills helps at least to redress some of the disadvantages. In the best case it may open up work opportunities not previously contemplated. The importance of this competitive edge should not be underestimated in a labour market where (it has recently been claimed) many IT skills have a half-life as short as 3 years and that up to 80% of computer users have not received formal training (Virgo 1996). From the point of view of training provision, it is of prime importance to detect growth areas in skills requirement quickly enough to implement training solutions which give the trainees this competitive advantage.

Surveys conducted by trade and management organisations are useful sources of information about skills shortages at a national level or within the 'computing industry' but do not necessarily clarify IT skills requirements at a local level, or over a range of occupations. Consequently we decided to conduct a survey of IT skills demands as represented in job advertisements in the local press. The aim was to see whether this 'snapshot' approach could provide relevant information on the nature of contemporary IT skills demands and the pattern of IT usage in traditional and non-traditional areas of women's employment.

2. Background, Scope and Methodology of the Survey

The *Coventry Evening Telegraph* is one of the most penetrative of the UK's daily local newspapers, claiming to reach more than 90% of the adult population in some areas. The Thursday evening edition carries a large number of job advertisements and is widely consulted by local job-seekers. This edition was analysed at three to four week intervals over a period of five months between June and November 1996. Details of all posts which required some form of IT or computing skills were entered in a database. These details included: Employer Name; Title of Post; Salary ; IT skills required; non-IT skills required; any qualifications or specific experience required.

Some posts where the requirements were highly coded (e.g. teaching and nursing posts) were excluded from the analysis as were Agency adverts, very small or uninformative adverts, and casual work.

For the sake of comparison, about one hundred 'IT professional' jobs were analysed from several editions of the *'On-Line' Guardian* over a similar time-period.

For the purpose of salary analysis, starting salaries were divided into four bands: Band 1 = <£8000 p.a., Band 2 = £8000 – £11500, Band 3 = £11500 – £15000 and Band 4 = >£15000. The choice of these bands was mainly arbitrary, but the £8000 p.a. upper limit for the lowest band was chosen because this represents around £4.40 per hour. The West Midlands Low Pay Unit (Flanagan 1996) have calculated that a wage of at least £4.50 an hour is necessary for an unemployed married woman (*without* children) to have any hope of escaping the poverty trap.

Salaries were quoted in just over half of the local advertisements. Where a range was quoted, the minimum 'over-21' salary was recorded. Salary information was not analysed in posts where only a maximum was quoted.

3. Survey Findings

3.1. Local Demand for Different IT skills

A total of 949 jobs were scrutinised in eight editions of the *Coventry Evening Telegraph* over a five-month period and the proportion of jobs which required IT/ computing skill(s) averaged 38.65%. All subsequent analysis of skills were conducted on this 'IT-requiring' subsample.

The relative demands for specific IT skills are listed in Table I. The highest demand was for skills in word-processing (34 % of 'IT-requiring' jobs), followed by spreadsheets (19 %), databases (11 %), networks (8 %), desktop publishing/graphics (8 %), CAD (7 %), accounting software (7 %), programming (5 %) and UNIX (4 %). In addition there was a small number of posts requesting Internet, Multimedia, GIS, TCPIP or Systems Analysis skills.

The greatest local demand, in purely numerical terms, is clearly for end-user application skills. In contrast, in 'Computing Jobs' in *The Guardian* (see Table I) the greatest demand was for skills in areas such as programming (predominantly C and C^{++}), database (especially development and administration), networks, UNIX and Internet. Similar patterns of demand have been reported recently in direct surveys of the IT industry (Virgo 1996, O'Neill 1996). The local demand for these computing 'infrastructure' skills mimics this pattern although they represent only a small proportion of the local job market.

3.2. Qualifications asked for

For the purposes of this study, qualifications were viewed in broadly two categories: a) qualifications related to IT skills, and b) general educational or professional qualifications related to other aspects of the job specification.

Of all the jobs analysed, 28 (about 8%) required a degree/HND level qualification, but only one specifically requested a computing-related degree. Other jobs cited requirements for HNCs, ONCs, 'A' Level, GCSE or Accountancy qualifications. RSA Word-processing (occasionally text-processing) qualifications were requested for 31 jobs. IT-related National Vocational Qualifications (NVQs) were requested for only three jobs.

Although the various vocational Examination Boards offer (and award) large numbers of

Table I. Comparison of demand for IT skills in posts advertised in the local press and in a national newspaper (expressed as % of all jobs requiring IT or computing skills)

IT skill	Coventry Evening Telegraph (340 Posts)	The 'On-Line' Guardian (101 Posts)
Word-processing	34%	6%
Spreadsheets	19%	3%
Database	11%	25%
Network skills	8%	17%
Desktop Publishing/Graphics	8%	6%
Accountancy software	7%	0%
Computer Aided Design (CAD)	7%	0%
Programming	5%	34%
Technical/Hardware expertise	5%	17%
UNIX	4%	28%
TCPIP	<1%	5%
Internet	<1%	15%
Multimedia	<1%	4%
Systems Analysis	<1%	6%
Geographical Information Systems (GIS)	<1%	3%

qualifications which recognise competence in a variety of computer applications at different levels, employers in this survey did not articulate their IT skills demand in terms of these qualifications (at least not at this level of job specification).

In the absence of competence indicators, and in the era of ubiquitous *Microsoft Windows*-based applications, it is not easy to deduce whether the post-holder will simply be required to perform data entry, or whether they will need to invoke the full problem-solving potential of the software. Occasionally 'advanced' or 'extensive' were used to describe the level of IT skill required. Advanced knowledge of databases was usually flagged by reference to development, administration or management of *relational* databases. 65 % of *The Guardian* 'database' jobs and 17 % of local 'database' jobs specified this level of knowledge.

3.3. IT Skills in Relation to Salary

A large number of factors influence salaries offered, including length of experience, range of capabilities and qualifications required, not to mention the nature of the employer's business and the sector it functions in. Consequently it is difficult to isolate an individual trend such as the correlation between IT skills and salary in such a multi-factorial relationship. Nevertheless many women aiming to re-enter today's labour market are mothers of small children – often single parents – for whom earning potential and the capacity to afford childcare and escape the benefit trap are very real issues. For this reason, it seemed relevant to attempt to establish which IT skills are particularly associated with either low- or well-paid work, and what co-requirements of skills and qualifications are required for the better paid areas of work.

The relative demand for different types of skills in the four different salary bands are shown in Table II. It is clear that the demand for word-processing skills bore an inverse relationship to salary offered, accounting for around 60% of the skills demand in the lowest two bands but for only 15% of the demand in the highest Band 4. Demand for *user* skills in other applications such as spreadsheets, databases, accountancy software, desktop publishing and presentation graphics tended to peak in the intermediate salary bands.

The best paid computing-related jobs (i.e. salary >£15000) were particularly associated with computing infrastructure skills (75% of '*Guardian*' jobs and 58% of local jobs in this band). The most sought after infrastructure skills were programming, networks, advanced relational database skills and UNIX.

The demand for *multiple* IT skills rose with salary. Demand for three or more IT skills rose from 8% of all jobs in the lowest paid band to 30% of jobs in the highest two salary bands.

20% of the jobs in Salary Band 4 required a Degree or HND qualification (not necessarily in IT) compared with only 9% of jobs in Band 3 and 2 % of jobs in Band 2.

The demand for RSA word-processing qualifications was almost exclusively associated with Band 2 (requested in 22 jobs (i.e. 25%) in this Salary Band, but only once each in Bands 1, 3 and 4).

3.4. IT Skills and Different Types of Occupation

Some types of specialist IT skills have a very obvious link with a particular profession, e.g. more than 85% of posts requiring CAD skills were either titled 'engineer' or required an engineering qualification. In these cases, the IT skill is a secondary but necessary requirement and the

Skill	Band 1 <£8000 pa	Band 2 £8000 - £11500	Band 3 £11500 - £15000	Band 4 >£15000
Word-processing	61%	57%	31%	15%
Spreadsheets	23%	27%	29%	9%
Database	8%	16%	20%	6%
Accountancy software	0%	8%	9%	6%
Desktop Publishing	0%	9%	17%	3%
Presentation Graphics	0%	6%	8%	3%
Networking	0%	2%	17%	18%
Programming	0%	1%	8%	9%
UNIX	0%	1%	8%	6%
'User skills'	92%	93%	89%	45%
'Infrastructure* skills'	8%	6%	23%	58%
1 IT skill	77%	64%	49%	52%
2 IT skills	23%	36%	51%	45%
3 IT skills	8%	17%	31%	30%

Table II - Demand for skills in different Salary Bands (expressed as % of Jobs in Band)

message for women returners in these professions is clear. About a quarter of posts requiring accountancy software skills also required an accountancy qualification; a similar number of posts which required DTP skills were for graphic designers/artists.

About one quarter of all IT-required jobs in the survey were overtly secretarial/clerical (i.e. the post title included the words 'clerk', 'clerical' or 'secretary'). In the UK 97% of secretarial work and 70% of clerical work is carried out by women (Wilson 1994) and the work historically attracts low pay and status (Werneke 1984).

Table III shows the pattern of IT skills requirement in jobs labelled 'clerical' or 'secretarial'. As expected, word-processing is the most sought after skill, followed by spreadsheets and, in the case of secretarial posts, presentation graphics. Interestingly, 28% of clerical posts and 40% of secretarial posts required two or more IT skills. Average annual salary was £8095 for clerical posts, and £10261 for secretarial posts. This compared with £11738 for the whole survey and £19330 for the IT professional jobs in *The Guardian*.

In her recent book, *Shaping Women's Work: Gender, Employment and Information Technology,* Juliet Webster (1996) has extensively reviewed research on the impact of technology on secretarial/clerical work. Some studies have indicated that the introduction of technology produces *deskilling* effects (Crompton and Jones 1984; Crompton and Sanderson 1990), particularly in the financial services and public service sectors where work tasks have been extensively rationalised and 'parcelled out'. Other studies have shown that the introduction of word-processing has *enskilled* some office jobs, freeing their incumbents from the more routine typing tasks, while allowing them to retain autonomy particularly in areas where they exercise their interpersonal skills (Fearfull 1994, Virgo 1994). However there is little evidence that the acquisition of IT skills is recognised by regrading or in terms of remuneration (Liff 1993). The current survey confirms that most clerical and secretarial jobs continue to be poorly paid but carry a requirement for an ever-increasing range of IT skills.

It has been suggested that IT support represents a possible career progression route for women in secretarial posts with an aptitude for IT. Table III shows the skills requirement for 'support' posts identified in the current survey. Salaries in this category covered a wide range (£8000 - £25000) with a mean of £13615. However, more than 80% of them of them carried a requirement for computer *infrastructure* skills such as networking, relational databases or UNIX.

An attempt was made to identify whether there was a category of 'miscellaneous', reasonably well-paid IT-required jobs which were not in the clerical, secretarial or support categories and which did not require advanced educational or professional qualifications. 34 such jobs were identified (about a third of which carried a co-requirement for some kind of specialised experience). IT skills required were diverse being divided, approximately equally, between user applications such as word-processing, spreadsheets and databases.

In addition to IT skills, 40% of jobs requested good 'communication', 'team-working' or 'interpersonal' skills. The demand for these types of skill was largely independent of salary and job category, except in engineering jobs where they were rarely requested.

Table III. IT Skills Requirement in Different Job Categories

Type of post	No of posts in category	Average Salary	Most frequently asked-for IT skills		No. of IT skills required	
Clerical	40	£8095	*word-processing*	62%	1 skill	86%
			computer literacy	26%	>or= 2	28%
			spreadsheet	26%	>or= 3	5%
Secretarial	43	£10261	*word-processing*	86%	1 skill	60%
			spreadsheet	26%	>or= 2	40%
			presentation graphics	12%	>or= 3	14%
IT Support	17	£13615	*network skills*	59%	1 skill	12%
			UNIX	29%	>or= 2	88%
			word-processing	24%	>or= 3	75%
			database (mainly Oracle)	24%		
			spreadsheet	24%		
Miscellaneous, better paid jobs (Salary Bands 3/4)	34	£15565	*word-processing*	23%	1 skill	60%
			computer literacy	20%	>or= 2	40%
			spreadsheets	17%	>or= 3	20%
			database	17%		

4. Discussion and Conclusions

It is clear that IT training is a necessity for women re-entering the labour market, otherwise they are effectively excluded from up to 40% of salaried local jobs.

Word-processing skills are in high demand but, taken on their own, mainly provide access to low-paid clerical/secretarial work irrespective of the degree of skill required. RSA word-processing (Levels 2 and 3) was the only vocational IT qualification which was frequently cited by local employers and appeared uniquely to differentiate between jobs in the lowest and second lowest salary categories. Clearly employers have faith in this type of qualification as an arbiter of standards for a certain type of work. The message for women seeking to improve their workplace position through training is, however, ambiguous. On the one hand, working towards these qualifications motivates trainees, in that they represent a passport to a certain (albeit not very well paid) position in the labour market. On the other, these examinations reproduce a stereotyped view of women's role in IT – namely the fast and accurate reproduction of text and layout specified by third parties. Furthermore, once women enter the labour market in these roles, they easily become trapped in low-paid, low-status jobs since there are few internal promotion routes which might allow them to progress. It could be argued that NVQs, and other awards based on their model, at least have the merit of encouraging creative and innovative IT solutions to work problems. However, the current survey tends to reinforce trends reported elsewhere – that NVQs are not yet widely sought by employers.

Outside word-processing, the highest demand was for user skills in spreadsheets, databases, desktop-publishing, presentation graphics, accountancy software and CAD. (The demand for CAD was almost exclusively associated with engineering qualifications and presumably has little currency in its own right. Nevertheless it is an important skill for women returners in the engineering area to acquire).

There were a significant number of reasonably well-paid posts which were not dominated by demand for word-processing skills. For women who want to avoid clerical/secretarial work, it would seem to be a good strategy to acquire a wide range of IT skills (although demands for two or more IT 'user' skills were also fairly common in secretarial posts). There was also considerable evidence that multiple IT 'user' skills increase eligibility for better paid jobs – though many permutations of skills are possible.

Insofar as our study looked at job details at the level displayed in job advertisements, employers seldom specified the extent of IT knowledge required (with the exception of word-processing). We intend to carry out more detailed studies to examine the putative skills gap between the use of IT applications in low-paid jobs and well-paid jobs – with a view to embodying these skills in higher level training courses and qualifications.

4.1. Implications for women's IT training

Many women first 'discover' IT on a Returners' course, and a proportion of them rapidly develop a facility and enthusiasm for IT which motivates them to explore further training options, either in the pursuit of wholly IT-related jobs or as valuable tools in their professional area. However, although short IT training courses are abundant, they concentrate mainly on a relatively small number of common office application skills (such as word-processing, spreadsheets and simple databases). This prevalence coincides with the relative demand for these skills observed in our study. Clearly such courses fulfil a labour market need at one level and a plethora of vocational qualifications exist to acknowledge achievement at basic skill levels.

The situation becomes more problematical at higher skill levels or areas of emerging skills demands. Funding for most courses for unemployed people (including women returners) is dependent on outcomes expressed in terms of recognised qualifications. The relative dearth of such qualifications at higher skill levels, and delays in validating qualifications in new skills areas, often prove strong disincentives for training organisations to run courses even where a training need is perceived. For example, there are currently few vocational qualifications which recognise skills in Internet working, relational databases, networks or presentation graphics – to mention just some of the skill demands we encountered in our study. Moreover, many of the IT skills required for support roles and the best paid jobs in our study (aside from those requiring a degree or professional qualification) were computing *infrastructure* skills including skills in networks, programming, relational databases, UNIX and TCPIP. In reality, opportunities to acquire these kinds of skills are relatively few outside computing degree courses, expensive commercial training providers or 'on-the job' training – each of which may be in different ways unattractive (Grundy 1996), unaffordable or inaccessible to unemployed women.

It could also be argued that three-year courses are not the most effective way to train women in the use of skills which are reputed to have a life-span of only six years in the workplace (Virgo 1996). The pedagogical feasibility of using short intensive courses to teach selected 'high level' IT skills deserves some consideration.

Lastly, training providers themselves need to recognise the importance of providing higher level IT skills training for women, with the associated implications for the staff development of 'traditional' IT trainers/tutors.

References

Crompton, R. and Jones, G. (1984). *White Collar Proletariat: Deskilling and Gender in Clerical Work*, 137-148. London: Macmillan.

Crompton, R. and Sanderson, K. (1990). *Gendered Jobs and Social Change*. London: Unwin Hyman.

Fearfull, A. (1992). 'The introduction of information and office technologies: The great divide?' In *Work, Employment and Society*, 6: 423-442.

Liff, S. (1993). 'Information Technology and Occupational Restructuring in The Office'. In E Green, D Pain and J Owen (eds) *Gendered by Design: Information technology and Office Systems*, 95-110. London: Taylor and Francis.

Grundy, F. (1996). *Women and Computers*, 13-25 and 75-84. Exeter: Intellect Books.

O'Neill, W. (1996). 'The workers who put the I back in IT'. In *The Wave*, Harris Research / The Guardian: 5.9.96.

Flanagan, H. (1996). *Fairness, security and Prosperity: The Case for a National Minimum Wage*, 34-35. Birmingham, UK: The West Midlands Low Pay Unit.

Virgo, P. (1994). 'The Gathering Storm: 1994 Skills Trend Report. *Institute of Data Processing Management/ Computer Weekly.*

Virgo, P. (1996). 'Apocalypse Soon: 1994 Skills Trend Report'. *Institute of Data Processing Management/Computer Weekly*, 24.10.96.

Webster, J. (1996). *Shaping Women's Work: Gender Employment and Information Technology*.: London and New York: Longman Sociology Series.

Werneke, D. (1983). *Microelectronics and Office Jobs: the impact of the Chip on Women's Employment*. Geneva, ILO.

Wilson, R. A. (1994). 'Sectoral and occupational change: Prospects for Women's Employment'. In R. Lindley (ed) *Labour Market Structures and Prospects for Women*, 25. Manchester: Equal Opportunities Commission.

Involve: Inclusive Teaching in First-Year Computer Science Course

Wendy Nightingale, Andrew Halkett, Kevin Hammond,

Colin Mason and Fiona Wilson

Division of Computer Science, School of Mathematical and Computational Sciences, University of St Andrews, North Haugh, St Andrews, Fife KY16 9SS.

Abstract

The Involve project is one of a number of projects funded under the SHEFC WISET (Women into Science, Engineering and Technology) initiative. It aims to identify and implement gender-inclusive teaching practices with the primary objective of improving female participation in the first-level Computing Science courses at the University of St Andrews. This project is primarily practically oriented: we aim to make the best possible use of existing research findings rather than necessarily generating new findings ourselves. This paper describes the status of the project, outlines the actions that have been taken to date, and discusses future directions.

1. Introduction

The primary aims of the Involve project are:
- to identify and implement best practice in inclusive teaching and learning in the St Andrews first level courses based on an awareness of different learning styles;
- to enable all students to feel ownership of, and competency in, the aims and outcomes of their courses;
- to develop a culture of inclusive teaching and learning throughout the division.

  In addressing these issues, we have tried not to treat women as a 'special case', since this can have a negative effect on the 'experimental subjects' (Cronin 1997). Rather we have attempted to adapt general best practice to gender-related differences in the student's experience (Seymour 1995).

2. Background

In common with other Computer Science departments in the UK, there is a significant gender imbalance among those taking our courses (Figure 1). Only the Vocational Information Technology (VIT) course has a roughly even gender balance, and this is largely due to a deliberate recruitment policy. The ratio in the Information Technology (IT) course is explained by the fact that this is mainly taken as an elective course by first- and second-year students from the Arts faculty.

Module Name	Code	Semester	M	F	% F
Scientific Information Technology	ScIT	1st	68	25	27%
Computer Science	CS	2nd	48	7	13%
Information Technology	IT	2nd	66	52	44%
Vocational Information Technology	VIT	Both	29	30	51%

Figure 1. Student intake into first–level modules for the academic year 1995–1996.

The normal route of progression for Computer Science honours students is through Scientific Information Technology (ScIT) in the first semester and Computer Science (CS) in the second. They must then survive a further year of sub-honours Computer Science, during which only half their courses will be in Computer Science and the remainder will be in other subjects, before starting their honours degree. The overall rate of progression is consequently low, though casual inspection reveals it to be much lower for female than male students. The course structure does, however, provide the opportunity to attract first year students into the division in the first semester (ScIT) and encourage them to continue in the second semester (CS) and beyond.

3. Teaching interventions

The interventions that have been taken were based on existing literature and the experience of our two teaching consultants. The problem of gender equity in the classroom has been recognised (Spertus 1991; Cottrell 1992) and addressed by institutions in North America (New England Consortium for Undergraduate Science Education 1996) and elsewhere in Europe (Svensson 1996). Whilst we have adopted some of these techniques we have sought to adapt them to our particular needs. Each intervention, outlined below, will undergo post–implementation review.

3.1. Study Skills

Effective studying is a key transferable skill. We have piloted the use of an integrated package called 'Personalised Advice on Study Skills' (PASS), developed by the Centre on Learning and Instruction, University of Edinburgh under the Teaching and Learning Technology Programme (TLTP). This package provides the students with study advice and allows staff to identify students who are using techniques associated with academic failure. Students who used the package found that the advice given was accessible and relevant. Their automatically generated learning profiles corresponded to their strengths and weaknesses as identified by their tutor and by themselves.

3.2. Group work

We recognise that group work is a vital and necessary skill in the workplace. Co-operation and communication has been identified as a key learning strategy for female Computer Science students (Svensson 1996) and recommended as a means for attracting women into technology courses by the Equal Opportunities Commission (Dain 1992). In order to prepare students for group work a set of 'Guidelines for Group Work and Group Report' were produced and distributed to students before a group practical. The guidelines were developed from the collective experience of tutors teaching on the VIT course, the Group Work section of the PASS Package and other sources (Race 1994; Race and Brown 1995). A sub-set of these guidelines and group-based assessment are now being adopted for the first-year Computer Science course.

3.3. Workshops
We are experimenting with the use of self-evaluating workshops as a practical means to raise awareness of issues through interaction within groups, with tutors involved only in the final feedback session taken at the end of the session.

3.4. Tutorials
Tutorial groups at St Andrews are small, typically five or six students chosen on the basis of their other academic commitments. Current practice is to bunch women in tutorial groups as far as possible in order to ensure that no group has a lone female or male. We have also experimented with different techniques to empower students and offer them greater ownership of the tutorial, e.g. allowing students to chair the session and explicitly allocating questions to individuals who are then expected to present the answer to the group.

In an attempt to match staff and student expectations, we have attempted to discover tutors' attitudes towards tutorials. The survey has been extended to students on the VIT course and is currently undergoing analysis. We will use this information to heighten awareness of the variety of benefits, identify any serious mismatch of expectation, clarify the purpose of tutorials and to address different student needs, including those which are gender-based.

For those students experiencing difficulty with course work, remedial tutorials are advertised on a drop-in basis for ScIT and CS while the VIT course provides extra tutorials ondemand: these can be one-to-one or small group sessions.

3.5. Novel lecturing techniques
There has been a shift from the traditional lecture theatre to a computer laboratory setting with high resolution video projectors used for demonstrations or as visual aids. This arrangement has facilitated a move from a traditional chalk-and-talk (or OHP-and-talk) environment to one that is more interactive and student-centred. Examples of non-traditional sessions we have tried include:
- short lecture followed by working through self-paced worksheets
- a traditional lecture with a break half-way through for individual or group work
- a lecture which requires students to work in tandem with the lecturer at the computer either individually or in small groups.

4. Staff training and on-going support
The project was launched at the beginning of the academic year in 1996 with two workshops; one for lecturing staff the other for tutors and demonstrators.

4.1. Tutors and Demonstrators

The Tutors' and Demonstrators' workshop identified a need for mutual support and raised many questions about teaching techniques. The group has continued to meet to discuss these issues. One of the objectives is to create our own WWW-based handbook of inclusive tutoring techniques.

4.2. Lecturing staff

The initial session for lecturers explored inclusive teaching practice in a broader setting, itself using a variety of inclusive teaching techniques, including pyramiding, buzz groups, pairing, horseshoe groups and cross-over groups. The objective of the session was to demonstrate inclusive teaching techniques in practice and to suggest how these techniques could be applied to particular modules within the division.

Since most of the lecturing staff also act as tutors (though much less intensively than the full-time tutors), a follow-up session was arranged to allow the tutors' experience to be exploited so as to provide the lecturing staff with input on good tutorial practice.

4.3. Staff self-assessment and observers

We have conducted pilot sessions in video taping lectures and tutorials. The tape is solely for the personal viewing of the member of staff. The adage that the 'camera never lies' is extremely useful in providing the basis of self–assessment.

We have also devised two checklists: a Checklist to Inclusive Lecturing and a Checklist to Inclusive Tutorials. The checklists provide the basis for the criteria used by independent observers to provide a confidential assessment of lecturing or tutoring technique.

4.4. Screening material

All of the electronic and printed material distributed in our first-level courses has been screened for gender inclusive language and sex stereotype roles. Feedback has been given to the course planning team, which has then taken action as appropriate. We are also liaising with the Division's Publicity and Recruitment working group in order to ensure that the best possible impact is obtained from our publicity material and contacts with prospective students, whether through direct personal contact or through letters.

5. Monitoring

We are designing and implementing an evaluation programme to assess where our interventions have been useful, where they are worth continuing and what further changes should be made. The evaluation procedures are outlined below.

5.1. Statistical profile

The nature of our project means that we are unable to easily *quantify* our success, although we can report qualitative effects. An increase in intake and retention of female students is the most directly measurable indicator of success and remains the primary long-term objective of the Division. We are in the process of gathering statistics which relate to the enrolment and completion of our first level courses with respect to gender. We will recommend that such a record should be maintained within the Division in order to permit longer-term analysis.

5.2. Student response

We have devised a questionnaire that is intended to gauge the attitude of ScIT students to computer science and their feelings of inclusion within the course and Computer Science Division. Face-to-face interviews were subsequently conducted with the same group of students. Results from these activities are described elsewhere in this proceedings (Wilson 1997). A revised questionnaire will be administered to the Computer Science students. A questionnaire has also been devised to gauge the attitude of VIT students to novel lecturing techniques and group work. The results are currently being analysed.

Students on the VIT course keep personal diaries which are submitted to their tutor each week. The diaries serve as a channel for immediate feedback on the student's experience in lectures, tutorial and practical sessions. Students tend to give a direct and, at times, a disarmingly honest response. This immediate feedback (cf. course assessment sheets at the end of each module) permits a quick response from the teaching staff and the students feel that they have greater ownership of the course which is changing to suit their needs.

In addition to the more formal contacts that are outlined above, we have also frequently discussed the issues both with individual students and with small groups. This has led to heightened awareness of gender issues amongst these students.

6. Conclusions and Further Work

The issue of women's under-representation in computer science is now firmly on the Divisional agenda. The Involve project has legitimised the problem and provided the necessary resources to allow us to make a start on tackling it. External speakers have offered different perspectives and strategies to the Division and kept alive the debate surrounding what changes we can and need to make in the Computer Science Division. Within this framework we believe that the Involve project has formed the basis for long-term positive change within the Computer Science Division.

The main focus of our future work will be to evaluate our current interventions and, where appropriate, apply them to other modules. The long term aim is to review the curriculum with a view to improving retention and progression and to apply similar changes to the second year Computer Science courses and beyond.

References

Cottrell, J. (1992). 'I'm a Stranger Here myself: A Consideration of Women in Computing'. in Learning from the Past Stepping into the Future. In *Proc. 1992 ACM SIGUCCS User Services Conference*, 71-76. Cleveland, OH.

Cronin, C. (1997). 'Winning Women: Participation Guide'. DBMS, University of Stirling. In press.

Dain, J. (1992). 'Person Friendly Computer Science. In Teaching Computing: Content and Methods'. *Proc. Women into Computing: 1992 National Conference*, Keele University, 1–12.

New England Consortium for Undergraduate Science Education (1996).
    'Achieving Gender Equity in Science Classrooms'. http://www.brown.edu/Administration/

`Dean_of_the_College/homepginfo/`
`Equity_handbook.html` (as of January 1997)

Personalised Advice on Study Skills User Manual (1995).
Centre on Learning and Instruction, University of Edinburgh.

Race, P. & Brown, S (1995). *500 Tips For Tutors*. Kogan Page.

Race, P. (1994). *500 Tips For Students*. Blackwell Publishers.

Seymour, E. (1995). 'The Loss of Women from Science, Mathematics and Engineering Undergraduate Majors: An explanatory account'. *Science Education* 79 : 437–473.

Spertus, E. (1991). 'Why are There so Few Female Computer Scientists?'
MIT Artificial Intelligence Laboratory Report. `Anonymous ftp from ftp.ai.mit.edu as womcs*.ps in directory pubs/ellens.` (as of September 1996).

Svensson, B. (1996). 'Reforming a Computer Science and Engineering Degree Programme: Operative Goals and Learning-related Strategies'.
`http://www.dtek.chalmers.se/Dpp/Publikationer/reform.html` (as of November 1996)

Wilson, F. (1997). 'Computing, Computer Science and Computer Scientists: how they are perceived', (in this volume).

Why do they never talk about the girls?

Minna Salminen-Karlsson

Department of Education and Psychology, Linköping University, Sweden

Abstract

The paper examines the process of planning a new computer engineering education programme at a technical university. In spite of the expressed aim of making the programme attractive to female students, gender issues are seldom considered. Analyses of the meetings and interviews with the team members demonstrate that

1) the interest in gender reform is overshadowed by the interest of overall pedagogical reform which is experienced as more pressing;
2) the female members of the planning team who are supposed to represent the needs and wishes of the female students do not fulfil this task;
3) there is an overall lack of knowledge about the existence of relevant research results in gender and technology and gender and education;
4) there is an ambivalence as to the image of the programme as being 'female-friendly'. This planning process is briefly compared to similar reforms at two other technical universities.

1. Background

How computer engineering education is created in the male-dominated environment of a technical university and, particularly, how and why it is still created to suit male students became my research question in 1993, when processes aimed at reforming computer engineering education were started concurrently at three technical universities in Sweden.

Two of the universities (here called SIT and TIT) obtained a sizeable state grant to reform computer engineering education with the aim of making it more attractive to female students. A third university (here called UIT), which had also applied for the grant and did not get one, set about making the proposed reforms anyway. The reform ambitions and procedures were formulated by the universities themselves, and even those with state grants were given a free hand. The only expressed directives were that the universities should reform an existing programme, or create a new one which would attend to women students' interests better than present measures. In practice, a condition for the state grant was also an introduction of problem-based or project-oriented teaching methods.

The background for this grant can be described as emanating from the conception of women as an untapped talent reserve for the needs of technical industry. Computer engineering education in particular is very male dominated, with the percentage of women having been around five to seven for several years. There was an array of projects during the 1980s aimed at showing girls what technical education and engineering is actually like, based on the assumption that girls just have many prejudices about both education and the profession, and where the problem is seen to be one of information. But as the percentage of women in computer engineering has stayed low, obviously the measures were not enough.

During the 1990s the problem has in part become more acute. Following the economic recession and increasing unemployment, the technical sector of higher education in Sweden has been augmented with the aim of both increasing the competence of the export industry and of providing education for unemployed youth. However, the interest of the 'masses' of young men has not increased correspondingly. The 1993 grant was the first one based on the assumption that the problem might not just be one of information, but there might be something wrong with the education itself.

SIT got the grant for creating a whole new educational programme (with 30 enrolments) in computer engineering, while TIT intended to reform its present computer engineering education (with 100 enrolments). UIT applied for the grant to introduce two special introductory years for 30 female students with a social science background from secondary education.

This paper is mainly based on my observations of the planning process which took place at SIT prior to the start of the new computer engineering programme. I expected that statements about female students would abound in the planning meetings, but this was not the case. The aim of adjusting engineering education to suit the needs and wishes of female students better did not play a significant role in the planning process. This made me curious about the mechanisms that were at work in the creation of the new programme.

My aim is to describe how the task of creating a female-friendly educational programme in computer engineering is performed by faculty at a technical university and to point to some factors which complicate the work.

2. Theoretical background

The process of creating a female-friendly computer engineering programme can be described by the concepts of feminist theorists and educational sociologists. I have chosen mainly to use theorists who elaborate the concepts of 'power' and 'reproduction'.

One of my theoretical points of departure is the concept of 'gender contract' as formulated by the Swedish researcher Yvonne Hirdman (1988). The bases of her theory are two underlying principles which she sees as affecting every instance of our social environment:

1) the separation of sexes so that characteristics, tasks, locations, etc. allocated to one sex are deemed unsuitable to the other, and

2) the normativity of the male, so that of these allocations the one reserved for males is constantly considered more worthy than the one allocated to females.

Success in increasing the percentage of female students in computer engineering would compromise both of these. As these principles, as seen by Hirdman, are the foundation of the (patriarchal) society, this is not easily managed.

As an education researcher I also use the concept of 'reproduction', the tendency of education to reproduce the prevailing societal conditions. The Swedish researcher Ulf P. Lundgren (1983) writes about two kinds of reproduction: vertical and horizontal. Vertical reproduction refers to the wish of the state authorities (backed by 'capital') to get citizens, and manpower, educated so as to fill their roles in society and in production. However, the educational institutions implementing reforms tend to reproduce their own structures and cultures – and gender contracts, and this is called horizontal reproduction by Lundgren. New curricula and educational reforms are created in the interplay and tensions between these two spheres.

I also use the concepts of 'field' and 'habitus' of Pierre Bourdieu (Bourdieu and Wacquant 1992). The world of technical universities (of which there are only five) in Sweden can be described as a special 'field', forming the behaviour, attitudes, traditions, values and perceptions (or 'habitus') of those people enclosed in this field. Perpetuating this 'habitus' is what the horizontal reproduction is about. One part of it is keeping up a certain kind of gender contract, which has as its consequence the reproduction of men's power over computer engineering in the society by means of education.

As to the position of the female members of the reform team, I have as my point of departure the theory of Kanter (1993) on women in a minority position being tokens, easily distinguished individuals in a, mostly negative, special position. Kanter enumerates several mechanisms that can be seen as affecting females in a technical university, for example, making them 'conceal' their femaleness.

3. Method

My basic material consists of notes and recordings from meetings with the reform team at SIT during the first year of its existence. I have also used interviews with 15 of the group members made during the first few months of that year. My material from TIT and UIT consists of interviews with the persons who have participated in the corresponding processes at these two universities. These data have been collected after the period in question was ended, which makes them less reliable compared with the observations at SIT. These data are used as a contrast and a complement to the data from SIT. The method of analysis has been inductive, with inspiration from grounded theory (Glaser and Strauss 1967).

4. Results

In analysing the material from SIT, four central areas of interest were found, each of them with a complicating impact on the ambitions of creating a female-friendly educational programme:
1) the interests of the reform team
2) the position of the female members in the team
3) the lack of knowledge on gender-related issues, and
4) ambivalence regarding the image of the new programme.

4.1 The interests of the reform team

The reform work had its beginning when the head of the computer engineering programme was informed of the possibility of applying for a state grant to recruit more female students. He was interested both in educational matters and in introducing more female perspectives into technology. He had been experimenting with problem-based learning for some time and wanted to try it out on a larger scale. Thus, he wanted to create a new educational programme with problem-based learning throughout, and more social sciences and communication skills than the present computer engineering course offered. This kind of education, he believed, would attract more female students.

The original reform team was personally recruited by the project leader and was formed mainly from academic staff in the departments concerned. Half of the members were female. In the interviews practically everyone said that their reason for engaging in the reform work was the wish to create a pedagogically sound educational programme, rather than to recruit female students. Many told of a long-lasting frustration over the teaching methods used in engineering education and welcomed the possibility of doing something about the situation. They hoped that this new approach would attract female students. As for problem-based learning, the main topic of the meetings, its female-friendliness was never officially questioned. However, in the interviews many team members said that they actually did not know whether problem-based learning would be better for girls than traditional teaching methods and three of the interviewees were negative about it. The main topic of the discussions, and the focus of the reformers' interests, was thus not directly related to the official aim of the programme.

4.2 The position of the female team members

The reform team and the working groups were set up with what became to be known as 'Noah's principle': an informal quota of 50% for male and female members, respectively. This principle was stressed in the beginning, and talked of proudly by the project leader. It was expected that a high percentage of female members would guarantee that female students' interests would be taken into account. The project leader talked (with the other group members quietly consenting) about the new aspects which the female members brought into the work of the team. However, what these aspects were was never really specified. Rather, it seemed as if the team members expected them to be there rather than actually seeing them there.

When asked why they had been put on the team, male and female members gave different answers. The female members almost always mentioned their sex as an important factor, apart from their professional qualifications and, sometimes, their previous connections with the project leader; while the men only mentioned their professional qualifications and connections with the project leader. This is hardly surprising, but is the first indicator that Noah's principle was not a guarantee for a balanced situation: both sexes were not represented on an equal basis, but the women felt they represented their sex on the team.

Even had the situation been balanced, the needs of the female students might have been left out of the discussions. The wish to recruit female students was not necessarily greater for all the female team members, compared with the males. The women in the team expressed in the interviews the further problem of not seeing themselves able to represent those female students who would be recruited owing to the reform, as they felt themselves as belonging to another category – they had not needed any such reforms to encourage them to apply for the computer engineering course and had accepted it as it was. As gender issues were rarely discussed in the meetings, any discussion of them did stand out as something special. One of the female members who actually took up gender issues spoke of her feeling that if she reminded the team too often about these issues she would be seen as a militant feminist.

The interaction of the team members was never discussed. Because there were as many female members as males the women were not seen as a weaker group. However my analysis of excerpts sent five meetings (with guidelines from Schlyter 1985) gave me insights into the dynamics of the group:

The project leader talked often and at length. After him, the other male team members spoke most often. They also referred to each other. The female members took fewer and shorter turns and were more often interrupted by questions, while the male members were more often allowed to finish their point before being asked questions. The female members' contributions were mainly commented on by other female members. Some of the female members reinforced the male members' comments with 'mmms' and positive appreciation, while the opposite did not occur.

Thus, while in numbers the group was balanced, the communication, while unbalanced, was not to an extreme even if men dominated in the discussions. However, the women did not fulfil the task implicitly allocated to them – seeing to the needs of the female students. The equality in numbers, which was expected to lead to a gender-balanced view of the course, did not have this effect.

4.3 Lack of knowledge

To be a woman was thus seen as a qualification for being appointed to the team for planning the female-friendly programme. This qualification was applied instead of needing to be knowledgeable or interested in gender issues.

In the original vision of the project leader, the programme would have two basic elements: a comprehensive view of computer technology, which would be acquired by problem-based learning, and 50% of the students being female. The project leader's base of knowledge was related to the first element, while his knowledge of gender issues in relation to technology and technical education was more fragmentary and did not include very many personal experiences. As for the other team members, almost all of them were more interested in the educational reform than in recruiting women, and so their knowledge interests were also directed that way. The unquestioned basic assumption was that problem-based learning is good for female students and, thus, was all that was needed.

After the work had been going on for about a year without gender issues being considered, a special working group devoted to gender issues was established. This meant that the requirements of being more interested in and possessing more knowledge on gender issues were not made of all team members. The working group on gender then began to discuss the social climate of the university, rather than the curriculum of the programme, which was very much in line with the way gender issues had been taken up in the previous team meetings. The need to integrate gender aspects into the subject matter was acknowledged, but there were hardly any suggestions as to how this should be done.

The team also lacked knowledge in social science, which was supposed to interest female students. While the technical and mathematical curriculum content led to lively and frequent discussion, the social science content was accepted without discussion as it was suggested by the social science representative.

Neither did the team strive to obtain any first-hand knowledge about the girls they were going to attract. When the team could not agree on what to call the programme, a representative visited three classes in secondary schools to present the programme and ask the girls what they thought a suitable name would be. This representative presented reports on the visits at one of the meetings, but they were not discussed.

This lack of knowledge can partly be blamed on the lack of interest in the issue of recruiting female students. However, as these members of faculty normally cherish (scientific) knowledge, it is surprising that they set about planning a female-friendly course without studying and reflecting on what is known about women and technical education and gender and technology. In general, there seemed to be much ignorance about this area of research. The group members seemed to lack awareness of the existence of relevant knowledge of scientific quality.

4.4 Ambivalence
None of the team members was opposed to the goal of the programme of recruiting 50% women, but there was an ambivalence about how this should be done. The question of how much this goal should be stressed when marketing the programme was a tricky one. At one of the earliest meetings it was agreed that efforts to make the programme attractive to female students should not be stressed when marketing the programme. The common view was that girls were not interested in applying for a programme conceived as feminine, and neither were gifted boys. There was also an apprehension about the programme becoming conceived as less 'serious' by students, colleagues and the computer industry if its female-friendliness was emphasised. Thus the female-friendly image was toned down both at the university and in marketing. This succeeded so well that the governing board of the university, at a hearing before taking the final decision about the start of the programme, asked what its aim really was. Was it to recruit female students or to produce a new kind of computer engineer? The hearing might have shown that the university was less concerned about the female image than the reform group itself – in any case, a working group for gender issues and plans for direct marketing of the programme to female students were begun after this hearing.

4.5 TIT
TIT made fewer far-reaching curricular reforms but managed to keep gender issues on the agenda during the planning process more effectively than SIT. The position of women was similar to that at SIT, but the competing interest of making a reform in the curriculum was somewhat weaker and there was slightly more knowledge – not among all team members but among a few of them. There was hardly any ambivalence about making gender-related reforms or creating the image of a female-friendly programme.

As TIT was reforming the whole of its existing computer science programme with its 100 new enrolments each year, the situation was quite different to that of SIT. TIT was opting for project-oriented learning, but the reforms were more moderate. However, compared with the stagnation with which the programme had been afflicted by over the previous few years, the reforms could be considered to be extensive. In addition to project work, the reformers at TIT reduced the number of obligatory subjects and restructured the first year of studies to give a 'comprehensive view of computer technology' with its social aspects. In addition, innovative measures to recruit female students were taken.

The interest in gender issues among TIT reformers at TIT resembled that of the reformers at SIT. There had been plans and wishes to reform the curriculum and the teaching methods long before the state grant for recruiting women was announced. Many considered the plan to recruit more female students as something connected to the grant rather than the programme's own need. To legitimise the absence of overt gender issues in much of the work, the stated aim was to create a better education for all. A better programme could be expected to recruit more female students, as female students were seen as more demanding about their education than the males. However, gender issues were kept on the agenda to a notably higher degree than at SIT. An important reason for this was that the governing board of the university had an influential and knowledgeable (female) member who took great interest in the reform.

At TIT women were a minority among the reformers but efforts had been taken to engage as many women as possible and there were female members in almost all working groups. On the basis of the interviews it is difficult to say anything about the modes of interaction in the groups. None of the female interviewees complained about having being ignored, but a couple of them told how other females (student representatives – of which there were relatively many) had had difficulties in their groups. It is reasonable to assume that the situation at TIT resembled that of SIT; that is, the interviewees assumed the patterns of interaction being gender-equal, while a closer look revealed that men were slightly dominating. Even at TIT the female reformers did not feel qualified to represent the female students-to-be for the same reason as at SIT – they saw themselves belonging to another category.

In terms of acquiring more knowledge in gender issues, the overall pattern at TIT was the same as at SIT. No notable efforts to improve the knowledge base on gender issues could be traced in most of the interviews, even if there were a few individuals with more knowledge. At TIT there seemed to be two, undiscussed, basic assumptions, which were regarded as solid knowledge and foundations of the programme: 1) female students are not interested in technical studies, if the (societal) use of technology is not carried along all the way and 2) female students demand a better pedagogy than the males.

While interests, sex-equality in the team and lack of knowledge were common features of both SIT and TIT, the aspect of ambivalence was not notable at TIT. Attempts to market the programme to female secondary-school leavers with arguments that the reform had especially taken their needs into acount were seen as positive. This difference may depend on the fact that TIT expected a relatively minor increase in the percentage of female students. Even if the percentage were to double (which was seen by the reformers as an acceptable result), it would merely rise from 7% to 15%, and this would not give the programme a female image.

4.6 UIT

While SIT and TIT were quite similar in many ways, UIT showed greater differences. Its approach of creating an all-female class – a very radical measure in the Swedish context – resulted in a different kind of ambivalence. As the only aim was to recruit female students, there were no competing interests. The reform team was more knowledgeable and continued to increase the members' knowledge on gender issues – among other things by making use of the experiences of the female members of the team.

The basic assumption at UIT was that pedagogy and the curriculum were not the problem but that girls rejected computer engineering education because of the dominance of males in computing, both at school and at the university. Thus pedagogical reforms were not perceived to be as important as at SIT and TIT. Instead, UIT went out directly to recruit female students. The idea was to find girls who had made a 'wrong' choice entering secondary education, by taking social science, but now had finished secondary school, changed their minds and could think of a technical profession. These girls were to be given a complementary year with secondary school mathematics and science and the first year of the computer engineering programme in an integrated manner. They were to form an all-female group during these two years to boost their self-confidence before they were integrated into the ordinary, male-dominated, computer engineering programme.

While there was a competing (and stronger) interest in educational reform at SIT and TIT, the reform at UIT concentrated on recruiting female students, and that was also the main interest of the reform team. Some pedagogical changes would be made to the benefit of the all-female group but they were regarded as comparatively unproblematic. The reasons for UIT focusing on the recruitment of female students were, partly, that the educational methods (which differed somewhat from those applied at SIT and TIT) were not conceived as needing any major reform, and partly, and most importantly, that UIT had suffered recruitment problems for years, which had become all the more acute. Put simply, there was a lack of academically competent male students.

As to gender equality within the reform team, it was notable that at UIT the interviewees stressed the importance of men in the planning team, while the importance of women was stressed at SIT and TIT. A female head of department had been one of the initiators of the project, but to lead the project a male professor was chosen – much for the sake of legitimating the project. The team members saw the project as being led by both of these persons on an equal basis. The team in itself was roughly gender balanced, but as to the modes of interaction, the interviews are not a trustworthy source.

Even with regard to the knowledge base of the team members, UIT differed from the other two universities. The female project leader had done a research project on gender and technology. Literature on gender issues was referred to more often. Seminars were arranged and attended. The experiences of the female students now on the programme were questioned, and female faculty members told of having started to recount their experiences more freely among colleagues. The preferences of the target group were investigated systematically.

There was a lot of ambivalence, but it was of another kind than that at SIT. The image of the programme was not a problem. But as single-sex education (as planned) does not exist in Swedish higher education and the idea is quite alien, many of the team members felt ambivalence towards the concept of an all-female class, as did their colleagues. Many of them did not like the idea. But when it became clear that there were many academically competent girls who could consider applying, practical necessity made it acceptable. Some of the reformers called it a temporary, emergency measure, taken in an acute situation.

The institutional context at UIT probably contributed to decreasing the ambivalence, as the reformers could expect positive feedback if they succeeded in raising the percentage of girls. At the university there had been several innovative measures to recruit female students, and the university is also conducting research in gender and technology. The university also agreed to engage in new exciting projects was also accepted at the university, its self-image being that of a 'pioneer spirit'. The possibility of reaching an important goal and the knowledge of institutional support balanced somewhat the hesitation caused by an unconventional and suspicious method.

5. Conclusions

The programme at SIT actually succeeded in recruiting almost 50% female students the first year, and was, naturally, regarded as a success in this respect. TIT doubled the percentage of its female students from 7% to 15%. I have no wish to belittle these achievements, which were made in spite of the absence of gender discussions during the planning process. My research question concerns solely the planning process itself. I am not only interested in the number of professional women entering the computer industry, but also in what possibilities they have for 'creating new areas combining what we want to develop with that which is unavoidable considering the political – and economic – climate' (Elkjaer 1989). All the programmes certainly recruited female students, but being basically traditional in their curriculum, would still socialise them to traditional values in computer engineering and not encourage them to create new areas.

Four aspects which stood out from the planning process to which can be attributed the failure to give due regard to gender issues during the planning process:

1) the imbalance in interests, where pedagogical reform from the start was more important than gender issues
2) the inability of the female team members to fulfil the roles allocated to them as spokes(wo)men of the female students
3) the ignorance on gender issues in general, as well as gender and technology and the target group, and
4) the ambivalence to the task itself of creating a programme which could be conceived as female-friendly.

Thus the team at SIT concentrated on creating a pedagogically innovative programme rather than a female-friendly one, even when they were in principle amenable to having more female students in engineering education and had the mission and the money to fulfil this. It is reasonable to assume that factors like this can often affect the process, if faculties at technical universities are to increase the recruitment of female students by means of educational reforms. In reforming computer engineering education the state had its aims and intentions and one kind of gender contract, while the aims and intentions and gender contract of the context of horizontal reproduction, the reform teams at the universities, were quite different (Lundgren's 1983). What could seem to be a straightforward task of finding out what girls wanted from computer engineering education and reforming the education to comply to these wishes became a complicated matter in the sphere of engineering education with its power relations and traditions.

To think of the processes in terms of Hirdman (1988), the task of the reformers at SIT and TIT was to change a separation of sexes on the societal level (prescribing computer engineering as a male task and computer engineering education as a male location) by breaking the normativity of the male on the institutional level (by creating educational programmes where the male would not be the norm). However, none of the teams was willing to really break with male patterns and traditions in favour of female ones. The needs that female students were assumed to have were accepted only in addition to male students' preferences. The reform teams' expressed ambition to create gender-equal education meant supplementing the education with something additional (female values), rather than profoundly changing the technological content which in itself can be seen as patriarchal (Wajcman 1991).

The need for educational reforms in Swedish engineering education is acknowledged both by state authorities and the technical universities themselves. For faculty who experience this working environment as frustrating, a grant which makes it possible to reform both education and the curriculum is welcome, whatever condition is attached to the money.

At SIT a high percentage of female students was the aim - but the realisation of the programme was not dependant on whether this would be achieved or not as the programme was expected to attract enough gifted students in any case. Thus, planning for female students had lower rewards for the faculty than planning educational reforms.

The case was the opposite at UIT, where problems of recruiting academically competent male students were more acute and the academic deficiencies of the present student body often encountered by the teachers. Thus a notable increase in the proportion of female students did in itself carry a reward.

Technical universities often use female faculty members as representatives for female interests when something is to be planned for female students. A mixed group can be expected to do better than an all-male one on these occasions, but leaving too much for the women to accomplish in these groups can be a mistake. To start with, because of the scarcity of female faculty, they are usually a minority in the group. They also are often on lower levels in the academic hierarchy, which gives them a disadvantage in the interaction. Often they also have a double task: while the male faculty represent their departments or competence areas, the female faculty members are expected to represent both their departments and competence areas *and* their sex. This double burden can be handled in different ways but it is easy for the women, as they have learned during their career (as Kanter 1993, describes) to conduct themselves the same way as their male counterparts rather than stressing their role as females. This is even more probable, as they often do not feel representative of 'women' or 'girls' in general.

The knowledge base on gender issues among the faculty in general seemed to be insufficient. Instead, some basic assumptions were used:

1) women's lack of interest in technical education is due to their wish to see technology in its societal context (all the three universities, but especially TIT ascribed to this)
2) women are much more interested in working in groups than men are (both SIT and TIT, but especially SIT)
3) women are scared away from engineering education because of the dominant behaviour of the male students (at UIT, but hardly at all at SIT and TIT, where female students do a lot of group work in mixed groups).

Research supports all three assumptions, which thus can be said to be realistic (Bruvik-Hansen 1984; Göransson 1995; Kvande 1984; Rasmussen and Håpnes 1991). However, when only one or two of these assumptions are used as guiding stars for the reforms, something will be lacking. Even other assumptions can be derived from research, for example that women do not share the overall view of technology and technical progress which is predominant at technical universities – of which the prestige attached to innovative 'hacking' is an example (Rasmussen and Håpnes 1991), or that women more often than men wish to be able to combine their studies with interests outside the university, which is very difficult when going through an engineering programme (Bruvik-Hansen 1984). Those research results which were exalted to guiding stars were those which could easily be combined with the reformers' pedagogical interests.

The ambivalence about the mission itself was only experienced at SIT. There were three reasons for it:

1) the team was creating a whole new programme, which could be criticised and categorized as being 'feminine', 'soft' and inferior

2) the percentage of female students was expected to be considerable, which would make this categorising all the easier, and

3) uncertainty about the attitudes of the institutional context – even if the reformers assumed that the central institutional authorities were positive about recruiting female students, there was no direct encouragement on their part, as was the case at TIT and UIT.

At TIT reform of the computer engineering programme to satisfy female students' needs was not seen as a risk to its reputation. The programme has a 'guaranteed' student body of young men from the region and this was expected to continue.

The ambivalence of the SIT reformers is understandable against the background of the field (in Bourdieuan terms) of technical universities in Sweden, where reputation and status are very important for both the universities and the single programmes. All technical universities in Sweden have taken some measures to recruit female students, so it could be expected that success in this would raise the status of a programme. However, there are signs of the opposite. The new programmes which often attract a higher percentage of girls are normally ranked lower than the traditional theoretical and technical, and male ones. UIT, which as an institution has a very high percentage of female students compared with the other universities, has not gained a higher status because of this – rather, one can ask whether the percentage of female students has been a contributing factor in UIT having the lowest status among the technical universities. Thus, there are reasons to suspect that a high percentage of female students actually draws down the status of a programme, and that the anxiety of the reformers was well-founded.

The question of status and reputation is also one of the explanations as to why UIT managed to make a radical reform: apart from having an acute need to recruit students, UIT reformers did not have very much status to lose, as computer engineering at UIT already was lowest in the status hierarchy of Swedish computer engineering programmes. With the interests of UIT as a whole in recruiting female students, the reputation of the programme would probably be even better at the university if they managed to get many girls.

To summarise the four aspects, the following can be concluded.

Competing interests: Recruiting female students does not seem to be the most urgent need when technical universities get a chance to make reforms in their programme. Other interests easily take over.

Women's position in planning teams: Including women in reform teams does not guarantee that the interests of presumptive female students will be taken up sufficiently. There are several reasons for this:

1) the women most often are in a minority

2) the women most often are on lower levels of the academic hierarchy, and thus have less influence

3) the women often have a double task of representing a department or competency area *and* their sex – and given the socialisation these women have undergone during their careers, the latter

easily gets less attention

4) common modes of speech interaction, where men dominate in meetings, can be assumed to occur even at technical universities.

    Lack of knowledge: There are at least three reasons why reformers in general do not seem to know very much about research in gender and technology or gender and education:

1) competing interests, as stated earlier
2) the commonly superficial knowledge of social science in general among faculty at Swedish technical universities – and gender research being apprehended as even more controversial, and thus not reliable, than social science in general
3) any knowledge except disciplinary is generally not required of teachers at university level – they are supposed to be able to plan their lectures, courses and, obviously, whole educational programmes on the sole basis of their disciplinary competence.

    Ambivalence: While technical universities are interested in recruiting female students, they still rank each other according to the technological content of the education and the technological research done at the institution. Because technology is seen as a male domain, too feminine an image may involve a risk of losing status, which is a most important asset among technical universities.

    Several of these aspects were not notable at UIT, where the reform concentrated on gender issues. This is reminiscent of other circumstances (wartime being the most commonly referred to) where women are allowed to enter male areas because of the scarcity of men. If men are really scarce, the faculty of a technical university can be expected to be more interested in recruiting women, which, in turn, should increase the interest for acquiring relevant knowledge and diminish the degree of ambivalence. Having an incentive to think about the education as gendered should somewhat change the relationships between male and female faculty members, too.

    This leads to a provocative notion: Thus far, computer engineering programmes in Sweden have been extended to the degree that students with fairly ordinary academic qualifications can come in to fill the programmes. To shift the gender balance, perhaps only those with good qualifications should be allowed on computer engineering programmes. This would discredit many male applicants and create a state of shortage, which would encourage the universities to make real efforts to attract female students.

References

Bourdieu P. and Wacquant, Loïc J.D. (1992). *An Invitation to Reflexive Sociology.* Cambridge: Polity Press.

Bruvik-Hansen, A. and Billing, Y.D. (1984). *Ærlig talt. Om kvinders forhold til ingeniøruddannelserne.* Forskningsrapport nr 6. Institut for samfundsfag, Danmarks Lyngby: Tekniske Højskole. [Honestly speaking. Women's relation to engineering education]

Elkjaer, B. (1989). 'Myth and reality about women and technology', in Tijdens, K. et al (ed.)*Women, Work and Computerization: Forming New Alliances.* 199-206 Elsevier Science Publishers B.V..

Glaser, B.G. and Strauss, A.L. (1967). *The Discovery of Grounded Theory. Strategies for Qualitative Research.* New York: Aldine de Guyter.

Göransson, A.G. (1995). *Kvinnor & män i civilingenjörsutbildning* Pedagogiska enheten vid Forsknings- och utbildningsbyrån, Göteborg: CTH.

Hirdman, Y. (1988). 'Genussystemet - reflexioner kring kvinnors sociala underordning'. *Kvinnovetenskaplig tidskrift*, 9 (3): 49-63.

Kanter, R.M. (1993). *Men and Women of the Corporation*. New York: Basic Books.

Kvande, E. (1984). *Kvinner og høgere teknisk utdanning. Delrapport: Integrert eller utdefinert. Om kvindelige NTH-studenters studiesituasjon og framtidsplaner*. Trondheim: IFIM Rapport.

Lundgren, U.P. (1983). 'Utbildning och arbete', in Bernstein, B & Lundgren U.P. *Makt, kontroll och pedagogik*, 9-21. Lund: Liber.

Rasmussen, B. and Håpnes, T. (1991). 'Excluding women from the technologies of the future? A case study of the culture of computer science'. *Futures* December: 1107-1119.

Schlyter, S. (1985). 'Makt och kön i språklig interaktion', in *Makt och kön. Rapport från ett seminarium 17-18 oktober 1985*, 51-68. Stockholm: Delegationen för jämställdhetsforskning.

Wajcman, J. (1991). *Feminism Confronts Technology*. Cambridge: Polity Press.

Positive Action: Promoting Technology and Science through Female Role Models

Ita Richardson

Dept of Computer Science & Information Systems, University of Limerick, National Technological Park, Castletroy, Limerick, Ireland

Ita Kavanagh

Dept of Science & Information Technology, Regional Technical College, Moylish Park, Limerick, Ireland

Abstract

Role models are key influencers in the career choices which students make. Female students in particular have problems identifying role models in newer and less familiar disciplines like computing, and a lack of suitable role models has been identified as one of the main reasons why female students do not pursue careers in science and technology (Murphy 1996). Authors of this paper are members of Women in Technology and Science (WITS), the Irish association for women technologists and scientists. One of the aims of WITS is to encourage the participation of young women in science and technology. One method used to do this is by organising Role Model days throughout Ireland.

This paper describes the organisation of one of these Role Model days, its impact on the students' consideration of career choices having attended the day and future initiatives in this area.

1. The Problem

Computer Science is a new discipline, and when the field of computer science emerged, it was hoped that this would 'break new ground in professional access and equity for women' (Pearl 1995). This has not been the case. In the Irish context, as globally, the number of females entering the science and technology professions is still very low (O'Dubhchair and Hunter 1995, Klawe and Levenson 1995). In fact, owing to the low numbers of women accessing computing careers, many women's organisations and individual women feel it necessary to promote technical careers among other women.

Many young women are capable of pursuing computing careers but because they have not the encouragement or the information to even consider these careers, they do not pursue them. This is the problem we try to address.

Examining the Irish situation, particularly in Limerick, where both authors are based, we present figures from the two third-level colleges based in the city (Tables 1, 2, 3). Departments and courses presented are computing-based courses within both colleges.

From Table 1 it can be seen that the percentage of women lecturing to students on computing-based courses is very low at 5% in the University of Limerick. However, at Limerick Regional Technical College, there are 42% women lecturing on computer-based courses. This is the exception rather than the rule in Irish Regional Technical Colleges, as can be seen in Egan (1995). The number of females currently studying on computer-based courses is given in Table 2. At the University of Limerick, 17% of students on computing-based courses in academic year 1995/1996 are females. This figure varies, for example, in the College of Informatics and Electronics at the University of Limerick, where 25% of 1995 graduates were young women. That year was exceptional, in that 35% of Computer Systems graduates were women. In 1996, the number of female Computer Systems graduates had decreased to 21% of the class. In the degree in Information Systems at Limerick Regional Technical College, the percentage of female graduates rose to 50% in 1996 but again this was the exception rather than the rule. In 1995, 25% of graduates were female and in 1997 we expect 39% of the graduating class to be female.

Table 3 shows figures for the three software-based courses within both colleges. It should be noted that these courses have a higher percentage of women studying than on more hardware-based courses, such as those run by the Department of Electronic and Computer Engineering in the University of Limerick (Table 2). From the overall total in Table 3, it can be seen that the percentage of women on these courses has decreased slightly over the four years, which would imply that the number of women joining the software profession within the next three years is not going to change significantly. In the two of the three courses given, there is a significant decrease in the percentage of female students from year 4 to year 1. In the remaining course, the percentage of females has only slightly improved from year 4 to year 1, and no difference occurs between year 3 and year 1.

2. WITS Initiative

One of the core aims of Women in Technology and Science (WITS), the Irish Association of female technologists and scientists is to increase the number of girls considering science, technology and engineering as a career. WITS was launched in November 1990 and the association currently has 300 members throughout Ireland from a broad range of scientific and technological backgrounds including computer professionals, engineers, industrial scientists, technicians and journalists. WITS members range in age and experience from third level students to some of the country's most senior scientists and academics.

Major influences on students making career and subject choices are peers, parents, teachers and role models, not necessarily in that order. Research has shown that many girls considering a scientific, technological or engineering career can be put off by people who are just not familiar with current careers and hold stereotyped views, perhaps of an engineer in oily overalls, with filthy hands who of course is male, or of the 'mad scientist' of Hollywood fame. A lack of suitable

UL: University of Limerick
LRTC: Limerick Regional Technical College

Department	College	Staff Total	Female	%Female
Computer Science & Information Systems	UL	18	3	17
Electronic & Computer Engineering	UL	26	0	0
Mathematics & Statistics	UL	17	0	0
Science & Information Technology	LRTC	19	8	42

Table 1. Permanent Full-Time Academic Staff in Third-Level Departments, November 1996 (Limerick Regional Technical College 1996, University of Limerick 1996a)

Department	College	Student Total	Female	%Female
Computer Science & Information Systems (UL)	UL	280	58	21
Electronic & Computer Engineering (UL)	UL	579	58	10
Mathematics & Statistics (UL)	UL	105	47	45
Science & Information Technology (LRTC)	LRTC	223	82	37

Table 2. Full-Time Students in Third-Level Departments, Academic Year, 1995/1996 (Limerick Regional Technical College 1996, University of Limerick 1996b)

Department / Course	Y1	F	%	Y2	F	%	Y3	F	%	Y4	F	%
B.Sc. Computer Systems (UL)	94	22	23	63	9	14	65	15	23	58	12	21
B.Sc. Applied Mathematics & Computing (UL)	35	14	40	32	14	44	17	8	47	21	11	52
B.Sc. Information Systems (LRTC)	118	40	34	58	22	38	31	12	39	16	8	50
Overall Total	247	76	30	153	45	29	113	35	28	95	31	32

Table 3. Full-Time Students in B.Sc. Degrees, Academic Year, 1995/1996 (Limerick Regional Technical College 1996, University of Limerick 1996b)

role models has been identified as one of the main reasons why female students do not pursue careers in science and technology (Murphy 1996). In a more recent study of Irish women in management, 47% of respondents quoted lack of female role models as a reason for the failure of women to break into managerial ranks (McGann 1996). In 1990 a study sponsored by the American Association of University Women (AAUW) concluded that one of the major problems with attracting and keeping women and minorities in computer science is the lack of role models at all levels, particularly senior levels (Pfleeger and Mertz 1995). During a study compiled with 50 WITS members in Ireland by Allen (1995), 88% of those interviewed identified meetings between school girls and people working in science and technology careers as a need. These studies indicate the importance of role models to schoolgirls when making their career choices.

Acknowledging that second-level female students do not pursue careers in science and technology, as evidenced from the statistics in the Tables 1, 2, 3, and that a lack of suitable role models was one reason for this imbalance, WITS produced a role model booklet in conjunction with the Department of Education in 1992. The booklet detailed the career paths of 20 women technologists and scientists and was distributed to every second level girl's school in Ireland. This booklet is currently being updated.

As a result of the success of the role model booklet, the idea of a role model day was suggested. Such a day would provide transition, fifth and sixth year female students with an opportunity to meet working women scientists, technologists and engineers. To date, four successful role model days have been organised – one in Dublin in Mount Temple School in 1993, two in Cork RTC in 1994 and 1995 with the support from the NOW project and one in Limerick RTC in 1996. Three more days are currently in the planning stages. This paper concentrates on the Limerick Role Model Day experience.

3. Organising a Role Model Day

Role Model days are about students meeting working women rather than a dedicated schools' promotion. They are not aimed at providing generic career information, specific information on points, courses and colleges or 'hands-on-taster' sessions. The women talk to small groups of schoolgirls about what is involved in their jobs on a day-to-day basis, the qualifications they required, the choices they have made, etc. Students also have an opportunity to meet the role models informally over lunch. The speakers at the Limerick Role Model Day included a localisation engineer, software programmer, electronic engineer, quality manager, apprentice tool fitter, mechanical engineer, database administrator, marine rescue pilot, and a cardio-technician.

With feedback and experience the general structure of the day has evolved during the years. Approximately 160 students attended the Limerick Role Model Day. It began at ten o'clock on a Saturday morning with an introductory session. This session was attended by all participants and lasted about 35 minutes. It included a short address by a career guidance counsellor and a speaker from the food industry on the wide variety of careers available in the food industry in Ireland today. The students were then divided into groups of approximately 40 and each group attended two workshops, with a short coffee break between workshops. Each workshop had four speakers, who each described her own career path and answered questions. The chairwoman of each workshop proved very useful in initiating discussion and creating a relaxed atmosphere. Workshops lasted approximately 45 minutes each. The students were then given an opportunity to ask the speakers questions informally over lunch. Posters were displayed and videos shown during the informal sessions.

A number of parents and teachers also attended the day. If parents and teachers wished to attend they were made welcome but primarily the day was aimed at second level girls. It was decided to limit the attendance to girls only, as these were our target audience and we felt that this would make best use of limited resources. This was emphasised in the advertisements for the day, which included national and local radio and newspaper coverage as well as mailshots to 128 schools within a 60-mile radius. The mailshot to each school included information for the principal, career guidance counsellor, transition year co-ordinator, science teacher and parents' council.

The three basic requirements for a Role Model day are speakers, a venue and administration. To date, WITS has organised the speakers, the host organisation has arranged the venue and WITS and the host organisation have worked jointly on the programme and administration. None of the Role Model days would have been possible without the support of the host institutions who provide valuable administration and financial support.

4. Choosing Role Models

When choosing role models for the Role Model day in Limerick, a number of criteria were followed.

The women were all local, living or working within a 50-mile radius of the city. It is important for students to see that women in the locality can become involved in the non-traditional careers, and not assume that those who pursue are from further a field.

Secondly, while it is important that the role models who speak are good at presenting themselves to the female students, we do not require the women to be over-achievers. The role models should reflect what women usually cope with while holding a job outside the home – the experience of being women in non-traditional roles, in jobs usually associated with men; coping with childcare facilities (and the lack of them); managing 'two jobs' and other issues. In fact, one role model was not available to attend at short notice, owing to childcare problems.

A range of careers was presented to the female students. The careers in Limerick spanned apprenticeships and jobs requiring certificates, diplomas and degrees. From a computing standpoint, they covered careers such as software programming, hardware engineering and database administration. Emphasis was placed on the different routes to each career, and on the need for students to examine all the options before they eliminated a career. They had the opportunity to meet role models who reached their position through a variety of career ladders.

Finally a range of experience must be presented. Some of the role models who spoke were recent graduates, others had up to 10 years' experience in their jobs. There were role models who changed jobs on a regular basis for various reasons and some who had changed direction in their careers. Role models who had reached management level also presented.

While we aimed to present an ideal variety of role models to female students, and we believe, succeeded in doing so, the fact was that all the women who spoke did so on a voluntary basis, on a Saturday morning. Contact was made through the Women In Technology and Science membership list, and through personal contact.

5. Feedback from Students

Feedback on the Role Model day was taken at two different times. At the end of the presentations, before students went home, they were asked to fill in comment sheets. Nine months after the event, we visited a school and received feedback from 14 students who attended the Role Model day.

5.1 Immediate Feedback

All participants were asked to complete a questionnaire before they left and 54 students completed it. The majority of students were informed of the day through their schools, with 17% hearing about the Role Model day outside of school.

Workshops were successful, with 48% of students identifying the individual workshops as the best part of the day, while 21% of students identified the 'informal session' or 'talking to speakers' as the best part. Thirty-one percent of respondents identified the introductory session as the worst part of the day, but 19% indicated that there was no worst part. Fifty-six percent of respondents stated that too few areas were covered by the talks, with no one indicating that too many areas were covered. Only 17% thought that the range of careers was 'wide enough'.

Overall the comments were very positive, with 87% of respondents saying that they would recommend the day to others. We also received requests for more information on particular careers and courses and requests to visit schools.

Some of the comments from students included:

It has made me feel even more confident that I can succeed in my career options.

. . . very supporting and encouraging to women who are interested in Science, Engineering and Technology.

Definitely worth going to.

It has encouraged me to work hard at my science subject.

It has given me direction and helped me to realise that all these careers are available for women.

I never realised all the different opportunities for each career.

5.2 Feedback – Nine Months Later

At the school we visited for follow-up feedback, we spoke to 14 students, 9% of the attendance at the Role Model day. Since the Role Model day, these students have been required to choose subjects, or will make college choices within the next three months. Seven (50%) of the students have since requested information from other sources either about careers discussed on the day or careers similar to those discussed. Three students changed the careers that they had been considering to science or technology options

A few interesting comments made were:

I was turned off Food Science because what she talked about was uninteresting.

It was nice to know that someone cared about our careers.

The day was very informative and I felt that it did open up new possibilities and avenues for me.

It cleared a lot of my 'woolly' thinking about technology.

Examining why students have decided to pursue a particular career, be it in science or technology or otherwise, role models influenced nine (64%) of the students. This figure demonstrates why it is important for students to meet with women who have pursued careers in the non-traditional areas.

6. Conclusion

It is proposed that the Department of Education will fund future Role Model days. Initially, during a pilot scheme WITS will work closely with both the Department of Education and host institutes in the development of generic material, programme and administration. WITS will organise the speakers. At the end of the pilot scheme, the Department of Education and the host institutes will assume responsibility for the venue, administration and programme, but WITS will continue to organise the speakers.

In addition, as part of its educational brief, WITS has developed a series of display boards featuring photographs and short narratives of working women scientists and technologists. These boards are used extensively at Role Model days, College Open Days, information evenings and science exhibitions. The association also maintains a list of women who are willing to go to schools in their locality to speak to students about their careers. This list is circulated to all schools via the career counsellors network.

It is hoped that all these initiatives will continue to encourage young women at least to consider careers in Science and Technology.

Acknowledgements

The authors would like to thank other members of Women In Technology and Science who helped in the organisation of this and other Role Model Days; all speakers at the Role Model Days; sponsors - Limerick Regional Technical College and the University of Limerick Women's Studies Course Board; staff and students of Colaiste Mhuire, Limerick who participated in feedback sessions.

References

Allen, J. (1995). Presented at *Forfas STI Awareness Campaign*. Dublin City University, Dublin, Ireland.

Egan, O. (1995). Proceedings of Conference on *Women Staff in Irish Colleges*. University College Galway.

Klawe, M. and Levenson, N. (1995). 'Women in Computing: Where are We Now?' *Communications of the ACM* 38 (1): 29-35.

Limerick Regional Technical College (1996). *Census Returns*. Limerick.

Murphy, C. (1996). 'Limiting Choice- The Least Productive Course'. *The Irish Times*, 9 January.

McGann, K. (1996). *Irish women who have broken through the Glass Ceiling in Business.* M.B.S. Thesis, Michael Smurfit Graduate School of Business, University College Dublin.

O'Dubhchair, K. and Hunter, N. (1995). 'Gender Issues in Computing', in Proceedings of *3rd Annual Conference on the Teaching of Computing"*, 244-49. Dublin.

Pearl, A. (1995). 'Introduction to Women in Computing'. *Communications of the ACM* 38 (1): 26-8.

Pfleeger, S. L. and Mertz, N. (1995). 'Executive Mentoring What Makes it Work?' *Communications of the ACM* 38 (1): 63-73.

University of Limerick (1996a*). College of Informatics and Electronics Annual Policy Review.* Limerick.

University of Limerick (1996b). *Admissions Office Internal Report.* Limerick.

Post-Beijing and Beyond: Gendered Perspectives on Access

Leslie Regan Shade

Constructive Advice, 221 Patterson Ave., Ottawa ON K1S 1Y4, CANADA

Abstract

This paper provides a gendered perspective on access to the emerging information infrastructure within the international context. It briefly discusses international public policy work on gender equity in national information infrastructure initiatives; and provides preliminary actions towards gender equity in the information infrastructure within the global information infrastructure.

1. Introduction: Public Policy and Gender Equity in the Information Infrastructure

Public policies concerning access to and equity in the emergent information infrastructure are of compelling importance now. Within the North American (and more specifically, Canadian) context, policy statements and declarations on gender equity in the new information technologies have been recently formulated.[1]

Despite the significant activities surrounding the Global Information Infrastructure (GII)[2], issues surrounding gender have not been considered. Global strategies that encourage gender equity in the information infrastructure are underway, however, thanks to the initial and follow-up efforts of the Fourth World Conference on Women held in Beijing in 1995.

This paper looks briefly at these activities, considers a gendered perspective on access within both the developed and developing world, and provides some preliminary actions towards achieving gender equity in the information infrastructure.

2. Access Issues

Several recent demographic surveys on the Internet reveal that women's participation on the Internet is not as high as their male counterparts, but that their access is slowly increasing.[3] This is especially true in North America, where studies indicate that women comprise over a third of Internet users. However, the situation changes for women in Europe. According to GVU's Sixth WWW User Study, while the gender ratio in North America is 31.4% female and 68.6% male, in Europe users are still predominantly male (80.2%).
(See <URL: http://www.gvu.gatech.edu/gvu/user_surveys/survey-10-1996/>).

At this point, statistics are not available on the specific demographics of users in the South or developing countries.

Access to the information infrastructure encompasses not just physical and technical mechanisms but a myriad economic and social factors. Public policy discussions on access, including those surrounding the GII, mainly discuss the technical barriers to access; for instance, the hardware and software to support communication, resource discovery tools, and issues surrounding standards, interoperability, privacy, security and intellectual property protection.

It is assumed, and advocated, that private industry will take the lead in developing and building the diverse technical components that go into making the 'information highways'. Furthermore, advances in developing and deploying the GII will depend on deregulation and the fostering of a competitive marketplace. Public policies, both national and international, have been therefore promoting the removal of regulatory, trade and policy barriers that could possibly impede competition and limit widespread deployment of the GII. In the current fiscal and policy climate, the mantra of the marketplace as 'driving' both availability and affordability (and hence, meeting universal access goals) is presumed.[4]

Some of the particularities of gender which can influence access include: access to the hardware and software to support communications; access to a user-centred design; access to online gender issue information services; and workplace issues. The following section sketches these access variables, with the differences in perception between the needs of women in developed versus developing countries given.

2.1 Access to the hardware and software to support communications

In developed countries, professional women in the corporate mainstream, academics and students at colleges and universities, and financially-advantaged women can more easily access Internet resources, either through institutional or private avenues. One of the biggest challenges is widening access to the information infrastructure for women who are not institutionally affiliated in industry, unions or academia. As governments and corporations downsize, it becomes increasingly difficult for new entrants to gain a foothold in various institutions.

The North American community networking movement plays a vital role in promoting public access (Schuler 1996), along with the creation of public access sites in public libraries, community centres, laundromats and cafes. Many public access sites have become community information and resource centres with training and community content creation as a mandate.

In developing countries, the use of networking technologies as a tool for international dialogue and information exchange is increasing, but their development should allow for equal participation by women and men of all incomes, linguistic groups and geographic bases.

The Panos Institute (1996) examined Internet access in developing countries in the South and concluded that the gap between developing and developed countries is considerable. Internet technology is both more scarce and more expensive in the South. An information gap already exists, in that at least 80% of the world's population still lack the most basic telecommunications: 'The information revolution has only reached a few universities, companies, journalists, researchers and governments in developing countries. There is a danger of a new information elitism which excludes the majority of the world's population.'

Obstacles to Internet access include physical factors such as inadequate telephone and electricity supply; the lack of computer and other technical equipment; outdated or defunct software packages; and the high cost of general telecommunications infrastructure, such as telephone connections and equipment. Social factors include the lack of adequate training and the staff necessary to support such training; and the absence of information and resources in local languages.

2.2 Access to a user-centred design

Design of the information infrastructure must be easily accessible to the broad population, including people with disabilities. Multiple access methods will be necessary to account for differences in both human capacities and cultures(Shneiderman 1995). These issues become more salient when we consider providing access to developing countries, where there are key barriers to access in terms of poverty, literacy, education and training, and a multiplicity of languages.

Participatory design (PD) practices, where the users of the technology initiate active participation in the systems design of the computer systems (Schuler and Namioka 1993), has not explicitly addressed gender as a factor. Balka's research into designing computer networks for North American feminist non-profit organisations has introduced an analysis of gender as a factor in PD projects (Balka and Doucette 1994; Balka 1997) by suggesting that notions of PD be expanded from considerations of business norms to encompass a wider range of organisational settings, including organisations that are unstable, poorly capitalised, and that include a wide range of learners.

Nor has participatory design focused on the needs of developing countries. A key component of this would involve recognising and promoting the knowledge and daily work practices of indigenous people and local communities. This obviously includes the recognition of the value of women's indigenous knowledge and skills.

2.3 Development of Online Gender Issue Information Services:

Use of the World Wide Web for women's content has increased substantially. Within North America, content covers a diverse topical range – for the academic, the activist, and the anarchist. As well as solid and indispensable information and resources, there is a sense that information can be empowering and have a playfulness and zestful irony.

The development of online gender issue information services will create added benefit. As universal access policies and the notion of essential services develop, the kinds of information and resources that can and should be provided for women needs to be recognised. Should this be information that resides at the government and community level? What should be considered 'basic content services', and how can one ensure that balanced perspectives be featured (i.e. information on childbirth options)?

Within the developing world, the promotion of women's indigenous knowledge and skills is vital. This also includes allowing women to identify the information that they want and need and assisting them in determining the appropriate delivery mechanism (i.e. a combination of online and offline modes). Also, the repackaging of information (i.e. from hardcopy to electronic, and vice versa) is a way of making sure that all alternative media can be disseminated in as many forms as possible.

2.4 Workplace Issues

In developed countries, the current rhetoric is that society and jobs are moving towards a 'knowledge-based economy' fuelled by the information infrastructure. Particular issues with respect to gender and the knowledge-based economy include:

- What jobs are being de-skilled by the introduction of computerisation and networked communications? In particular, how are women's jobs being de-skilled? For instance, if libraries and Kindergarten–Twelfth-Grade educational institutions are being wired, how is this affecting a workforce predominantly staffed by women?
- How are women using networked technologies in entrepreneurial ways? Given the increase in self-employment amongst women, how are they involved in the commercial end of networking (i.e. as consultants, owners of businesses, content creators)?
- What are the obstacles, including educational barriers, and family support mechanisms such as childcare, for women in entering and thriving in the high technology field?

In particular, the impact of telework on women needs to be explored. So far, public policy has not addressed the broader social issues of telework (Borowy, Johnson 1995). Although telework has been promoted as a way for women to work at home while combining childcare responsibilities, the added stress that juggling these dual roles can create for the teleworker, the employer and family dynamics is often left unrecognised. The creation of flexible childcare arrangements that benefit the teleworker needs to be addressed; but, given the retreat in North America from investing in quality childcare at the government level, this seems unlikely.

Economist Juliet Schor (1992) has documented an average increase in working hours (the equivalent of an extra month a year) for most full-time employed people. This concomitant erosion of leisure is particularly acute for working mothers, with estimates of time spent on domestic responsibilities ranging from 25 to 45 hours per week. One of the questions to ask is whether or not new information utilities will lead to an expansion of everyday tasks, raise standards of work or efficiency, or increase or decrease women's leisure time.

The issue of work (and more particularly, gendered work) within developing countries raises a host of issues related to women as supporters of their family and their informal role in the production, reproduction and distribution of material goods. The feminisation of poverty as a global phenomenon also reflects a prevailing gender bias in research and policy for the use of science and technology in developed and developing countries (Missing Links 1995). In addition, access to appropriate technologies and educational and technical training needs to be increased and sustained.

3. Post-Beijing Actions

The final Beijing Declaration and Platform for Action from the Fourth World Conference on Women reiterated the need for women, especially in developing countries, to enhance their skills, knowledge and access to information technology. (Item 237, Beijing Declaration and Platform for Action 1995).

Strategic objective J.1 of the Beijing Declaration identified the need to 'increase the participation and access of women to expression and decision-making in and through the media and new technologies of communication'. A series of actions called on governments, NGOs, the media and private industry to encourage and recognise women's electronic networks; to promote and develop educational and training programmes for women in new communication technologies; and to encourage the use of computer networking as a means of strengthening women's participation in democratic processes and as a means of encouraging alternative media that promotes women's voices.

On 26–8 June 1996, an Expert Workshop on Global Information through Computer Networking Technology in the Follow-up to the Fourth World Conference on Women (FWCW) was held at the United Nations headquarters in New York. The Workshop, sponsored by the UN Division for the Advancement of Women (DAW), the UN Development Fund for Women (UNIFEM) and the International Research and Training Institute for the Advancement of Women (INSTRAW), looked at how to facilitate global information exchange for monitoring the implementation of the Beijing Platform for Action through the use of computer networking technology. The Expert Workshop devised a series of recommendations to implement a World Wide Web site, WomenWatch. The Workshop also looked at issues surrounding access and training issues; best practices with global networking for women; and principles for cooperation between NGOs and the United Nations in the design and implementation of the WomenWatch project.

In conceptualising WomenWatch, several salient questions arose:
1) How can an Internet site mobilise, build coalitions and offer a space to share experiences and lessons learned?
2) How can women in the South play an active role as both producers and creators of content on the Internet?
3) What partnerships can be developed to increase women's presence on the Internet, particularly in the South?, and
4) How can a Web site 'ensure that the commitments made in Beijing become reality for women everywhere?'

Advocacy and mobilisation through electronic communications via three related activities was considered:
1) providing vital information resources
2) serving as an organising tool, and
3) facilitating outreach activities.

Partnering and partnerships was also another important activity identified. This would include advocacy and mobilisation with: diverse media – mainstream and alternative; the private sector; non-governmental organisations (NGOs); diverse women's organisations; the United Nations; various governments; the academic community; specialised libraries and new users.

Another important area of action which WomenWatch identified was to influence telecommunications policy issues surrounding access, security, privacy and intellectual property: 'It was recommended that the WomenWatch initiative play a pro-active role in the telecommunications and information policy process within the United Nations system and *vis a vis* other multilateral and regional organisations, to ensure that gender considerations become and remain an integral part of those discussions and decisions. This would include a voice with groups like the World Bank, the International Telecommunications Union, European Union and the United Nations Commission for Science and Technology.'

Other areas identified by WomenWatch included the development of a 'hospitable' online environment for women, the development of software; and the conceptualisation of a broad World Wide Web strategy regarding issues surrounding interoperability, interactivity, navigation tools and language.

4. Preliminary Actions Towards Achieving Gender Equity

The International Development Research Centre (IDRC) Gender and Information Working Group suggests that policy recommendations should account for several factors, including the information needs of both men and women to 'foster an understanding of the mutual benefits to be gained by society' (IDRC 1995, 279), and that approaches should be participatory, encouraging community-wide participation in the design and management of initiatives. Public policy formulations on universal access should consider the following actions with respect to ensuring gender equity in the information infrastructure.

4.1 Access to the Technological and Social Infrastructures

Access to computers and the Internet is a major difficulty for women, especially in developing counties. Access is multi-faceted, including access to both the technological and the social infrastructure. How the information needs of a diverse public, in both developed and developing worlds, can be met is a particular challenge.

Although explorations on how to assess and subsidise universal service to basic network services are underway in North America, the needs of women and women's groups must be considered as these universal provisions are deliberated. Likewise, the coordination of national and international efforts, particularly with respect to initiatives that provide training, access to hardware and software, and mentoring opportunities, within the context of the Global Information Infrastructure, should be expedited.

- The promotion of community-based computer networks and a strategy to encourage more women and women's groups to take an active role in participating in content creation, training, mentoring and management of community networks should be facilitated.
- The development of online gender information services and the creation of a 'hospitable' environment should be encouraged. Identification of the kinds of information and resources can and should be provided for women should be made, with a plurality of viewpoints respecting the tenets of free speech represented. This can include information that resides in the federal, state/provincial, municipal and community level; and, in developing countries, attention given to the promotion of women's indigenous knowledge.
- Funding mechanisms for the creation of content by women and women's groups, and the provision of training programs in basic and advanced HTML and networking skills should be encouraged. To expand upon the recommendation of the Beijing Platform for Action, training and assistance in direct use of the Internet within developing countries needs to be broadened.
- The development of public access sites in public libraries, community centres and women's centres should be facilitated.

4.2 Privacy and Security:

Technical means that can guarantee the privacy and integrity of information must be encouraged. In order to protect computer systems, networks and information, information security and privacy protections are of vital importance. Infrastructure-wide security services include:

identification and authentication (the ability to verify a user's identity and a message's authenticity); confidentiality (the protection of information from unauthorised access and disclosure); integrity (the protection of information from unauthorised modification or accidental loss); nonrepudiation (the ability to prevent senders from denying they have sent messages and receivers from denying they have received messages); and, availability (the ability to prevent denial of service).

- Cryptography can improve identification and access control through password encryption; protect confidentiality and data integrity by encrypting the data; and improve nonrepudiation services through encrypted electronic signature and related means. The use of public key cryptography such as Pretty Good Privacy (PGP) and Privacy Enhanced Mail (PEM) is advocated.
- The development of harassment guidelines, in coordination with commercial online services, Internet Service Providers, K-12 schools, universities, and the private sector, should be advanced.

4.3 Employment and Workplace Issues:

Networked technology is dramatically changing work and the high-tech global economy. At the same time that it is creating innovative opportunities for time and cost-efficient collaborative endeavours, it is also leading to both de-skilling and job losses in many industries.

- The de-skilling of work (particularly those in pink-collar ghettos traditionally occupied by women) by information technologies should be explored.
- Issues surrounding telework, including childcare, employee benefits, and ergonomics, should be researched more thoroughly.
- The obstacles (educational barriers, lack of affordable childcare) for women in entering and thriving in the high-tech fields should also be a priority consideration.
- The concept of lifelong learning as it applies to women (from young girls to seniors) should be explored.
- The effect of a knowledge-based economy on developing countries needs to be addressed and assessed. How can women's indigenous knowledge be transferred to this milieu?

McCorduck and Ramsey enthuse that the new information technologies flatten hierarchies, provide flexible work and social arrangements, and because of this '. . . women will flourish. This technology means brawn no longer matters. Brains do, and have we got brains!' (McCorduck, Ramsey 1996, 7).

Although it is important to present positive and glowing perceptions about the possibilities and outcomes of the information infrastructure in order to stimulate and promote the activities of women, it is also important to keep in mind that constructive and socially redeeming policy-making needs to be effected. Such policy-sparity in access (technological and social) to the information infrastructure, as well as providing practical solutions regarding issues surrounding work and employment, and privacy and security. Given the fast pace towards the implementation of a global information infrastructure, it is urgent that women in developing countries have a voice in the development, dissemination, and deployment of the technology, and that women in developed countries assist them in reaching these goals.

Notes

1. In Canada, the public interest group The Coalition for Public Information (CPI) included gender equity recommendations in its final report. See *Future-Knowledge: a public policy framework for the information highway*, 1995.
http://www.nlc-bnc.ca/documents/infopol/canada/cpi-fk.txt
    Canada's Information Highway Advisory Council's (IHAC) final report recognised that gender and social barriers need to be removed to ensure equitable and universal access to the information infrastructure. In May 1996, IHAC released its response to the Council's final September 1995 report, wherein it reiterated its commitment to ensuring universal access to all Canadians, with particular attention paid to the needs of a multicultural and bilingual society. The need to examine gender as one factor affecting access was also emphasised. See IHAC, *Building the Information Society: Moving Canada into the 21st Century*, May 1996; and *Connection, Community, Content: The Challenge of the Information Highway*, September 1995. URL:http://strategis.ic.gc.ca/ihac.

2. US Vice President Al Gore has been instrumental in promoting the GII. He exults that the GII 'will forever change the way citizens around the world live, learn, work and communicate . . . The GII is a historic undertaking. It is strengthened by participation, bolstered by openness, and fortified by strong nations and talented people pursuing dreams of a better tomorrow.' (See *Global Issues, Electronic Journals of the U.S. Information Agency*, 1 (12), September 1996.
http://www.usia.gov/journals/itgic/0996/ijge/ijge0996.htm).
    To promote the US vision of the GII, the telecommunications sector has been liberalised and there is a movement to work with international governments to eliminate obstacles that stand in the way of communication and information industries competing in foreign markets. Critics (non-US citizens) have remarked that GII stands for 'Global Information Invasion'. See Kahin, B. and Nesson, C. (eds.) *Borders in Cyberspace: Information Policy and the Global Information Infrastructure*, Cambridge, MA: MIT Press 1997.

3. O'Reilly and Associates put the US Internet male to female ratio as 67% male and 33% female. See O'Reilly and Associates. 1 October 1995.
http://www.ora.com/research/users/charts/net-gender.html.
    A survey conducted by Matrix Information and Directory Services and Texas Internet Consulting revealed a male to female ratio of 62.7% to 37.3% for the general Internet. See John S. Quarterman and Smoot Carl-Mitchell, May 1995, J. S. Quarterman, February 1996, Ages and genders, *Matrix News* 6(2).
http://www3.mids.org/ids3/ids3sum.603.

4. For a look at some of the myriad factors that comprise the social infrastructure (network literacy, and the diverse social variables affecting geographic, linguistic, income and class-based barriers) see Clement, A. and Shade, L.R. 'What Do We Mean By "Universal Access"?: Social Perspectives in a Canadian Context,' *Proceedings of INET96*, Montreal, 25–8 June, 1996. For a look at international public policy pronouncements on universal access, see 'Universal Access: The Next Killer App', by L.R. Shade, a paper produced for *Defining and Maintaining Universal Access to Basic Network Services: Canadian Directions in an International Context*. Invitational Workshop sponsored by Industry Canada and the Faculty of Information Studies, Toronto, 14–16, March 1996. Both are available at:
http://www.fis.utoronto.ca/research/iprp/ua.

References

Balka, E. (1997). 'Participatory Design in Women's Organizations: The Social World of Organizational Structure and the Gendered Nature of Expertise'. *Gender, Work and Organizations* 4(2): 99-115.

Balka, E. and Doucette, L. (July 26, 1994). 'The Accessibility of Computers To Organizations Serving Women in the Province of Newfoundland: Preliminary Study Results'. *Electronic Journal of Virtual Culture* 2(3).
http://www.inform.umd.edu/Educational_Resources/AcademicResourcesByTopic/WomensStudies/Computing/Articles+ResearchPapers/ArachnetJournal/balka

Beijing Declaration and Platform for Action. (1995).
http://women.usia.gov/usia/beijpg.htm.

Borowy, J. and Johnson, T. (1995). 'Unions Confront Work Reorganization and The Rise of Precarious Employment: Home-Based Work in the Garment Industry and Federal Public Service', in Schenk, C., and Anderson, J. (eds.). *Re-Shaping Work: Union Responses to Technological Change*, 29. Don Mills: Ontario Federation of Labour, Technology Adjustment Research Programme.

FCC Documents on the Telecommunications Act of 1996.
http://www.fcc.gov/telecom.html

IDRC Gender and Information Working Group. (1995). 'Information as a Transformative Tool', in *Missing Links: Gender Equity in Science and Technology for Development*, 267. Gender Working Group, United Nations Commission on Science and Technology for Development. Ottawa: International Development Research Centre.

McCorduck, P. and Ramsay, N. (1996). *The Futures of Women: Scenarios for the 21st Century.* Reading, MA: Addison-Wesley Publishing Co..

Missing Links: Gender Equity in Science and Technology for Development. (1995). Gender Working Group, United Nations Commission on Science and Technology for Development. International Development Research Centre: Ottawa.

Panos Institute (1996). *The Internet and the South: Superhighway or Dirt-Track?*
http://www.netural.com/lip/file_a03.html

Schor, J. B. (1992). *The Overworked American.*.New York: Basic Books.

Schuler, D. (1996). *New Community Networks: Wired for Change.* New York: ACM Press/Addison-Wesley Publishing Company.

Schuler, D. and Namioka, A. (1993). *Participatory Design: Principles and Practices.* Hillsdale, NJ: Lawrence Erlbaum Associates, Publishers.

Shneiderman, B. (January 1995). 'The Information Superhighway: for the people'. *Communications of the ACM* 38: 162.

United Nations. *Report on The Expert Workshop on 'Global Information through Computer Networking Technology in the follow-up to the Fourth World Conference on Women (FWCW)'*, 1996.
gopher://gopher.un.org/00/sec/dpcsd/daw/REP

WomenWatch Homepage
http://www.un.org/dpcsd/daw/dawwatch.htm

Women, the Information Revolution and the Beijing Conference. *Women2000* Issue No.1/1996 - October 1996. United Nations Division for the Advancement of Women (DAW).
http://www.un.org/dpcsd/daw/w2ww.htm

The Internet - a 'feminine' technology?

Margit Pohl

Department for Design and Technology Assessment, University of Technology Vienna, Moellwaldplatz 5/3, A-1040 Vienna, Austria

Abstract

There are contradictory opinions amongst feminist researchers as to whether the Internet is a more 'feminine' technology than more traditional computer technology. On the one hand, the more communicative character of the Internet might be better adapted to women's needs: on the other, pornography and aggressive interaction styles might deter many women from using it. Further, it can be argued that the ambiguous character of the Internet makes it impossible to categorise it along the male-female continuum at all. The following paper addresses theoretical and empirical aspects of this discussion.

1. Introduction

Women are supposed to have a rather holistic and 'soft' style of interacting with computers whereas men are thought to be more analytic and 'tough'. This assumption has led scientists to believe that it would be appropriate to develop gender specific computer programs which make allowances for the different cognitive styles of women and men (see, for example, Rada 1991, Shneiderman 1992). There are theories about different cognitive styles in cognitive psychology based on similar dichotomies: mind/body, reason/passion, nature/culture (see e.g. Witkin et al 1962). One of the main problems with these theories is that they do not question the female/male dichotomy. Gender differences seem to be given and natural. Women's choice is restricted either to adapting to male values, or to developing a completely different model of computer usage based on what is traditionally assumed to be female: emotion and person-centredness.

My argument against such cognitive theories does not suggest that differences between women and men cannot be observed. Apparently, they can be observed. The question rather is whether categories are defined in such a way that inherently accepts the female/male dichotomy as given, or whether they make the formation of gender differences transparent. The first is a rather static approach, whereas the second implies that the historical development of categories and their permanent construction in interaction processes has to be taken into account. The important point about the dynamic approach is not the existence of gender differences as such but the question of how the concept of gender will develop in the future. It is quite well known by now that the first computer programmers were women. This work was quickly redefined as a typically male kind of occupation. After the introduction of the Internet, discussions about the character of computer systems started again. The Internet has much to do with communication between people. Is it, therefore, a 'feminine' technology or at least a technology that is adapted to women's needs?

I think it is necessary to analyse the conditions for the implementation of a specific technology and its effects in great detail before trying to find an answer to the question of its overall character. Therefore, I want to discuss the 'feminine character' of the Internet by using a concrete example – the World Wide Web (WWW). Sherry Turkle, a well known scientist from MIT, argues that the Internet supports a more feminine style of computer usage which she calls 'soft mastery'. I would argue that the character of the Internet is more ambiguous and that it also supports masculine strategies. In addition, I doubt that the concept of gender specific computer usage will make it easier for women to become computer experts. When computer usage is seen as gender specific, the expertise of women will, by definition, always be limited.

2. Gender and the Internet

Contrary to popular belief, the Internet is not a homogeneous technology but provides many different services. Among the most important of these are email and the World Wide Web. Sherry Turkle also mentions MUDs (Multi-User Dungeons or Multi-User Domains) which are (predominantly) text-based adventure games. MUDs enable the players to assume any identity they want, which also means that women can pretend to be men and men can pretend to be women (Bruckman 1993). To a certain extent this also happens with email. There is a very popular Internet myth about a male psychiatrist who posed as a disabled woman for years and developed very close relationships with many women on the net (gender swapping).

Email, in a narrow sense, is a rather private form of communication which can convey the impression of great intimacy, a mixture of the telephone and the traditional letter. Based on email technology, mailing lists enable multiple participants to discuss various topics, which is a public form of communication. It can be assumed that there are visible distinctions between these two forms of communication, although there is still not very much empirical evidence about this topic. The WWW is something completely different. Basically, direct interaction between people is not possible. MUDs, on the other hand, support direct interaction in a public form. The most important difference between MUDs and mailing lists is that MUDs are usually fictitious. They are the ideal forum for the projection of one's fantasies and wishes. It is quite obvious that the various services of the Internet have different effects on gender relations in the Internet.

So far the Internet has been a very fluid technology which can still be shaped to a certain extent but it is an open question how it should be shaped to support women and their particular needs and interests. Well-known feminists express contradictory views about the Internet and its potential influence upon the status of women. For Sherry Turkle, the Internet is, to a certain extent, a female technology which supports special female abilities. Dale Spender's attitude is more critical although she also points out that the Internet supports the communicative skills of women.

Turkle's ideas about the Internet are based upon the categories of soft and hard mastery (Turkle 1990, Turkle 1995). She is especially interested in the concepts or images people form about technology. In the course of her research she found that women and men have different attitudes towards computers. She conceptualised these attitudes using the terms of 'hard' and 'soft' mastery. Hard mastery is, for example, the standard, rule-driven, top-down approach of structured programming. In contrast, soft mastery or bricolage is bottom-up and consists of playing with the elements of a program or with bits of code. These approaches are not only relevant for programming but for computer usage as a whole. Hard mastery is, for example, based on the analytical style of 'Western' philosophers. On the other hand, there is a similarity between soft mastery and the more intuitive and holistic style of 'non-Western' science. The distinction between soft and hard mastery is, to a certain extent, related to the female/male dichotomy although Turkle points out that no style is unique to either women or men. She argues that skills which are typical for soft mastery are an important part of girls' socialisation in Western societies – negotiation, compromise, give and take. Typical male behaviour – decisiveness and the imposition of will – are more appropriate for hard mastery. It must be mentioned, however, that what Turkle describes as a feminine style of computer usage is again a style which is only typical for white, middle-class women. It is by no means clear if her results hold for other groups of women who up until now have had no access to the computer.

It is important to note that Turkle uses interviews as her main source of data. This means that she investigates the images people form about the use of computers rather than the concrete practices they adopt. It must be mentioned, however, that there is evidence that the actual differences in cognitive style between women and men are less obvious than the images people form about them. Research on gender differences in cognitive abilities shows that differences are usually restricted to rather narrow skills and that these cannot be observed on a very general level. The only cognitive abilities for which rather significant gender differences can be shown are visual-spatial abilities. These abilities consist of at least four factors – spatial perception, mental rotation, spatial visualization, and spatiotemporal ability. Even in this area results are often ambiguous, and fairly consistent differences can only be found for three of the four factors (Halpern 1992). Stepan analysed the programming styles of women and men and could not find any significant differences between them, although there are pronounced differences among programmers in different institutions (Stepan 1994). Sherry Turkle's work, on the other hand, shows that most people have the impression that these differences are considerable. People try to make sense of the world which surrounds them, and in this process they probably overrate these gender differences.

Turkle points out that modern networked computer systems do not require analytical programming skills anymore. The users do not have to follow a predefined set of rules but rather can try out different solutions and choose the one which suits them best. Modern computer networks support holistic and intuitive strategies:

> The computer culture is close to the point where full membership does not require programming skills, but is accorded to people who use software out of a box. Bricoleurs function well here. Recall that they like to get to know a new environment by interacting with it. When all the computer culture offered were programming environments, the bricoleur wanted to get close to the code. Now when dealing with simulation software, the bricoleur can create the feeling of closeness to the object by manipulating virtual objects on the screen. (Turkle 1995, 61).

It should be noticed that Turkle's argument only applies to certain services of the Internet – WWW and MUDs, but not to email. Furthermore, a certain amount of analytical or programming skill is still necessary, e.g. for those persons who want to develop their own WWW documents. If women concentrate on their bricolage skills, it will be men who provide information on the

WWW. This is already the case. The authors of WWW-pages are predominantly male. This shows that it is necessary to be very careful about any argument concerning the 'female' nature of the Internet and to avoid over-generalisations.

Dale Spender, another feminist researcher who writes about the Internet, is more critical. On the one hand, she points out that cyberspace can be a very agreeable place for women:

> After all, when you stop to think about it, the medium is more attuned to women's way of working in the world than to men's. Cyberspace has the potential to be egalitarian, to bring everyone into a network arrangement. It has the capacity to create community; to provide untold opportunities for communication, exchange, and keeping in touch. In other words, it is like an enhanced telephone (Spender 1995, 229).

On the other hand, Spender points out that there are still many barriers which prevent women from participating fully in the Internet culture. This does not mean that women lack the skills to use and shape the Internet. There are many examples in computer science and adjacent fields which show that this is not the case. Still, an explanation has to be found for the fact that female users of the Internet are a small minority. The most obvious barrier is the fact that access to the Internet costs money and requires training and plenty of time. Apart from that, female socialisation does not prepare women for the use of technology. Most of the Internet users are students, university staff and employees of large and technologically advanced companies. Housewives, shop assistants or secretaries are seldom found on the Internet. The style of communication prevents many women from participating in the Internet. It is well-known that the most important topic in cyberspace is pornography, a fact which does not make women very comfortable. Spender also quotes several researchers who found that the educational system discourages girls from using the computer. Generally, a male culture of computer usage developed which excludes women.

> It's the masculine relationship to the machine, which seems to bring out the worst in some men. It's been there with cars (the biggest, the brightest, latest, fastest) and it's there with computers as well (Spender 1995, 183).

There is evidence that there are female and male styles of interaction on the Internet, especially in mailing lists (Herring 1994, 1996), just as there are in face-to-face communication. Susan Herring argues:

> Women's messages on both lists tend to be aligned and supportive in orientation, while men's messages tend to oppose and criticize others. Further, the lists themselves exhibit an overall aligned or opposed orientation, depending on whether the majority of participants are women or men (Herring 1996, 104).

This does not mean that all women behave in a female style. Nevertheless, expectations and interpretation of communicative acts on the Internet are influenced by these styles. Gender-specific behaviour can be found on two levels. The first is the actual behaviour of the Internet users, and the second focuses on the stereotypes and images people have.

Generally, it can be said that there are still many barriers which prevent women from using the Internet. Various strategies have been proposed by female scientists to overcome these. Some of them suggest that women should exploit allegedly female features of the Net (virtual microworlds which support bricolage, email which supports communication, etc.) to overcome these barriers. The idea of a feminine style of computer usage is very important in this context. There are certain features of modern computer technology which might support a feminine style of computer usage. Nevertheless, it is debatable whether the empirical evidence concerning a feminine style of computer usage can be generalised. Furthermore, such an approach restricts women to certain areas of the Internet. Important aspects of the systems are still under male control (technical support, information structuring on the WWW, questions of privacy, etc.). Another possible strategy is for women to adapt to masculine forms of computer usage. It can be argued that women are as well able to think analytically as are men. Women should behave in a competitive manner to conquer cyberspace. The danger of this strategy is obvious – adaptation to male values which have proven to be problematic in many ways.

3. WWW - surfing the net

The WWW is one of the fastest growing areas of the Internet. The idea is that all the knowledge of the world is at the fingertips of the netsurfers. In reality, the WWW poses serious problems. As the number of documents increases exponentially, access is getting more and more difficult. This is partly a technical and partly a conceptual problem. The technical problem is that the response times of the system are much too long, therefore the WWW is often called World Wide Waiting. As the number of users becomes larger every day, this problem will not be solved in the near future. Nevertheless, the conceptual problem of structuring the information on the Web is the more serious one.

Every user of the WWW is allowed to add his or her own document to the Web. This has been welcomed by many users as an increase of democracy and equality in this very small section of society. On the other hand, the uncontrolled and chaotic addition of documents has also led to confusion and increasing search times. We have all the unnecessary information of the world at our fingertips, but the information we really need is almost inaccessible. The demands for quality control become louder and louder. But it is by no means clear who will set the standards and how these standards should look if quality control is to be exerted. If ever access to the WWW is controlled, women will probably suffer from these measures as they are generally not supposed to be computer experts.

As the WWW is rather chaotic and will remain so in the near future, it is necessary to develop appropriate search strategies to profit from the Web. There are basically two strategies – database-like search and search via links. In databases, the user has to choose appropriate search terms and the system then looks for these words, either in the title of the document, in the keyword list or in the full text of the document. This search process is highly structured. Nevertheless, very often it does not lead to useful results, especially not on the WWW. It is usually very important to find the right search terms, which can be an extremely difficult process. The other method – following links – is more associative and resembles Turkle's soft mastery. Links are connections between two documents which have been created by the author of the current document. If you follow a link in the Web, you are entirely at the mercy of the authors of Web documents. This can be either an advantage or a disadvantage. Sometimes you get surprising insights when you follow a link, but more often, links lead you to documents which are either under construction, have been removed to another (unknown) location or are entirely useless. It is more or less a law of the Web that you usually only find things you were not looking for (which can also be quite exciting sometimes).

I am not sure if these processes can be described by Turkle's terms of bricolage.

And bricoleurs are more comfortable with exploring the Internet through the World Wide Web. Exploring the Web is a process of trying one thing, then another, of making connections, of bringing disparate elements together. It is an exercise in bricolage (Turkle 1995, 61).

In educational theory, there is an ongoing discussion whether such unstructured search processes, as Turkle describes them, lead to positive results. The majority of researchers found that such undirected behaviour, which only follows intuition, very quickly leads to frustration (Hammond 1992). Every search process in large and unstructured collections of documents must be embedded in a sensible task. This task to a certain extent determines and at the same time restricts the explorative behaviour. In this sense, it cannot be called bricolage, even if it leads to less frustration.

In my university department many students use the WWW to search for information. In the course of a lecture, we asked a group of students to write reports about their experiences with the Web - whether they found what they were looking for and whether they felt confused by the huge mass of information. The group consisted of 28 students. Three of these were female, a number which is quite representative of the whole group of computer science students at my university. Generally, both female and male students complained that the Web was extremely time-consuming and that it was difficult to find what they were looking for. The few women were not especially enthusiastic about the Web although they all mentioned that under certain circumstances it can be a very useful tool.

Although we left it to the students to use the strategies they found appropriate, almost all of them started with search engines. It is debatable whether the use of search engines really is supported by a bricolage approach. Intuition and the creation of connections are not very important for this activity although it does not use a top-down approach. To a certain extent, it is rule-based even if it is often necessary to try out many different search terms. A possible conclusion from this discussion would be that neither hard nor soft mastery alone are a sufficient precondition for successful search via search engines. The search via associative links was often not very successful either. One of the female students, who looked for information for a holiday trip, used a link which was called 'Roads less travelled' and got to a document about conspiracies and hoaxes, crystal balls, UFOs, mysterious creatures, etc. Links like that were the rule not the exception – a phenomenon which frustrated her greatly. Many students (male and female) complained that documents were overloaded with information and were confusing.

A strategy which all the women used in this situation was to ask friends for addresses of interesting WWW sites or to look up such addresses in journals. A development in this direction are 'search directories'. (This term is quite arbitrary. So far, there is no common term for this phenomenon.) There are already search directories especially for women who are interested in feminism and related topics. They have been set up by women who were annoyed when they got results like 'blonde women with long legs (jpeg)' as a result of a query for information about women. Such search directories collect WWW addresses which are relevant for specific topics whereas search engines usually give access to every document that contains a certain search term. Again, it is not obvious if the use of such search directories is soft mastery or hard mastery.

4. Conclusion

As a result of theoretical considerations and the (still scanty) empirical evidence, I tend to assume that search methods on the WWW are (still) not gendered. This hypothesis contradicts Turkle's view that soft mastery (which is similar to many typically female skills) is the appropriate approach for search processes on the Web. At least for the World Wide Web, Sherry Turkle's assumption that the Internet supports soft mastery is, to a certain extent, misleading. Apart from that, the absence of stereotypes can be advantageous for women as it does not restrict their behaviour to specific forms of using the Web. The development of the category of soft mastery can be used as a justification to deny women access to important parts of the Internet. The technical basis of the Internet, questions of privacy or the development of sophisticated documents on the Web still require something which Turkle calls hard mastery. On the other hand, it cannot be denied that many elements of male computer culture are threatening to women. Pornography and 'flaming', which can be understood as forms of behaviour related to hard mastery, are phenomena which can be seen as typically male. In this context, the conception of soft and hard mastery seems plausible.

Ultimately, it is difficult to generalise empirical results in this area so far, and it makes more sense to analyse the various technologies separately. In some areas of the Internet gender differences can be observed, in others not. Therefore, further research should concentrate on questions concerning specific services of the Internet rather than on the Internet as a whole.

References

Bruckman, A. (1993). 'Gender Swapping on the Internet'. Proceedings of the INET '93 (International Networking Conference). San Francisco.

Halpern, D.F. (1992). Sex Differences in Cognitive Abilities. Hillsdale, NJ: Lawrence Erlbaum Associates.

Hammond, N. (1992). 'Tailoring Hypertext for the Learner', in Kommers, P.A.M., Jonassen, D.H., Mayes, J.T.(eds.) Cognitive Tools for Learning. Berlin, Heidelberg, New York: Springer.

Herring, S. (1994). 'Gender Differences in Computer-mediated Communication. Bringing Familiar Baggage to the New Frontier'. Keynote talk at panel entitled 'Making the Net*Work*: Is there a Z39.50 in gender communication?', American Library Association annual convention, Miami.

Herring S. (1996). 'Two Variants of Electronic Message Schema', in: Herring, S. (ed.) Computer-Mediated Communication. Linguistic, social, and cross-cultural perspectives, 81 -106. Amsterdam: John Benjamins.

Rada, R. (1991). Hypertext. From Text to Expertext, London, New York: McGraw-Hill.

Shneiderman, B. (1992). Designing the User Interface, Reading,MA: Addison-Wesley.

Spender, D. (1995). Nattering on the Net. Women, Power and Cyberspace, Melbourne: Spinifex.

Stepan, F. (1994). Untersuchung zur Geschlechtsabhängigkeit des Programmierstils, Institut für Gestaltungs- und Wirkungsforschung, Technische Universität Wien (master's thesis).

Turkle, S. (1990). 'Style as Substance in Educational Computing', in: Berleur, J., Clement, A., Sizer, R., Whitehouse, D. (eds.). *The Information Society: Evolving Landscapes,* 145-160. Berlin, Heidelberg, New York: Springer.

Turkle, S. (1995). *Life on the Screen. Identity in the Age of the Internet,* New York, London, Toronto: Simon and Schuster.

Witkin, H.A., Dyk, R.B., Faterson, H.F., Goodenough, D.G., Karp, S.A. (1962). *Psychological Differentiation,* New York: Wiley.

Politicizing the Internet: Getting Women On-Line

Barbara Crow

Faculty of General Studies, University of Calgary

Abstract

Most of the feminist analysis regarding the Internet has focused on why feminists should go on-line; little attention has been given on 'how' to do it. This paper explores one attempt to translate feminist theory into praxis through the development and provision of workshops on how to get women on-line.

1. Introduction

Feminist analysis has consistently revealed the historical gendering of technology. Balka 1992; Benston 1989; Bleier 1986; Brecher 1989; Prioux and Prioux 1989; Bush 1983; Cooper and Selfe 1990; Franklin 1990; Hacker 1990; Haraway 1991; Herring 1993; Keller 1985; Menzies 1996; Perry and Greber 1990; Rothschild 1988; Taylor, Kramarae and Ebben 1993; Turkle and Papert 1990; Wajcman 1991). This analysis not only reveals women's limited opportunities and conditions surrounding technology but also provides us with insights on how to challenge and resist this gendering. It has been my task to translate the feminist analysis on gender and technology into the feminist practice of getting women on-line. The Internet has been defined in several different ways. My definition comes from Heather Menzies' *Whose Brave New World*: 'The highway is a webwork of powerful (high capacity) computer-communications networks capable of handling everything from video to voice, text to computer data and graphics, interchangeably, interactively, and at lightning speeds.' (1996: 7) The terms Internet, on-line and information highway, I use interchangeably in this paper.

In an examination of the Internet, feminism has taught us to ask important questions about the relations of power — Who benefits from the Internet? What are its origins? Who has access to the Internet? Whose language shapes the Internet? How can we intervene - do we want to intervene in this technological practice? But in order for any of these questions to be addressed, a more primary intervention has to occur: we must provide the conditions and opportunities to get women on-line. This paper describes one approach on how to commit this feminist intervention.

As well as being a parent, an assistant professor in Women's Studies and an anti-racist, feminist activist, I am a self-taught computer user. Over the last decade, I have been assisting women with everything from purchasing a computer, loading software, to how to get on-line. As computers arrived with software, the request changed in nature with the majority focusing on how to get on-line. After several one-to-one meetings teaching women how to get on-line, it became apparent that what was holding many women back from exploring the machine themselves was the perception of the computer as a complicated instrument. Many women expressed 'fear' of breaking the machine and felt 'stupid' after reading the manuals or asking for technical help. This revealed, yet again, the legacy of the gendering of technology and particularly, women's ambivalence to computers (see Frenkel 1990 and Turkle and Papert 1990). It was through these one-on-one experiences that I was able to identify what was holding women back from their participation on-line. I named and translated these fears and concerns into a series of Internet workshops for women only.

2. The Workshops: For Women Only

I have offered workshops on university campuses in the United States and Canada. While I recognise that this is a privileged site, it is a community where I spend most of my time as an academic. It is in our local communities where we must begin with 'community-based needs'. Also, while the assumption is that universities have the 'latest' and most 'sophisticated' digital technologies, the availability of computers, on-line services and resources vary dramatically across campuses.

It is in these contexts that I have developed a variety of workshops pertaining to the Internet. The workshops I will address specifically are 'Exploring the Internet' and 'Creating your own Home Page'. The workshops are generally three hours long. The content of the workshops takes approximately two hours to deliver and the extra hour is available for questions. The following is a description of what I do in the workshops and how I conduct them. Before I offer the workshops, there are two important steps that need to be taken. The first is a discussion of how to notify and invite the various women's communities to the workshops. The workshops are an excellent opportunity to develop and build ties in the women's community. Diversity is ensured by advertising the event to all of the women's groups on campus – these include students, staff and faculty. I have also been asked by specific women's groups to tailor a workshop for their needs. For example, I have been asked to provide workshops for the University of Calgary's female staff association Women's Council and Network, the Academic Women's Association and Studio XX (artists' collective). This attention to how to best reach the women's communities in universities has meant that the participants in the workshops have ranged in age from 17 to the early 70s; they are white women, women of colour and First Nations women; and they are students, staff and faculty.

The second step is to visit the facilities where the workshops are to be offered. I check out what kind of computers and software, Internet services and computer resources are available. It is also time to find a computer lab that will allow each participant to be in front of her own terminal. Depending on the facilities, numbers in the workshops can range from 15 to 45, but the smaller the better. If the participant numbers extend beyond 15, I ask for some names of women in the community who are Internet literate if they can assist with the workshop. This step allows one an opportunity to assess the computer culture within which the communities operate. I also try to find a friendly technical person whose name I can pass on during the workshops. I then tailor one of the working Internet documents developed by Linda Tauscher and myself to the particular institutions. Once these two steps are completed, I begin the workshops.

Before any one puts fingers to the keyboard, I relay my own personal narrative around computers and contextualize the Internet. This is the important work of demystifying computer technology. I do this first by providing a brief history of the Internet - the story of its origin. This allows participants to see why they may not have been interested in this technology and reveals how computer language operates as a barrier. It is also important to note that there are many women who are innovators in this technology (two recent publications include Cherny and Weise (1996) and Sinclair (1996)). We then move to a discussion of the location of women in the computer science profession and the numbers of women on the Internet.

I try to address and dispel the fear many women report regarding their interactions with computers. I reassure them that they will not break the machine – and if they do they should see it as an act of resistance! I dispel the fear of 'being stupid' – that they do not understand how computers work. In particular, I discuss how the technical delivery of the technology is politicised. I discuss the power of computer technicians and try to break down the barriers on how participants can make technical support work for them. I finish this section by framing the workshop around the tension between the Internet's capacity for surveillance and control and it being a place for feminists to subvert and resist. Most importantly, I state at the end of this section that I am sharing with them this information so that they may decide whether or not they want to participate in the technology.

Once the intellectual tools are made available, we move to the technical dimension of the workshop. There are two factors to be considered. The first is how to use this technology with an emphasis on problem-solving. The second is in regard to computer needs.

3. How does this technology work?

I provide a variety of tools for participants to learn about computers and the Internet. This variety of tools provides a range of materials and strategies to assist with problem-solving. A lengthy verbatim account of the workshop is handed out. I encourage participants to write down steps that may have been forgotten in the preparation in the hand out or to jot down responses to questions that are raised. I make explicit throughout the workshops – 'what do you need to know for problem-solving?' An overhead is connected to a computer so the women can look to a larger screen to match up with their own. Finally, I encourage them to consult with their peers during the workshop. This develops their skill for asking questions and begins the work of constructing themselves as 'experts'. They have a hard copy of the workshop, their own terminal, a projected version of the screen, pen and paper, my talk and their peers.

4. What do I need to go on-line?

Part of the workshop is dedicated to the provision of technical information: what kind of computer equipment is needed to get on-line from home, what they need to get access to services and where, if any, can they get this kind of information on campus. Finally, there are two other important dimensions that operate throughout the workshop. One is that I never touch anyone's keyboard without the permission of the user. After years of assisting with computer technology, many women have told me that when they have asked for technical help, the technician (most were male) has taken over their keyboards. In this situation, the women either abdicated responsibility for solving the technical problems – they hoped that through observation they would be able to reproduce the corrective measures and/or they were afraid to ask for fear of seeming 'stupid'. When a problem arises, I get the participants to invoke strategies for addressing the problem. Second, and related to the first concern, is that we do not move forward in the workshop until everyone is at the same place. This dimension is critical as it reveals to the participants that they are not always responsible for why a computer may not be responding to the seemingly 'correct' commands. It also provides an opportunity to invoke problem-solving strategies by asking participants to turn to the screen(s) at hand and make suggestions. The workshops are concluded with my hope that participants will modify the workshops to their own specifications and that they will pass on this knowledge to other individuals and groups.

5. Reflections on the Process

This is just one kind of feminist foray into digital technology on university campuses — it must be recognised along with other initiatives such as groups like Women in Science and Engineering (WISE). While I have been involved in teaching hundreds of women on the Internet, my intervention works in the system as it currently exists and only for the women who take these workshops. Our task is how to reach women who do not avail themselves of these services – who continue to have an ambivalent relationship to computers.

We also have to be concerned by the ways our interventions are co-opted by the university. While we have used university resources for the workshops, the workshops were not offered or funded by the various academic computing services - we are providing a service many universities are not prepared to offer. At one institution, a computer technician wanted to place a sexual harassment charge. The technician argued that workshops for women only discriminated against men.

Finally, I am not developing the software, the crucial dimension of how we 'navigate' the 'information highway', nor am I addressing the material conditions required to facilitate access outside of the university. I would suggest that these tasks must be more fully addressed and pursued in our political work with digital technology. I hope that you are able to use these suggestions for designing and implementing Internet workshops in your community. It is a labour intensive process, but one that provides the conditions and opportunities for one kind of feminist intervention on the Internet and develops another resource for women's communities.

Acknowledgement

I would like to thank Jeanne Perreault for her insightful comments and Linda Tauscher who assisted with the development and delivery of the workshops 'Discover the Cyborg in You: Feminists Going On-Line', sponsored by the Women's Resource and Collective Centre, University of Calgary 1995.

Note

The documentation for these workshops is available at the following web site: http://www.ucalgary.ca/~crow/internet.html. These have included, for example, how to use email, how to search the Internet, and how to become part of a user group. The hand outs are also available on-line at this web site. Therefore, if participants wish to offer the workshop later the documents are available for them to consult, modify or reproduce. For examples of women taking control of their technology, visit the following web sites: 'Cybergrrl' http://www.cybergrrl.com and 'Feminist Activists Resources on the Net' http://www.igc.apc.org/women/feminist.html.

References

Balka, E. (1992). *Womantalk Goes On-Line: The Use of Computer Networks in the Context of Feminist Social Change.* Ph.D. Dissertation. British Columbia: Simon Fraser University.

Benston, M. (1989). 'Feminism and Systems Design: Questions of Control', in. Thom, W. (ed.). *The Effects of Feminist Approaches with Tomorrow,* Calgary: University of Calgary Press.

Bleier, R. (1986). *Feminist Approaches to Science,* New York: Pergamon Press: New York.

Brecher, D. (1989). *Women's Computer Literacy Handbook,* New York: Plume.

Brunet, J. and Prioux, S. (1989). 'Formal versus Grass-Roots Training: Women, Work and Computers'. *Journal of Communication* 39 (3): 77-84.

Bush, C. (1983). 'Women and the Assessment of Technology: To Think, To Be: To Unthink, To Free', in Rothschild, J. (ed.). *Machina Ex Dea: Feminist Perspectives on Technology,* New York: Pergamon Press.

Cherny, L. and Weis, E. R. (1996) (eds.). *wired_women: Gender and New Realities in Cyberspace,* Seattle, WA: Seal Press.

Cooper, M. & C. Selfe, C. (1990). 'Computer Conferences and Learning: Authority, Resistance, and Internally Persuasive Discourse'. *College English* 52 (8): 847-69.

Franklin, U. (1990). *The Real World of Technology:* CBC Massey Lectures Series, Concordia, ON: Anansi Press Limited.

Frenkel, K. A. (1990). Women and Computing. *Communications of the ACM* 33 (11): 34-46.

Hacker, S. (1990). *Doing it the Hard Way: Investigations of Technology and Gender,* Boston: Unwin Hyman.

Haraway, D. (1991). 'A Cyborg Manifesto: Science, Technology, and Socialist-feminism in the Late Twentieth Century', in *Simians, Cyborgs and Women: The Reinvention of Nature,* 149-182, New York: Routledge.

Herring, S. (1993). 'Politeness in Computer Culture: Why Women Thank and Men Flame', in Bucholtz, M. and Sutton. L. (eds.). *Communication Across Cultures: Proceedings of the Third Berkeley Women and Language Conference,* Berkeley, CA: Berkeley Women and Language Group.

Keller, E. (1985). *Reflections on Gender and Science,* New Haven CT: Yale University Press.

Menzies, H. (1996*). Whose Brave New World: The Information Highway and the New Economy,* Toronto, ON: Between the Lines.

Perry, R. and Greber, L. (1990). 'Women and Computers: An Introduction'. *Signs,* 16 (1): 74-101.

Prioux, J. and Prioux, S. (1989). 'Formal versus Grass-Roots Training: Women, Work and Computers'. *Journal of Communication,* 39 (3): 77-84.

Rothschild, J. (1988). *Teaching Technology from a Feminist Perspective: A Practical Guide,* New York: Pergamon Press.

Taylor, J., C. Kramarae, and Ebben, M. (1993). (eds.). *Women, Information Technology, and Scholarship,* Champaign-Urbana, IL: Board of Trustees of the University of Illinois

Sinclair, C. (1996). Netchick: *A Smart-Girl Guide to the Wired World,* New York: Henry Holt and Co.

Turkle, S. & S. Papert. (1990). 'Epistemological Pluralism: Styles and Voices within Computer Culture'. *Signs,* 16 (1):129-57.

Wajcman, J. (1991). *Feminism Confronts Technology,* Pennsylvania, PA: Pennsylvania University Press.

Gender on the Internet: Are Styles Changing?

Amina Znaidi

Centre for People and Systems Interaction, South Bank University, London SE1 0AA

Abstract

Surveys of Internet users (e.g. Resnick 1995) reveal that the number of women users is increasing rapidly. This may have implications for the Internet culture which, we are told, is largely male dominated (e.g. Spender 1995). The small number of studies on gendered styles of communication on the Net (e.g. Herring 1994) report that males and females exhibit different linguistic behaviour. The study in this paper suggests that this may not be so and that in some circumstances the culture of gendered communication may be changing.

1. Introduction

Most of the work on gender and language on the Internet claims that communication styles on-line mirror those in face-to-face communication. The aim of this study to verify such claims. This involves analysing messages posted to three mailing lists and comparing the results with the work of both Tannen (1994) in face-to-face and that Herring (1994) on CMC.

2. Background

The study was based on Tannen's (1995) work on face-to-face communication and Herring's (1994) work on on-line communication. Although the work on gender and the use of computers is now extensive, most of it is concerned with access and pays only secondary attention to communication style (e.g. Kramarae and Taylor 1992; Shade 1993; Truong 1993).

Tannen describes two poles of gendered communication styles, in which women *tend* to approach communication with an emphasis on 'rapport' while men *tend* to approach it with an emphasis on 'report'. Consequently women speakers are generally more concerned with establishing a personal link with the other person, and men often seem to be keener on problem-solving and establishing status. Herring examined five mailing lists in which some were mixed and others were single gender lists and got broadly similar findings to Tannen. Herring concludes that while women take a 'cooperative' approach to on-line dialogue, men take an 'adversarial' approach.

3. The study

This study is a pilot which examined postings to three mailing lists: *ARNIB-L*, *MAROC-L* and *WISENET-L*. The first two lists discuss topics of general interest and tend to be male dominated.

WISENET-L is for discussion of women's issues and is dominated by women. An important reason for choosing these lists is that, at least in the case of two of them, I am confident of the gender of participants. This is crucial for analysing the data, particularly given the fact that some Internet users disguise or swap gender when participating in Internet discussions (e.g. Rheingold 1994). Although working with lists with equal participation is desirable, such lists could not be found.

4. Collecting and categorising the data

The data were collected over a period of three months and an average of 160 message per list were analyzed. In the case of *ARNIB-L* and *MAROC-L* the ratio of male/female participation is approximately 1 female to 20 males, whereas for *WISENET-L* it is 1 male to 30 females.

In order to categorise the messages I developed a list of linguistic styles based mainly on reports from Tannen (1994) and Herring (1994) and from my own observations of the data. Table 1 shows the list of linguistic features.

As is the case in most lists some participants post more messages than others and so I recorded linguistic categories from frequent participants once only. That is to say, if a frequent poster used advice giving more than once, I recorded it once only so that this would not influence the amount of advice giving done by all participants in the list.

Table 1: Linguistic categories with examples. H is for Herring; T is for Tannen

Linguistic category	Example
advice giving	You should go to your supervisor and explain the situation to him
agreeing	I agree with x, we should keep the name *ARNIB-L*..
apologising (H,T)	I am sorry I did not make myself clear
assertions (H)	This is a case about money, power and the sorry state of our honour and pride
disagreeing	I disagree; the original idea was that Aranib has a meaning for EVERY combination of three consonants.
flaming (H)	He should have kept his trap shut instead of being so stupid
hedging (H)	you probably know more than I as I am not an expert in the field
Use of personal experience (T)	When I was working in France, I came across similar conditions
praising (H,T)	I enjoyed reading your post, keep up the good work!
question asking	Could you please let me know if you are willing to help on this project
supporting	I encourage you to stand up to him; you
self-promotion (H)	As an expert in the field, I
thanking	Thank you all for your help...
use of personal opinion/feelings	I think, I feel, I wish, I hope, etc.

5. Results and discussion

Results in Table 2 show equal instances of advice giving from males in both *ARNIB-L* and *MAROC-L*, while the greatest number of advice giving is used by females in *WISENET-L*. This is because in *WISENET-L* women ask for advice and respond to requests for help very often. This would support the argument that women tend to aim at establishing 'rapport' when communicating with others. Agreement is also used mostly by women in WISENET, very few men in *ARNIB-L* and a fair number of men in *MAROC-L*. So it seems that overall participants in all three lists seem to express their agreement with each other. However, while disagreement features more or less the same in *ARNIB-L* and in*WISENET-L*, it features quite significantly in *MAROC-L*. This is because politics, which seems to stir peoples emotions, is a very frequent topic on *MAROC-L*. But one would expect that this would also lead to a high usage of flame, which is not the case. Flaming, which is not used by females on any of the lists, is used by a very small number of males on the three lists. Apologising is used more by males in *MAROC-L* than by either the females in *WISENET-L* or the males in *ARNIB-L*. This is also because in *MAROC-L* posters express their regrets for their frequent use of strong disagreement, while for the other lists there is little need for apologising.

Assertions are quite high in both *WISENET-L* and *MAROC-L*, and are almost double the number of assertions in *ARNIB-L*. This result seems to contradict those of Herring, who argues that only men seem to assert. However, since she argued that women are only active in lists where they are in the majority, it could be that in the case of *WISENET-L* women feel confident in asserting their views because they know they are not at risk of being intimidated by men. Very few participants in these lists hedge. However, females in *WISENET-L* seem to use hedging significantly more than men in the other lists. This seems to support Herring's findings, which indicate that women hedge much more than men when posting on the Internet. The use of personal experience seems to be used fairly equally among the three lists, with the biggest

Table 2: Data presentation, for each list: f is for female, m for male.

Category	List					
	Aranib		Maroc		Wisenet	
	F	M	F	M	F	M
advising	0	5	0	6	26	1
agreeing	2	10	1	24	38	0
apologising (H, T)	2	6	1	16	7	1
asserting (H)	0	50	0	110	90	0
disagreeing	0	12	0	110	31	3
flaming (H)	0	4	0	2	0	1
hedging (H)	3	1	0	1	5	0
use of personal. experience	6	51	3	63	77	0
praising (H, T)	0	4	1	9	4	0
question asking	2	24	3	5	55	1
supporting	0	0	0	0	9	0
self-promoting. (H)	0	0	0	3	0	1
thanking	0	17	1	19	22	1
personal opinion/feelings	6	31	1	44	61	5

number, however, in *WISENET-L*. This does not seem to support Tannen's claim that only women draw from their personal experience in discussion.

Praising, which might be expected to be used more by women as it supports a 'cooperative' approach to talk, is used very little but equally in all three lists. Question asking is used by very few males in *MAROC-L*, 24 times in *ARNIB-L* but by more than twice that in *WISENET-L*. Question asking results in *MAROC-L* and *WISENET-L* seem to agree with Tannen's claim that women find it easier to ask questions about things they do not know or understand while men are reluctant to do so. However, this does not seem to account for the significant number of question asking in *ARNIB-L*. On the other hand the type of questions asked and the way they are asked would indicate whether the act is a 'cooperative' or a competitive one. However in all three lists questions vary from a simple request for information to a challenge for an answer, a rhetorical question, or indeed a sarcastically asked question.

Only females in *WISENET-L* express support for each other's arguments. This clearly supports the claims by Tannen and Herring that, in conversation, women seek to establish a 'rapport' with others. Self-promotion, although used by males only, is however, used by very few of them and in one list only (*MAROC-L*). This does not support Herring's claim that men use self-promotion more than women. Thanking is shared fairly equally among the three lists and so it seems that many participants in the three lists show appreciation for each other's view.

Although females in *WISENET-L* have the highest instances of expression of personal feelings and/or opinions, a fair number of males in the other two lists use this feature as well. While participants on these lists use assertions frequently, they seem to prefix many of their assertions with an indication that this is their own personal feelings about issues rather than a clear-cut description of states of affairs.

For the small number of females who participate in *ARNIB-L* and *MAROC-L*, much of their linguistic behaviour clearly support the claim by both Tannen and Herring that women refrain from public speech, and that when they do, they tend to show a more 'cooperative' approach to communication. The Table shows that the females in *MAROC-L* and *ARNIB-L* use linguistic behaviour that is generally described as typical of female speech. The females in *ARNIB-L* agree, apologise, hedge, use personal experience, ask questions and prefix their assertions with expressions such as 'I think' 'I believe', 'in my opinion'. The females in *MAROC-L* exhibit the same linguistic behaviours except for hedging, which they do not use, and the single use of thanking. But since their participation is so low it is difficult to know how their behaviour reflects that of women on the Internet.

6. Conclusion

This study presents somewhat different results from the face to face communication studies carried out by Tannen and from the CMC studies carried out by Herring. One way to account for these differences could be that members of the lists in this study appear to exert some sort of self-censorship. Also, and at least in the case of both *ARNIB-L* and *MAROC-L*, 'rules' of reasonable behaviour are laid down by the members and the list owners, and those who do not adhere to such rules are threatened with expulsion from the lists. Therefore posters, who are mostly male, refrain from 'confrontational' behaviour. In the case of *WISENET-L*, which has a female majority, such norms of behaviour seem to prevail too, though without an apparent call to follow them.

It could be that while women usually opt for a 'cooperative' style of communication, men do so only when there are prescribed rules of behaviour. One way of verifying whether members on the lists in this study do indeed exercise self-censorship would be to conduct a study with a larger number of moderated and unmoderated lists in order to examine whether moderation is the most significant factor influencing communication styles.

References

Herring, S. C. (1993). *Gender & democracy in computer-mediated-communication*. Electronic Journal of Communication 3(2).

Kramarae, C. H. & Taylor J (1993). 'Women and men on electronic Internetworks: a conversation or a monologue?', in *Women, Information Technology, and Scholarship*. Urbana: Center for Advanced Study, University of Illinois.

Lakoff, R. (1975). *Language and Women's Place*. New York: Harper and Row.

Shade, L. R. (1993) 'Gender Issues in Internetworking'. Keynote presentation given at Community Internetworking: the International FreeInternet Conference, Carleton University, Ottawa, Canada.

Rheingold, H. (1994). *The Virtual Community: Finding Connection in a Computerized World*. London: Secker & Warburg.

Resnick R. (1995). 'A survey Of Women Online. Interactive Publishing Alert' (IPA) magazine, New York

Spender, D. (1995). *Nattering on the Net*. Melbourne: Spinifex.

Sproull, L. & Kiesler, S. (1991). *Connections: New Ways of Working in the Internetworked Organization*. Cambridge, MA: MIT Press.

Tannen, D. (1994). *Talking From 9 to 5*. New York: William Morrow & Company, Inc.

Truong, H. A. (1993). 'Gender Issues in Online Communication'. Paper presented at *Third Conference on Computers, Freedom, and Privacy*, Burlingame, CA, March 1993. [In conjunction with BAWIT-Bay Area Women in Telecommunications]